The Leadership Scorecard

By

Bryan Cambrice

ISBN: 978-0-578-29866-5

Cover design by: Get Covers
Library of Congress Control Number: TXu002308463
Printed in the United States of America

Dedication

This book is dedicated to my parents without whom I would be nothing.

Table of Contents

Preface

When I was a boy growing up in the 1980s, I used to watch shows on PBS about animals and many of these animals (e.g., rhinos and elephants) were facing extinction if something wasn't done drastically by humans to alter their course. They were an endangered species. I also remember Black adults referring to Black males as an "endangered species" because of our high levels of unemployment, poverty, addiction, incarceration, homicide, and shortened life expectancy. Today, Blacks in the United States, and perhaps globally, are an endangered species. We are bedeviled by a myriad of challenges and every time we start to make progress, someone (i.e., racists) snatches the rug right out from under us and we have to start all over. We're constantly dealing with new challenges while coping with existing ones and we're losing. We're like the Titanic, a ship that struck an iceberg and now's taking on water. We're sinking! We're like a patient on life support and we're dying. Soon, someone is going to pull the plug! We find ourselves in this situation because we are bereft of leadership.

I began researching for this book as far back as 2007 and I began writing it in December 2010. I was inspired, in part, by the 2008 election of Barack Obama and, in part, by conversations Black intellectuals were having about Black leadership. So, I came up with The Leadership Scorecard. The purpose of this book is to help Blacks independently assess, gauge, and rate our leaders. It also offers us ways we can develop leaders internally while rejecting those selected for us by outsiders. Finally, it gives suggestions on how we, as individuals and as a group, can be both better leaders and better followers.

The leaders profiled in this book will be judged using the following four categories: 1.) Leadership; 2.) Race Pride; 3.) Role Model; and 4.) Impact on the Race. The last category is the most important and it has twice the weight of each of the other three criteria. A score will be assigned in each category. Then, the sum of these four scores will be added together and divided by five instead of four because the Impact on the Race category is equal to two categories. For example, Jane Doe has a 3.0 in Leadership, a 3.5 for Race Pride, a 3.2 as a Role Model, and a 3.1 for her Impact on the Race. Her final score will be a 2.56, or a C-plus. (3.0 + 3.5 + 3.2 + 3.1 = 12.8. 12.8/5 = 2.56.) Some will say that's harsh because she got at least 3 points in every category. That's true. But, remember this individual's lasting legacy is her impact on the race and her numerical score is not the only thing she should be evaluated on. It is only a quantitative measurement. She is also being judged qualitatively which can't be measured by numbers alone. You, as the reader, also have her track record to go by which was painstakingly recorded in her profile. So, after reading each chapter you have both objective and subjective criteria by which to judge each leader. My assessments and scores of these individuals are not absolute. It's up to you, the reader, to decide whether you think these individuals are good or bad leaders and hopefully to come up with your own criteria, or scorecard by which you'll judge Black leaders.

Introduction

I wrote this book to enlighten and inform. I want you, the reader, to understand how and why we got here and what we can do to get us out of it. When I began looking for subjects to write about, I had over 100 people. But, I knew I couldn't write profiles about all those individuals and finish this book. So, I narrowed it down to 21 and then, 20. Eventually, I settled on 13. I thought an odd number would work best.

Since Black leadership is based more on an individual's prominence and less on his/her area of expertise, I pulled individuals from a variety of spheres such as entertainment, religion, education, civil rights, the military, or of course politics. Simply being a celebrity makes one a Black leader. That's why I chose Oprah Winfrey and Jay-Z. They are the wealthiest, most prominent, and celebrated Black entertainers today. They both have appeared on the Forbes 400 Richest Persons list. I selected comedian Richard Pryor because not only had he revolutionized comedy, but he greatly influenced popular culture in general. Dr. Kimberle' Williams Crenshaw developed the legal concept of Intersectionality. It is the most popular feminist theory and it heavily influences today's media and pop culture.

During the Obama years, Al Sharpton became the premiere civil rights leader in America and a Democratic Party boss in his own right. Vernon Jordan, another civil rights activist, became a successful corporate lawyer, investment banker, and political fixer. John Lewis was an activist turned politician. He marched on Washington with Dr. King and authored the bill that created the National African American History Museum.

Finally, I chose individuals who reached the highest levels of government and politics. So, I chose General Colin Powell because he was the first Black Chairman of the Joint Chiefs of Staff and the first Black Secretary of State. Maynard Jackson was

the first Black Mayor of Atlanta. Douglas Wilder was the first
Black elected governor of any state. Jim Clyburn was the first
Black House Majority Whip. Kamala Harris is the first Black and
the first female Vice President and of course, Barack Obama
became our first and only to date Black President. It is my
pleasure to have written this book for you and it is my sincerest
hope that you are better after reading it. Thank you.

Oprah Winfrey

Brief Bio

Oprah Gail Winfrey was born on January 29, 1954, to Vernon Winfrey and Vernita Lee in Kosciusko, Mississippi. Oprah spent her earliest years of life with her grandmother, Hattie Mae Presley Lee, while her mother moved to the North in search of better opportunities. Her grandmother taught her how to read and would take her to church every Sunday. Oprah grew up very poor even by Mississippi standards. Kids would make fun of her clothing which was made from potato sacks.[1]

When Oprah was six,[1] she moved to Milwaukee, Wisconsin to live with her mother. Life with her mom was rough. She endured poverty, neglect, and abuse. When she was 14, she became pregnant, but her son was born prematurely and died shortly after. In high school, she moved to Nashville, Tennessee to live with her dad. Life with her father was much better. Oprah, an honor student and a high school beauty queen, was voted most likely to succeed by her classmates.

Early Career

After graduating from high school, she attended Tennessee State University where she majored in Communication. While in college, she worked as a news reporter at WVOL, a local Black-owned radio station.[1] While attending TSU, she was offered a job to be a news anchor at a Nashville TV station. Oprah initially turned the job down because she was still in school, but after one of her professors had given her a stern lecture about how foolish she was being and about all the people who would die to be in her place, she went back to the station and accepted. She was hired to do the six o'clock news in Baltimore in 1976.[1] Later, she co-hosted a talk show called People Are Talking.[1] Oprah became the host of AM Chicago in 1984, a momentous opportunity that launched her into stardom. Two years later, she became the host of The Oprah

9

, an award-winning talk show that was on the air for 25 years!

The Color Purple

While she is most famous for her talk show, it was her role as Sofia in <u>The Color Purple</u> that may her a star! That film introduced Oprah to the nation and the world. It was the springboard that launched her nationally syndicated show a year later! Thirty-eight years later, it remains her biggest role. Oprah wasn't the film's only star, however. Audiences were introduced to both Whoopi Goldberg and Danny Glover. They're the only actors besides Oprah who have been riding on that purple gravy train ever since. It's led to plays and musicals, and now, there's going to be a remake of the movie. This movie has spawned an entire industry over the last 38 years. Think of all the billions this film has made White people at the expense of Black people!

To say this movie was controversial in 1980s Black America, which is when I grew up, is an understatement. All the men hated it and all the women loved it! My parents saw it. My teachers saw it. People at my church saw it. I must've seen it five or six times in my lifetime. I even read my mother's copy of the book! It was the first time that I became aware that there was a schism between Black men and women. One that's grown into a chasm over the last 38 years. It put Black men on the defensive and allowed Black women "to exhale" because at long last they got to read, speak, and see "their truth." It led to "Sister Circles" and book clubs. The backlash from Black men that followed led to the emergence of Shahrazad Ali, a Black female author who was red pill long before there had ever been a Red Pill/MGTOW (Men Going Their Own Way) Movement. Even Farrakhan commented on the film.

The movie, based on a novel of the same name, was set in the Deep South. It was about a poor Black woman, named Celie, who grew up being molested by her father. After she became an adult, her father forced her to marry an even worse man. Her husband, Mister, beats her every day and when he's not beating her or "doing his business" on her, he lays around the house and sleeps while she waits on him and his kids hand and foot. On top of that, she has to deal with constant insults from her father-in-law. While both the book and the movie belong to a literary genre called Realistic Fiction, they were definitely more fictional than they were realistic. The setting appears to be a huge mansion in the middle of a huge plantation in the early 20th Century. Except for a few scenes that occurred in the latter half of the movie, there were no Whites in a film about the segregated South! Even as a kid, I didn't find this plausible. How was a Black man supposed to have such a fine house and all this land without any envious, greedy White people trying to swindle him out of it or run him off of it? The only doses of realism that occurred in this film were when Oprah's character, Sofia, got arrested for hitting a White man and when she had to leave her family's dinner to chauffer a White lady around town.

Both, the film and the book are very entertaining, and you wind up feeling good for Celie at the end because she overcame Mister and finds out that the man whom she thought was her dad wasn't her dad, but her stepdad. So, the two children she bore for him were not her half-brother and sister. The problem with these two works of art, especially the film, is their insidiousness. They are pieces of propaganda designed to create a wedge between Black men and women and as we can see over the last 38 years that wedge has only grown exponentially. Not only are Black men and women not marrying each other, but they are also "going to war" with each other. Neither side is winning although Black women appear to be on the winning side of things. But, when Black men lose, Black women and children lose, too.

For those people who say it's a movie – it's just entertainment, I want them to ask themselves a few questions. Why was this novel, from a previously unknown author, adapted for a film? Why did it earn a Pulitzer and how many Black male authors have won Pulitzers versus Black female ones? Why would Steven Spielberg be interested in directing this film? Would he direct a film that

11

depicted Jewish men or Jewish people or White men or White people, in general, in this way? I don't think so. So, was he being an ally or an opportunist? A propagandist is more like it. Why was Oprah Winfrey, a host on a local morning talk show and an untrained actress, given such a pivotal role? Why was her character's stepson named Harpo which is Oprah spelled backwards which later became the name of her studio? Was there a subliminal message being sent? Were they preparing our minds to embrace this unknown Black figure whom they plucked out of nowhere to lead in much the same way they did with Barack Obama almost 30 years later?

Because she's made them tens of billions of dollars, Oprah became a big business to White people. She, like Michael Jordan, is very lucky that they let her have a piece of it because they didn't have to. She could've wound up like Dr. Dre only worth hundreds of millions of dollars despite being the face and the genius behind the brand "Beats by Dre," while his White "partner" Jimmy Iovine wound up being worth billions. Typically, the Black talent is allowed to become rich if the White manager behind him/her becomes much richer. But, the optics of a Black female billionaire is much more valuable and much less threatening than when a man became the first Black billionaire as was the case with BET founder, Bob Johnson. In the following sections, I'm going to show why Oprah has been so valuable to Corporate America aka the Establishment and why they felt somewhat obligated to pay her back by letting Forbes dub her a billionaire.

The Oprah Winfrey Show: 25 years of Anti-Blackness & Misandry

I, like a lot of Generation X'ers, grew up watching The Oprah Winfrey Show primarily because our parents did. Initially, Black folks watched daily with pride because she was the first Black person to have a national talk show. It was exciting! Just like every crossover Black celebrity before her and since, Oprah's original audience was Black. We made her; celebrated her; and supported

12

her! But, then, things took a turn for the worse. Every episode was about something salacious, tawdry, and ignorant, especially those dealing with Black people. During the first ten years of her show's run, frequent topics of hers were drugs, AIDS, domestic violence, child abuse, rape, homosexuality, infidelity, teen pregnancy, interracial relationships, sex, pornography, racism, poverty, and celebrities behaving badly. Because Oprah made sure that Black folks were almost always the face of all that, her Black fans started turning away while her White fans stayed and grew in number, titillated by all the tragedy porn they were watching. It wasn't until the mid-90s after people had gotten sick of the drama, that Oprah Winfrey became Oprah, the Saint of Materialistic Consumption where audience members were told, "You get a car and you get a car and you get a car!" That's when her Book Club became a staple on her shows and she'd bring on pop psychologists and spiritual advisers like Dr. Phil and Deepak Chopra.

Oprah knocked out the competition! Both, talk show pioneer Phil Donahue and the ever muckraking and scandalmongering Geraldo Rivera were sidelined by Ms. O., and the legion of clones that emerged after her like Ricki Lake, Jerry Springer, Jenny Jones, Gordon Elliot, Maury Povich, Rolanda Watts, Divorce Court's Mablean Ephraim, Judge Greg Mathis, Judge Joe Brown, and Judge Judy among others. Daytime TV became a cesspool! Guests of The Oprah Winfrey Show who have gone on to have their own daytime shows include Dr. Phil, Dr. Oz, Rachel Ray, Ellen DeGeneres, and Rosie O'Donnell none of whom are Black. Her bestie, Gayle King, was the only one who tried and failed. But, she gets to be one of the hosts of The CBS Morning Show and that's only because Oprah was an interviewer for 60 Minutes.

I watched numerous episodes of her show, but there were a few that stood out to me. The first one was about a Black couple who had a tumultuous relationship that involved infidelity and drug abuse. Her hosting a Whites-only audience in Forsyth County, Georgia was the second. She had an episode after Anita Hill came forward with her allegations of sexual harassment against Clarence

Thomas which threatened to derail his Supreme Court confirmation. I remember her hosting a show about interracial relationships and there were only Black men and women on the stage. It was either the late 80s or the early 90s. Before the show cut to a commercial, a Black male panelist in response to a question from Oprah declared, "The best sex I ever had was with a Black woman! But, the best time I have ever made love was with a White woman!" The audience, filled with women, both Black and White, just gasped with disgust! I'm absolutely, positively certain that episode and those comments had a deleterious effect on Black male-female relations in the decades since its airing.

Although Oprah relied less on sensationalism to gain viewers by the mid-90s, she never gave up on it completely. During a show in the late 90s, she introduced the country to the so-called "Downlow" phenomenon where closeted gay men married women knowing full well they were gay. Because "on the down low" was a phrase from Hip-Hop slang, that meant keeping something secret or to yourself, being "on the down low" was seen as "a Black thang." As if, White men and others don't practice this reckless behavior. The supposedly high levels of AIDS and HIV infections in the Black Community were blamed on these closeted gay Black men and Black ex-cons who engaged in homosexual sex while in prison in addition to supposedly high levels of promiscuity among Blacks in general. These men weren't on the down low; they just were lowdown! But, thanks to Oprah, the whole Black community got tarnished by it.

She once interviewed Halle Berry, whose man troubles are well-documented. She gushed over Halle's new White beau, a French-Canadian model named Gabriel Aubry, and told the actress to "Just have babies! Don't worry about getting married!" Now, why would anybody take relationship advice from the unmarried, childless Oprah? But, Halle, like a fool, did and we all know how it turned out with Aubry. She really showed her anti-Black misandry, or hatred of Black men, when she hosted an interview special with Michael Jackson at his home in the 2000s. When she saw

14

Michael's father, Joe Jackson, present in the home, she became indignant and muttered on camera, "What's he doing here?" Like the man who made the "King of Pop," shouldn't be by his son's side! Man, Oprah's got some nerve!

Her Other Projects

As if spending 25 years on a talk show trashing Black men – Black people wasn't enough for Oprah, she's either starred in, written, or produced movies and TV shows doing the same thing. She even founded a cable network dedicated to showing the worst of her people. Four years after her debut in The Color Purple and three years after the premiere of her show, Oprah produced and starred in the ABC miniseries The Women of Brewster Place. I watched it with my mother. After The Color Purple and a season or two of The Oprah Winfrey Show, my dad had had enough! Set in a Northern ghetto during the 1960s, the show proceeds to take us on a tour of the lives of these single Black women, from multiple generations, who live in this rundown apartment complex called Brewster Place located on a street that's made into a dead end by a brick wall. Oprah played an urbanized Sofia. Jackee' Harry, who played Sondra on the 80s sitcom 227, played a 60s version of the same character, a bubble-headed floozy who lets herself get taken advantage of sexually by a preacher. Lonette McKee played an out lesbian who winds up getting raped by some young hoodlum played by Glenn Plummer in an alley in full view of her neighbors who did absolutely nothing to help her not even calling the police. Famed actor Moses Gun played the apartment complex's drunken repairman. His character gets brutally beaten and killed with a crowbar while trying to render aid to Lonette McKee's character who having just been beaten, raped, and left for dead in an alley hates all men and is out for blood! All the Black men in this mini-series were portrayed as trifling, sorry ne'er do wells, or flawed in some sort of way who are always abusing, betraying, or messing it up in some way for Black women. This has been a steady theme in all of the projects Oprah has been associated with over the last 38 years from The Color Purple, The Women of Brewster Place,

15

Beloved, Selma, Greenleaf, Queen Sugar, and The Immortal Life of Henrietta Lacks.

In Selma, Oprah even felt the need to take the saintly Martin Luther King, Jr., down a peg. There was a scene in the movie where the Kings were at home and a package was delivered which Mrs. King opened. It contained a tape recorder that had a tape with a recording of Dr. King allegedly having sex with another woman. There was also a note from FBI agents, who illegally made the recording at the behest of President John F. Kennedy, Attorney General Bobby Kennedy, and FBI Director J. Edgar Hoover, calling King a hypocrite and telling him to kill himself. When Coretta confronts her husband about his alleged infidelity, she tells Martin "I know what you sound like." Oprah makes this college-educated, classically trained opera singer sound like a pickaninny off the plantation. Not only was this scene racially insulting and offensive, but it was also historically inaccurate. The march in Selma took place in 1965. The FBI sent the Kings that tape in1961. In addition to poisoning the minds of moviegoers against Dr. King, I'm sure it reopened wounds for his children and grandchildren. But, Oprah doesn't care about that. All she cares about is slamming Black men. The $3 million she gave to Morehouse will never wipe away her treachery.

Is Oprah Really a Billionaire?

In 2003, Oprah Winfrey, the Grande Dame of Daytime Talk, was added to Forbes' list of the 400 Richest Americans marking the first time that a Black woman anywhere in the world had become a billionaire. She also was the 2nd African American to become a billionaire after Bob Johnson, who became one after he sold BET to Viacom in 2002. I remember watching a video, either on TV or the Internet, where Forbes described how she made their list. In a nutshell, the narrator said, that it was because of her deal with syndication giant, King World. In the late 90s or early 2000s, her agent/business partner negotiated a deal between King World and Harpo Studios, Ms. Winfrey's company, to pay her $300 million a year for the right to distribute her show to TV stations across the country. After three or four years of receiving this amount annually in cash payments, Forbes determined that she was a billionaire and added her to their list. Seems simple enough. Of course, they don't include her taxes and personal expenses over those years, but let's just say Oprah had made over a billion dollars in the three or four years before 2003. She continued to earn roughly $300 million a year from her contract right up until the end of her show in 2011.

On June 26, 2012, Oprah, sandwiched between Bill Gates and Warren Buffet, appeared on the cover of Forbes. The imagery was powerful. Here was this Black woman, a billionaire in her own right, appearing on the cover of a very popular business magazine, with two of the wealthiest men in the world, both of whom were White as are the vast majority of the world's billionaires. But, looks can be deceiving. Oprah, according to Forbes at the time, was worth $3 billion while Gates was worth over $60 billion and Buffet was worth over $50 billion. Based on her net worth alone, Oprah didn't have any business being in that picture let alone in the same room with these two captains of industry. There's absolutely no equivalency between a single-digit billionaire and a double-digit billionaire. (Hell, Gates spent much of the Nineties worth over $100 billion as he became the first centi-billionaire 25 years before Jeff Bezos and Elon Musk even joined the ranks of multi-millionaires let alone billionaires!)

It was the 30th Anniversary edition of the magazine and the trio was attending the Forbes Summit on Philanthropy.[2] Also, she has nowhere near the power and influence that those two gentlemen have or even that of some less wealthy billionaires or multi-millionaires. Whatever power and influence she does have, she's chosen to use it to go over after other Black people or used it on frivolous or nebulous things. And please don't talk about her endorsement of Barack Obama. That is not political influence! That was a celebrity endorsement that may have yielded a candidate some votes, but that is not the same as hiring lobbyists; joining a trade association or a chamber of commerce; or funding a think tank or political action committee. These are the things that billionaires do!

On two separate occasions, Oprah has sold two major stakes in her cable channel the Oprah Winfrey Network (OWN.) The network started as a joint venture between the media personality and Discovery Communications with each owning 50%. But, in 2017 Oprah sold half of her share, or roughly 25% of the firm for $70 million to Discovery.[3] Oprah would remain CEO of OWN while Discovery gains a 75% stake in the company. In December 2020, she sold 80% of the remaining 25% of OWN that she owned or 20% of the company to Discovery for $36.5 million worth of Discovery's stock. But, this time, she only got half as much money for her relinquishing roughly the same amount of ownership.[3] Talk about a fire sale! Oprah would remain Chief Executive Officer while retaining just under 5% while "her partner" would now control roughly 95% of the cable outlet.[3] So, she went from a partner to an employee. What happened to everyone telling me Oprah was a BOSS? I don't know if they just didn't know or they just weren't paying attention, but they've been awfully silent.

Oprah almost immediately sold half of her $36.5 million worth of Discovery shares for $18.25 million.[3] But, if you're worth $2.6 billion,[3] $18 million in cash is a drop in the bucket. It seems like there's trouble in Paradise and her having seven homes and a luxury apartment all across the US and the Caribbean is causing Oprah to be cash poor also known as BROKE like a rapper or ballplayer who's spent too much of his earnings on ladies, liquor, rims, fancy clothes, and expensive cars. Seems like Lady O is struggling to finance that billionaire lifestyle and is now having to "ball on a budget." Apparently, she's been just as materialistic as the ghetto youth she once criticized when she explained once why she chose to build a school in South Africa instead of on Chicago's southside.

Oprah's not a billionaire, at least in a traditional sense. Bezos, Musk, Gates, Buffet, the Waltons, Koch, and most other billionaires all got their money by having near-monopolies over entire industries and sectors of the economy through the businesses they own. Oprah, Jay-Z, Tyler Perry, Kanye West, Rihanna, and the other Black billionaires and millionaires get their money the same way other Black people do – by working for White folks. They may own their own companies, but they do so through the support, sponsorship, grace, and sufferance of much wealthier White people and the companies they own. Have you ever noticed whenever you read about Oprah, Obama, or Jay-Z sailing on a yacht somewhere they are always on David Geffen's, Richard Branson's, or Jack Dorsey's and not their own? Oprah hosted Maya Angelou's birthday party at Donald Trump's Mar-A-Lago country club instead of her palatial estate.[1] Now, I wonder why?

Her Spearheading the Time's Up/Me Too Movement

On Sunday, January 7, 2018, while accepting the Cecil B. DeMille Award at the 2018 Golden Globe Awards, Oprah Winfrey invoked the name of Recy Taylor, a Black woman in Alabama who had been kidnapped while walking home from church and brutally raped by six White men and left blindfolded on the side of the road in 1944.[4] Although the men were arrested and confessed, two all-White grand juries failed to indict them.[4] Recy Taylor, who had died at age 97 just ten days before Oprah's speech, had lived for 73 years with the pain and anguish of knowing that her tormentors walked away Scott-free. To my knowledge, at no time before her acceptance speech in 2018, had Oprah Winfrey ever invoked Recy Taylor's name or the names of any one of the countless Black women who were victims of sexual violence at the hands of White racists. She's never depicted them in any of her films or television shows. Never interviewed any survivors on her talk show. But, for some odd reason, she decides to invoke this now deceased Sister's name in order to bolster a fledgling organization called Time's Up that says it's dedicated to fighting sexual assault and harassment in Hollywood.

Black folks often get mad about the appropriation, or theft of our culture, ideas, and inventions by Whites and others, especially by White celebrities, musicians, and artists. Well, what about historical appropriation where other people take our story and make it their own? This has been going on for a long time with the mostly White LGBT+ Community, White liberals, White Jews, Irish Americans, and other White ethnics. Now, other so-called People of Color (i.e., Latinos, East Asians, Middle-Easterners, South Asians, Native Americans, and recent Black immigrants) want to piggyback on African Americans' struggle. What's worse it's Negroes like Oprah who are giving it away! Giving them license and permission to steal our history! Our Struggle! That's exactly what she did when she invoked the name of Mrs. Taylor to give cover to washed-up White actresses looking to secure legal settlements over alleged sexual harassment by powerful White men in Hollywood. This was a new low even for Oprah. Unsurprisingly, unconscious Black people from the elite down to the masses were all celebrating this disrespect and defilement of our Sister and her memory.

Since her infamous "Time's Up" speech the only people who have gone to jail and/or paid settlements have been Bill Cosby and R. Kelly meanwhile Matt Lauer, Roman Polanski, Charlie Rose, Woody Allen, Les Moonves, and a whole slew of White male celebrities remain filthy rich and free as a bird. Oh, yes, one White guy did go to jail. That was Harvey Weinstein and the only reason he's in jail is because Black people pointed out that it was only Black men who were going to jail; being seriously investigated; fired; and/or being sued for proven or unproven acts of sexual harassment, sexual misconduct, or sexual assault. Oprah was accused of continuing to associate with Weinstein while ignoring the rumors about the famed producer's bad behavior.[5][6] Gayle King, stood behind Charlie Rose not only after he admitted to wrongdoing, but even after 27 women came forward and accused him of misconduct.[7] In addition to Cosby and Kelly, other famous Black men like Justin Fairfax, Russell Simmons, the late Kobe

20

Bryant, Cuba Gooding, Jr., Morgan Freeman, Nate Parker, Trey Songz, Nelly, Tavis Smiley, Will Smith, and Denzel Washington have been subjected to various forms of investigation, scrutiny, or criticism in the Court of Public Opinion because of the so-called Time's Up/Me Too Movement. The problem with those whose rallying cry is "Believe all women!" is that such thinking has led to a lack of due process for the accused and a presumption of guilt instead of innocence like what happened with Clarence Thomas, Brett Kavanaugh, Kevin Spacey, and Chris Noth among many others. Unfortunately, there's no presumption of innocence, no due process, and no statute of limitations in the Kangaroo Court of Public Opinion where Oprah is the Chief Justice.

Score

Leadership For almost four decades, Oprah has been world-famous. Whether it's to sell products and services or to support a particular agenda, she's used her voice to influence billions of people. In the process, she became a global celebrity. She gets a 3.0 in the Leadership category.

Race Pride On an episode of A&E's biography that came out in the late 90s, Oprah once admitted that she was scared of White people. She told a story about how she avoided getting beaten up by the White kids at school by talking about the biblical prophets Elisha and Elijah. Soon after, they left her alone because they thought she was crazy. Almost 50 years later, she's still scared of White people. Scared they'll take stop liking her. Scared they'll take her fortune and fame away which is why she is still tap dancing to racist tunes even though she's a so-called billionaire. No Black person with any race pride would do a hit piece on the late, great Michael Joseph Jackson, a man who was acquitted of child molestation and sexual abuse in a criminal court and who was found not liable of the same in a civil court. Even the FBI said they investigated him for 10 years and could find no evidence of wrongdoing. But, Harpo does not care about that! All she cares about is taking a Black man down and getting paid for it. Since she's a billionaire, why's she still working and doing interviews? Bill Gates, Steve Ballmer, and Jeff Bezos have stepped down from the day-to-day operations of their businesses to pursue other interests. Why hasn't Oprah? Perhaps, she can't afford to. She gets a 1.0 for Race Pride.

Role Model Oprah's an example of a person who did well in school; worked hard; spoke properly both on and off camera; used her voice to promote issues that were important to her; and gave money to noble causes like education. But, that's only part of what it means to be a role model. A role model, like any leader, has to set a moral example and I'm not just talking about morality in a religious sense. I'm talking about having self-pride, race pride, and a sense of obligation to others of your race or group. Oprah's missing that half of being a role model. As a result, she only gets half the total points available in this category and that's a 2.0.

Impact on the Race Despite her intelligence, charm, wit, projection of strength, and individual success, Oprah has had a deleterious impact on our race. From her first feature film to her talk show to her other movies and TV shows, there's been this constant need on her part to show the worst of our race, especially the worst of our men, sending the message to Black women and girls that Black men and boys are the reason you're being held back. You don't need them; so, get rid of them! For someone who claims to be spiritual, she seems to be fixated on the sensual. She loves to sensationalize. She gets off on titillating her audiences by feeding them their most prurient fantasies and confirming their basest stereotypes about Black people. Those Black women and men who blindly worship her are just as myopic, narcissistic, materialistic, and, in some cases, just as careerist as she is. For someone who has spent a lifetime in the business of presenting images, you'd think she'd be a good steward of her people's image. But, she hasn't been these last 38 years and for that, she gets an F. Her score in this category is a 0.9.

<u>Overall Score</u> Oprah's overall score is a 1.38, or D. (3.0 + 1.0 + 2.0 + 0.9 = 6.9)/5 = 1.38.

Kimberle' Williams Crenshaw

Brief Bio

Kimberle' Williams Crenshaw was born on May 4, 1959.[8] Her parents were Walter and Marian Crenshaw.[9] She's a native of Canton, Ohio.[9] After graduating from McKinley High School, she went to Cornell University in Ithaca, NY where she majored in Africana Studies and Government in 1981.[9] She graduated from Harvard Law School three years later. Then, she pursued a Master of Laws degree, or an L.L.M. from the University of Wisconsin and she clerked for Wisconsin Supreme Court Judge Shirley Abrahamson.[9] She's a law professor at both Columbia University and UCLA. She's also an activist and runs the African American Policy Forum, an organization dedicated to fighting for diversity and gender inclusion.[9]

What Is Intersectionality? (Her Original Theory and Usage)

While being interviewed during a video for the National Association of Independent Schools (NAIS,) Dr. Crenshaw had this to say about her theory, "Intersectionality is just a metaphor for understanding the ways that multiple forms of inequality or disadvantage sometimes compound themselves and they create obstacles that often are not understood within conventional ways of thinking about anti-racism or feminism or whatever social justice advocacy structures we have. *Intersectionality isn't so much a grand theory. It's a prism for understanding certain kinds of problems.*"[10]

Interestingly, the professor admits that her brainchild is not a theory based on rigorous research, but a political ideology or worldview that allows her and her acolytes to cherry-pick data as it suits them and their agenda. I believe this agenda has less to do with ensuring that Black women have equal access to education and employment and more to do with elevating Black Women in society to the exclusion of Black Men. They want to divest from

Black Men. They want to stop investing in Black men. They want to be seen by Whites and others as separate and apart from Black Men. It's almost as if they want to be seen as a different race altogether.

Intersectional feminists have no use for Black men. They care more about getting back at Black men than helping Black women. They deliberately conflate their failed or dysfunctional PERSONAL relationships with systemic oppression. They have made their PERSONAL lives POLITICAL instead of making their POLITICS PERSONAL. So, if some Black man or boy disappointed them; mistreated them; or broke their hearts, then, every Black man or boy did and he MUST PAY. Worse still, many of these young women and teenage girls haven't even been in a relationship or suffered any abuse, trauma, or hardship, yet they still feel the need to live vicariously through some other woman's pain or sorrow and take it on as their own. They have negative attitudes toward Black males despite not having any negative experiences with Black males to justify or explain such attitudes.

So great is their hatred for Black Men that they even create ahistorical characters in their films like the nonexistent Black slavecatcher, Bigger Long, from the 2019 movie Harriet. That name itself conjures up racist sexual stereotypes of Black Men as bucks, breeders, and studs (i.e., a Mandingo) and it bears an uncanny resemblance to that of Long Dong Silver, the Black 1980s porn star who was often filmed bedding White women. Bigger Long's sole motivation for catching Harriet Tubman is so that he can spend his reward money on sleeping with White whores. It's as if all Black men want to do is a fuck White women! The Black female producers and writers of this biopic let the real-life White slaveowners, slavecatchers, and bounty hunters who tormented Harriet off the hook just so they could tarnish the Black male image. They admitted to making it palatable for White consumption by calling it an *American story, not a slave story*. Excuse me, what? How can you have a movie about a slave and it not be about Slavery?

Crenshaw claims that she first postulated her theory after coming across the case of Emma DeGraffenreid, a Black woman who filed a lawsuit against a car company for both race and gender discrimination.[11] Mrs. DeGraffenreid and four other Black women claimed they were laid off because they were Black women.[9] But, according to Dr. Crenshaw, the judge threw these women's cases out because the automaker was able to prove that it hired both Blacks and women. Dr. Crenshaw said that the Blacks they hired were men who did factory work and the women they hired were Whites who did secretarial work.[11] She expounded on her point by saying, "In the context of employment discrimination, intersectionality was meant <u>to draw attention to the many ways Black women were being excluded from employment in industrial plants and elsewhere that were segregated by gender and race.</u>"[15] (This was her agenda.) Unfortunately for her argument, there was no segregation based on gender. But, it was based on race. Her argument is ahistorical and false. Rosa Parks was not made to sit in the back of the bus because she was a woman, but because she was Black.

Although Crenshaw developed Intersectionality with the intent of examining how Black women faced discrimination for being both Black and women, the concept has been used to examine other identities people may have and how those identities are used to oppress them. Examples include being a woman and a lesbian; being a transwoman who's also an undocumented immigrant; being a Muslim who is poor; or being an Asian woman who suffers from body dysmorphia. The concept wasn't popular among feminists until Obama became President. Now, it's the most commonly talked about feminist theory in both the news and social media thanks in large part to 4th wave feminists[12] who have embraced it with a vengeance. This cohort of feminists consists of late Generation X'ers, Millennials, and Generation Z women and teens who often belong to a wide variety of racial, ethnic, religious, or sexual minorities.

Counterarguments

While Intersectionality is perhaps the most popular "theory" explaining how society is organized, it's not without its critics both from within and without Feminism's ranks. Rekia Jibrin, Sara Salem, Barbara Tomlinson, and Lisa Downing are all feminist critics of the theory. Jibrin and Salem say Intersectionality is impractical, too complex, and focuses too much on conflicts within race (e.g., The Gender War among Blacks) instead of fighting specific forms of oppression like racism, sexism, classism, or homophobia "in society as a whole." Tomlinson disagrees with the way Intersectionality has been used to attack other feminists and feminist theories. "Lisa Downing argues that intersectionality focuses too much on group identities, which can lead it to ignore the fact that people are individuals, not just members of a class. Ignoring this can cause intersectionality to lead to a simplistic analysis and inaccurate assumptions about how a person's values and attitudes are determined."[12]

Dr. Tommy J. Curry, the Personal Chair of Africana & Black Studies at the University of Edinburgh in Scotland and a self-described masculinist, criticizes Ms. Crenshaw's use of racist and discredited theories about Black male sexuality to undergird her arguments about the discrimination faced by Black females. In his article entitled "Decolonizing the Intersection," Dr. Curry talks about how Kimberle' Crenshaw was deeply influenced by the 1981 book The Second Assault written by White feminist theorists Joyce Williams and Karen Holmes. According to Dr. Curry, these authors wrote in their book that Black men rape Black women solely to prove their manhood because White Racism prevents them from being men in other ways. Since White men have all the power, Black men have to rape Black women in order to feel like men or so the theory goes. Not only is this patently false, but the authors even admitted that they had no evidence to prove their theory's veracity, or truthfulness.[13] Yet, both they and Kimberle' Crenshaw pushed it anyway – turning legions of women of all stripes against Black men. It's now an article of faith in

Intersectionality that Black men are violent brutes who rape and abuse women in order to compensate for not being as manly as White men. Ironically, despite Black men being weaker politically than White men, they are viewed by intersectionalists as the greater threat.[14] Intersectionalists like Crenshaw love portraying Black men as hypersexualized brutes through news media, social media, and pop culture (i.e., movies, magazines, and TV shows) much like D.W. Griffith's film <u>The Birth of a Nation</u> did over a century ago.

Antonio Moore, an LA-based attorney and activist, focuses his criticism of Ms. Crenshaw and intersectionalists as a whole on their frequent failure to use data to prove or disapprove their thesis, and whatever little data (i.e., statistics) they do provide, is used to buttress their preconceived notions. By 1989, when Dr. Crenshaw wrote "De-Marginalizing the Intersection" which examined a Black woman named Emma DeGraffenreid's 1976 lawsuit against General Motors for both racial and sexual discrimination, there was almost 20 years of Bureau of Labor statistics that had shown a phenomenon that Moore described as "The Rise of the Black Female Professional."[15] According to Crenshaw, Black women were losing out to Black men (not White men) over factory jobs and to White women (not White men) over office jobs. According to Dr. Crenshaw, sometime in the past, all the Black jobs were going to Black men and all the women's jobs were going to White women. But, had she done her homework, she would've found that her assumptions about Black women not getting hired to do office work were false. According to the US Bureau of Labor Statistics, Black men made up 6.4% of those employed in Professional and Technical jobs in 1972.[16] Black women were employed in 10.6% of those jobs at that time.[16] By 1980, Black men made up 8.2% of those employees while Black women filled 13.8% of those jobs.[16] In 1980, 9 years before her journal article, Black women had roughly 40% more professional jobs than Black men did.[15][16] They were twice as many Black female accountants than there were Black male ones in 1972 and 1980.[16] By 1980, there were more Black female lawyers and judges than there were in 1972.[16] The opposite was true just 8 short years earlier.[15][16]

As far as Black men beating out Black women for opportunities for blue-collar jobs goes, they weren't winning much of a prize for participating in that type of competition. The jobs that Black men had were the most dangerous and grueling.[15] They were given those jobs because they were Black and they got the lowest pay despite doing the most dangerous work.[15] Are you saying Dr. Crenshaw that you want Black women to endure this type of discrimination, too, just to be equal to (Black) men and bring home a paycheck? Also, why are you blaming Black men for a situation that White men created?

There is a counterargument to Intersectionality called Social Dominance Theory (SDT)[15] that says societies are based on hierarchies of groups with one group being more dominant over the others. It was developed in 1992 by Jim Sidanius, Erik Devereaux, and Felicia Pratto.[17] Unlike Intersectionality, which is qualitative, speculative, and dogmatic, Social Dominance Theory is quantitative and empirical in its approach to collecting and analyzing data on discrimination. SD theorists let the data drive their conclusions rather than having predetermined conclusions and then, cherry-picking data that supports those conclusions. "For data collection and validation of predictions, the social dominance orientation (SDO) scale was composed to measure acceptance of and desire for group-based social hierarchy, which was assessed through two factors: support for group-based dominance and generalized opposition to equality, regardless of the ingroup's position in the power structure."[17]

While Intersectionality posits that females are automatically at the bottom of any society solely because they are female, Social Dominance Theory says that it is outgroup males who are actually at the bottom of society because they pose the greatest threat to ingroup males, their women, their children, their wealth, their society, and their way of life. Any objective and fair-minded person with half a brain knows this is true based on the despicably cruel way Black men and boys are treated in this society and the vast libraries of evidence that prove it. Because intersectionalists assume that anyone who is not a (White) heterosexual male is automatically at a disadvantage, any person belonging to two supposed outgroups has double the disadvantage such as a White lesbian. She's a woman and she's gay. A Black lesbian would have triple the disadvantages that a straight White male would because she's Black, a woman, and gay. The more disadvantaged identities intersect in a single person the worse off that person is. In the world of intersectionalists, a White trans female like Caitlyn Jenner is at a greater disadvantage than a Black heterosexual male simply because that heterosexual Black male's only disadvantage is being Black. Caitlyn, on the other hand, has more disadvantages due to being female and trans despite having spent over 60 years as a heterosexual White male and most of adulthood as a rich and famous White man.

Intersectionality also does not take into consideration the role that family plays in a woman's status. White women are reared by; related to; and married to White men. Their destinies are inextricably linked. When a White woman marries a White man, she benefits from that man's protection and provision. She bears his children and thus, is forever linked to him emotionally, financially, and biologically. When her husband, father, uncle, or brother dies, she stands to inherit his wealth. So, while she may have been subordinate to him as a woman, she's superordinate, or superior to all others in a White Supremacist society. Black feminists love to imagine they have a sisterhood with White women while White women are in complete solidarity with White men. They seem to have forgotten that Emmett Till, Mamie Till's 14-year-old son, was kidnapped, tortured, mutilated, and killed because a White woman told two White men to do that. However, we should never forget that almost all of the lynchings that took place were based on the pretext of "defending" White womanhood. To this day, almost all of the false rape claims made against Black men and boys are made by White women and girls. Lastly, almost 40% of all slaveholders were White women.[18]

Intersectionality doesn't take into account the mass incarceration of Black men that began during the 1970s and 1980s. In 2010, the Black male incarceration rate was 5,546 per 100,000 or 5.5% of the Black male population in the US according to the Bureau of Justice Statistics.[15] White males were incarcerated at a rate of 919 per 100,000 or 0.92%.[15] The Black female incarceration rate was 332 per 100,000 or 0.33%.[15] White females were incarcerated at a rate of 129 per 100,000 or 0.13%.[15] When you compare the incarceration rate of Black men to White men it's almost 6 times as high. When you compare the incarceration rate of Black women to White women it's 2.5 times as high. But, when you compare the incarceration rate of Black men to Black women's, it's over 17 times as high! I know Black men aren't committing 17 times as many crimes as Black women, but we're going to jail 17 times as much. I also know we aren't committing 42 times the number of crimes that White women commit and 6 times as many as White men considering that we only make up 6% of the US population while Whites make up 60% of this country's people. No, Black men aren't committing most of the crimes in this country. We are just targeted for destruction by this country's White elite and other racists. Why don't intersectionalists get that?

Feminists love to talk about the wage gap between men and women and particularly between White men and women of all races and Black men and Black women. There was a 2019 article written by Katharina Buchholz for <u>Statista</u> that talks about the Wage Gap between White men and all races of women in 2018.[15] It's been updated since to include 2020 statistics. "For every dollar white, non-Hispanic men earned in 2018," Asian women received 87 cents, women overall received 82 cents, Black women received 61 cents, Native American women received 58 cents, and Latina women received 55 cents.[19] The updated article didn't include White, non-Hispanic women, but the 2018 article reported that they received 77 cents out of every dollar a White, non-Hispanic man received.[15][19] In 2020, the New York Times published a story that showed data that Black men earned 67 cents out of every dollar that a White man made, or 6 cents more than Black women.[15][20] But, that same article showed that once you included the extremely large numbers of unemployed and incarcerated Black men the amount that Black men actually earned was 51 cents for every dollar a White man made which is exactly what they made in 1950.[15][20] Black men are at the bottom of society. Being male doesn't make you privileged if you're Black. Intersectionalists and so-called Black feminists like Kimberle' Williams Crenshaw don't want to talk about that. But, they do want to gripe about "My Brother's Keeper."

Intersectionalists talk a lot about Black women suffering abuse at the hands of Black men, who are just these brutes, but they never mention how bidirectional intimate partner violence is in the Black Community. Black women attack and kill Black men as much as Black men attack and kill Black women. They also never provide statistics to support their claims. They rely only on anecdotes, or people's stories. Tragically, they play on the same racist stereotypes and tropes about Black men being hyperaggressive, hypersexual brutes that D.W. Griffith did when making his film The Birth of a Nation over a century ago. But, instead of White women demanding that we be lynched, it's Black women doing it. Brittney Cooper aka Professor Crunk implied during an interview that it was okay for White people "to lynch" a guilty Black man after Bill Cosby's indecent assault conviction was overturned.[21]

Often, it's an unabused Black woman threatening to call 911 to keep her man in check or calling the police on an innocent Black man knowing full well that when they arrive they will shoot him first and ask questions later if ever. It appears that these Black gynocrats want the police to do their dirty work for them. The number of homicides among Blacks that were the result of intimate partner violence went "from a high of 1,529 in 1976 to 475 in 2005, for a total decline of 69%"[22] So, domestic violence is not rampant among Black people despite its sensualized depictions in news stories, TV shows, and movies and what Black feminists would have us believe. During this same period, "intimate partner homicides declined by 83% for Black men vs. 55% for Black women."[22] Also, domestic violence amongst Blacks is much more bidirectional, meaning both the woman and the man are fighting each other rather than one party being the aggressor and the other party being the passive victim, than is the case for non-Blacks.[15][22] According to a 2012 study, 61.8% of Blacks who were involved in a domestic dispute reported that both the female and the male were hitting each other as opposed to 50.9% of Whites and 49% of Hispanics.[23] That same study also showed that both Black and White women were almost twice as likely as Hispanic women to be the aggressor in the fight.[23] Why aren't intersectionalists lecturing and shaming these female abusers as much as they lecture and shame all men, abusive or not?

Intersectionality Today

Today's version of intersectional feminism seeks to include everybody as an oppressed class except for Black and White heterosexual males. Paradoxically, a legal concept that was supposed to help Black women combat discrimination is being used to silence, vilify, and destroy Black men. Adherents to Intersectionality, including Ms. Crenshaw, seem to view Black men as partners with White men in White Patriarchy. A strangely ahistorical and inaccurate view since Black men are the primary targets for destruction by White Patriarchs.

Originally designed to look at the roles that both race and gender play in the lives of Black women, Intersectionality metastasized during the Age of Obama to include LGBT+, immigrants, refugees, undocumented workers, Latinos, Muslims, Jews, and any combination of the aforementioned groups. Since talking about anti-Black racism has become passe' among White liberals and Democrats, talking about homophobia, transphobia, xenophobia, and Islamophobia has become all the rage. All of sudden "gay became the new Black." Latino was the new the Black."

33

Everybody was "Black" except Black people. It was like somehow we had arrived because a Black man was President. Blacks ain't never stopped being Black! If anything, we're Blacker, or more downtrodden than ever before.

It was also during this period that Blacks got tarred and feathered by "our friends" the Democrats as being more homophobic and transphobic than everyone else. On November 4, 2008, the same night that Obama was elected President, Proposition 8, an anti-gay marriage initiative passed in California. It was supported by every racial and ethnic group in the state, but somehow only Blacks got blamed for it. The retaliation by the mostly White LGBT+ community was swift and relentless. On MSNBC and other so-called liberal outlets, people of all shades labeled Blacks as homophobic. Black commentators would often apologize profusely on TV because of alleged homophobia "in the Black Community." The Black Church was painted as a hotbed of hypocrisy and hatred while homophobes in White churches were given a pass. Last time I checked, there were no Black pastors or church members holding picket signs at funerals to condemn people to hell who had died of AIDS or who died in combat while being gay.

The Black people who seem to get the most glowing attention from the media these days are those celebrities, pundits, activists, and journalists who are either gay males or trans females. The so-called liberal media even lied and reported that trans females were being targeted and hunted down by heterosexual Black males as if there was this anti-gay, anti-trans Klan of Black men running around in our neighborhoods. Black Lives Matter (BLM,) an organization that came to prominence off the backs of dead Black men and boys murdered by racists, spends most of its money and time on Black trans causes while spending the rest of its money on buying its founders luxury homes.

Black women have largely been forgotten about in intersectional discussions and analyses except to be placed in opposition to Black men. The most damaging or shall I say the most damning legacy of

Kimberle' Crenshaw's Theory of Intersectionality has been the Gender War raging between Black Men and Women in the United States. This conflict has sadly spread well beyond America's borders to include the UK, the Caribbean, and Africa thanks to the Internet.

Blacks are the least likely to get married and have a stable nuclear family than any other group in the United States. Once divorced, Blacks are more likely to stay divorced than people in other groups. Black men and women are the least desired partners by all groups including by other Blacks according to multiple surveys by dating apps and they are the least likely to date or marry interracially.[24][25] Despite this, there are groups of Black men and women who seek to date and marry interracially exclusively. Among the men, they're called Swirlers. Among the women, there's something called the Divestment Movement as in Black women who seek to divest from Black men. So, while nobody else wants us, we're doing everything in our power to keep ourselves apart. Hopefully, someday soon, we'll realize we're all we got.

Intersectionalists bear much of the responsibility for this situation because they have spent decades adding fuel to the fire by placing almost all of the blame for Black women's plight in America on the shoulders of Black men. Articles like The Root's "Straight Black Men Are the White People of Black People" and Jemele Hill's retweet of the same article have fanned the flames of this conflict. Supposedly, heterosexual Black men have all this power and privilege despite belonging to the demographic that's the least educated, the least employed, and the most likely to be homeless, mentally ill, incarcerated, or die from murder in this country. Turn on MSNBC, CNN, FOX, your local news or read the New York Times, Washington Post, Time, Newsweek, the Atlantic, or your local newspaper and you'll see a steady stream of stories about how (straight) Black men are losers.

The mainstream media aren't the only purveyors of this propaganda. Both, Black-targeted and Black-owned media like

Essence, Ebony, Black Enterprise, The Root, theGrio, Blavity, the Shade Room, OWN, and BET are just as guilty of pushing this same nonsense. These media outlets tell Black women and girls daily that Black men and boys are albatrosses around their necks. "You don't need them; get rid of them!" That's why so many Black women and girls always lead off with "I'm strong and independent" when they meet a new guy or introduce themselves to someone new no matter the situation. Millions of young Black women and girls have never heard of Kimberle' Crenshaw, bell hooks, Toni Morrison, Alice Walker, or Britney Cooper, but they do fear and loathe Black men and boys because of the work these women have done in collaboration with White racists in academia, media, entertainment, business, philanthropy, and politics.

As an educator, I've seen how this toxic femininity has become an impediment to our children's education. Because so many of my students come from single, female-headed households, they are not used to having an adult male around. They are not used to having men stick around long enough to develop a relationship with them. They balk at male authority as a result. A parent once told me that her daughter doesn't do well with male authority, including her own father's. She told me that she'd rather have her daughter taught by a woman than a man. Now, this is the same woman who also told me her daughter is smart she just doesn't know how to read. Part of the reason that she doesn't know how to read is because she doesn't have any structure or discipline at home. Her mother moves a lot and her children have frequently changed schools during the year. She needs positive role models – male as well as female. This child would benefit from some moral guidance even if it came from her teacher – her male teacher.

A multitude of books, plays, TV shows, and movies have emerged over the last 50 years that demonize Black men while lionizing Black women like For Colored Girls Who Considered Suicide When the Rainbow Wasn't Enough, Beloved, I Know Why the Caged Bird Sings, The Color Purple, The Oprah Winfrey Show, The Women of Brewster Place, Waiting to Exhale, Precious, For

Colored Girls, Greenleaf, Queen Sugar, and Self-Made. It's not lost on me that the majority of the aforementioned works are associated with Oprah Winfrey.

Thanks to what I call "Stripper Rap," THOT culture has invaded Hip-Hop and Dance with Meagan the Stallion, Cardi B, and City Girls being the most popular rappers, and twerking, a dance originating in Black strip clubs, being the most popular dance. Many Black women twerk everywhere no matter how inappropriate. You got Lizzo telling a White audience that it started in Africa and the President of BLM, Patrisse Cullors, leading a twerk off in the street as an act of Black feminist protest and sexual liberation. I guess twerking in public is the new slut walk or akin to feminists baring their breasts. Being a stripper, a prostitute, a gold digger, or a whore is no longer shameful. It's an aspiration for many young women these days. These girls aren't just selling themselves on the street; dancing in a strip club; taking calls through an escort service; working out of a brothel; nude modeling; or acting for a porn company. They are going completely and totally "renegade" by setting up "Only Fans" accounts and doing "private" shows there and elsewhere online; looking for sugar daddies on sites like "Seeking Arrangements," "Sugar Babies;" and "Ashley Madison." Prostituting themselves either part-time or full-time on dating apps like Facebook Dating, Tinder, BLK (BLACK,) Plenty of Fish (POF,) and other social media apps like WhatsApp, Instagram, or Snap Chat. Backpage, Craigslist, and Skip the Games will soon be put out of business by these apps if they haven't already been by law enforcement. YouTube and TikTok are also venues for racy videos. Even if they are not online, these women don't mind "doing something strange for a little change" every now, and then, to supplement their incomes and to add excitement to their lives.

Black women were told by liberal racists and their Black pawns that they had become the "Backbone of the Democratic Party" after Democrat Doug Jones became a US Senator from Alabama in 2017. He got 92% of the Black male vote and 97% of the Black female vote. It was his securing of 95% of the Black vote that got him over the top. But, somehow it was Black women alone who got him elected and it was Black women, independent of Black men, who won the Democrats the House in 2018 and the Presidency and both Houses of Congress in 2020 despite Black men voting 87% for Biden-Harris second only to Black women who voted 92% for the same ticket. (Latinas trailed far behind Black men at 3rd in their support for Biden at 65%.) The Democrats have convinced Black women that they did this all by themselves. Many of them ran for office and lost in the last two years naively believing the Party would have their back. The Democrats have already pivoted away from Black voters and Black candidates favoring those who are Latino, Asian, LGBT+, Native American, refugees, or immigrants over African Americans. Last December, New York City passed an ordinance to give over 800,000 non-citizens the right to vote which Democrats hope will soon displace the plurality that Black voters currently have in that city.

Even financial institutions are getting in on the divide and conquer act. Major companies like Google, Chase Bank, VISA, and MasterCard announced in 2021 that they were offering billions in loans and grants to Black female-owned businesses. 600 Black women in Georgia are going to be getting $850/month for 2 years starting in 2022.[26] Microlender Kiva announced over a decade ago that it would only give loans to African women because executives there believed African men, simply because they are men, would misuse the funds while the women were supposedly more trustworthy. Supposedly, these women would only use the money for their small businesses and farms and not for their self-aggrandizement.

Now, some might argue that Kimberle' Williams Crenshaw is not responsible for how people interpret and misappropriate her theory. I have to disagree. While it's true that she can't control how people think, act, or react, she does have clout. She does have influence and she can influence the direction that the

Intersectionalist Movement goes by using her voice and using her platform wherever she is – at the University, at a convention, during a speech, in her books, during interviews, and online to tell people what Intersectionality is and what it is NOT. She's failed to do that and therefore, as a leader, she's been derelict in her duty.

Her Role Today

While Kimberle' Williams Crenshaw is not the most visible or strident voice for Intersectionalism today, she doesn't criticize or critique it, either. She seems to have no problem with the anti-Black misandrist ideology that it's become. She, herself, pushes the lie being told over and over again, on social media and elsewhere that Black female victims of police brutality and racist violence are ignored while Black male victims hog all the publicity. Could it be that the overwhelming majority of victims of police brutality and racist violence are Black men and that's why you hear more about them? They'll be 200 cases of Blacks being killed by the police in one year. Five of them will be female and 195 will be male and we're not supposed to talk about the males? Only five of these cases will even make the national news, but we're not supposed to talk about the demographic that's most affected by racist police and vigilantes? Get out of here!

It's more likely that coverage of such cases is more of a function of numbers than a function of gender bias. There are simply many more male victims than there are female ones. So, many that they can't or won't all get national coverage. Ironically, she doesn't mention Sandra Bland or Renisha McBride, who before Breonna Taylor were the most famous Black female victims of racist violence in recent history. Ms. Bland, a recent graduate of Prairie View A&M University, was falsely arrested by a White Hispanic state trooper and died in her jail cell in Waller County, Texas in 2015. Ms. McBride, a young Detroit woman involved in an accident, was killed by a White man named Ted Wafer, who said he came to the door "filled with piss and vinegar," in 2013 for the crime of knocking on his door asking for help. How could she forget about them when both of their cases were all over the news? She didn't forget. She deliberately excluded them from the conversation because talking about them would poke holes in her story about nobody caring about Black female victims of police brutality.[11][27]

Dr. Crenshaw claimed during a speech at the Women of the World conference in 2016 that Black men have a monopoly on leadership within the Black Community.[28] Perhaps, she was referring to Dr. King and other civil rights leaders of the 1950s and 60s and to the fact that the majority of Black preachers are male. But, today there are thousands of Black women who are preachers, pastors, and bishops. Black Lives Matter, the organization, was founded and led by three women, and Tamika Mallory, Barbara Arnwine, and Sherilyn Ifill are all prominent civil rights leaders. To those female activists from the Sixties like Ella Baker who complained about Black male leaders hogging all the spotlight while they were relegated to secretarial work, my response is Dr. King, Malcolm X, Medgar Evers, and many, many, many other Brothers were all assassinated before they were 40 while Ms. Baker and many of her fellow female activists lived to be 83 and beyond. Now, I'll ask Ms. Crenshaw and all the other "nattering, nabobs of negativity" who have a problem with Black male leadership, would they trade places with these bold, Black Brothers?

She even had a problem with the milquetoast "My Brother's Keeper" program to help teenage boys who had fallen through the cracks.[28] But, it wasn't because it was more of a photo-op than it was a real program or that it came out at the tail end of Obama's Presidency. No, she was mad because it didn't include Black and Brown girls. She ignores the fact that girls of every race do better in school than boys and that the classroom is a much more inviting and stimulating environment for girls than it is for boys. Women have been graduating from high schools, colleges, and professional schools at much higher rates than men for decades since the passage of the 1964 Civil Rights Act. Title 9 of that Act ensures that women, all women, have equal access to a quality education.

But, somehow because the President's program didn't target the few girls who have fallen through the cracks it was an awful thing and an example of patriarchy. If you'd ask her, she'd probably tell you that Obama ought to be ashamed of himself.

Her fake outrage over "My Brother's Keeper" reminds me of the outrage and apprehension that many Black women expressed in 1995 over the Million Man March. Black women were telling their men not to go and breaking up with them if they did. For all their talk about men needing to respect the sanctity of women's spaces and the plethora of "Sister Spaces" that have cropped up online and off since the Nineties, it seems rather hypocritical to me for women, particularly Black women, to object to Brothers having a powwow and developing fellowship and communion with one another. Since men, especially Black men, spend so much time worrying about what women want, think, and feel, no woman should be objecting to Men Going Their Own Way every now and then.

She makes false equivalencies between individual acts of machismo and sexism on the part of Black males with White American Patriarchy which is systematic in its combination of racism, sexism, classism, and homophobia. There is no such parallel system on the part of Black men anywhere in the world let alone in the United States. Patriarchy is a system created by wealthy men to govern everyone not just women and children. Not only is it a legal and economic system like racism and White Supremacy are, but it governs descent and inheritance. It determines who gets a nation's economic and social benefits and who does not. It determines who rules and who is ruled. Even poor and middle-class White men are at a disadvantage within White American Patriarchy. Wealthy White men control everything. In this system, they are, in effect, everyone's "Daddy." The fabulously wealthy men who rebelled against the British Crown to form a new nation are called the "Founding Fathers" for a reason. We all have to do what they say to do even though they died a long time ago because of the Constitution they left behind. Also, there are strict constructionist judges and conservative politicians who enforce it. Liberal judges and politicians do, too. That's why when White male billionaires like the Koch Brothers, George Soros, Bill Gates, Warren Buffet, Sheldon Adelson, and Michael Bloomberg say, "Jump!" politicians reply, "How high?"

If patriarchy means "rule by the fathers," but there's a dearth of Black Fathers, where does this patriarchy of Black men exist? There's no patriarchy in Black America. If anything, there's a matriarchy or more properly described a gynocracy, or a patriarchy by women. Black women are the "men" in Black America. They are the providers. They are the heads of our households. Because Black men have been targeted for destruction in every conceivable way by this society, Black women have largely been left alone to rear the children and to take on the roles that were once reserved for men because there are no men. In many poor and working-class Black communities, there are very few productive men. They're either dead, in jail, addicted, mentally ill, or homeless.

In addition to that, Black women have been elevated to a very junior partnership within the White Establishment through education, work, welfare, and the criminal justice system. This was done by racist politicians to cause further divisions between Black men and women and to destroy the Black Family. Black women and girls are more likely to be praised and promoted in school; they are more likely to be hired than Black men and boys are; they can't receive welfare if they're married or live with their boyfriends; and they are less likely to receive jail time even for serious offenses than men are. So, while they exist near the bottom of society, Black women still rank higher than Black men on the totem pole. As a result, Black women learn at a very early age to have contempt for Black men. This is why so many Black women are so comfortable with saying, "All Niggas ain't shit!"

I've heard and read comments from Black women that I know and many more that I don't know where they have said they didn't "feel protected." Protected by whom? From whom? If the answer to the first question is by Black men and the answer to the second question is from White men, other men, and society at large, then why are you against Black Male Patriarchy? Why are you against Black men taking charge and being in charge? That's what other men do on behalf of their women and children. But, somehow it's wrong for Black men to do? Seems like Black women like Kimberle' Crenshaw want to have it both ways. They don't want to be controlled by or answerable to Black men, but they still want Black men to protect them from danger and to shield them from the consequences of their actions. If you want a man to protect you, then you have to respect his competence and authority and follow his lead.

Curiously, these same Black feminists have no such qualms about submitting to White male authority. Is it because they are self-haters who believe that the White Man's ice is colder; do they fear the consequences of disobeying White Daddy; do they simply loathe Black men; or could it be all three? I pointed this out once to a Black woman I had a conversation with and I used White male teachers, bosses, and policemen as examples. She replied that those men have "expertise," and that's why she respects them and submits to their authority. They had "earned her respect" and it wasn't just because they were White men. I'm not buying it! If that were the case, then she wouldn't submit to the authority of unfair teachers, less experienced bosses, or rude or racist cops. She submits to those men, however, because she knows she will suffer the consequences if she doesn't.

The 2016 Women of the World conference where Dr. Crenshaw gave the keynote address was sponsored by Bloomberg which is owned by Michael Bloomberg. This is the same Michael R. Bloomberg who's worth over $60 billion; who when he was the Mayor of New York terrorized its Black and Brown residents with his "Stop and Frisk" policing; and who bought off almost every Black Democratic politician including Stacey Abrams by spending over $500 million during his very brief and thankfully unsuccessful presidential run. For all their talk about the evils of patriarchy, the Women of the World didn't have any problem asking for money from their Big White Daddy. So, it seems like the only men they have a problem following are Black men.

Score

<u>Leadership</u> Kimberle' Crenshaw has accomplished much in her life. She graduated from Harvard Law School. She's a tenured law professor at not one, but at two very prestigious universities. She's written numerous articles and books and has won many awards including Professor of the Year twice at UCLA Law School. She was dubbed the #1 Feminist by <u>Ms. Magazine</u> in 2015.[9] She is the author of the most popular feminist theory today, Intersectionality. Millions of people have been influenced by her, whether they have heard of her or not. But, Black America doesn't need another celebrity academic producing crackpot theories so she can become rich and famous. It's a shame that this legal eagle hasn't used some of her brilliance to fight against police brutality, racial discrimination, wage theft, or for fair housing, a living wage, Affirmative Action, or dare I say it – Reparations. Kimberle' Crenshaw, the feminist icon and heroine, turns out to be just another selfish careerist. She gets a 2.5 in the area of Leadership.

<u>Race Pride</u> By all outward appearances, it would seem that Dr. Crenshaw is a Race Woman. She wears dreadlocks and African garb. She's a Black feminist and Critical Race theorist. She's the head of the African American Policy Forum so she must be fighting for Black people, right? Not quite. Her organization focuses primarily on milquetoast issues like "gender and diversity"[9] That, in and of itself, is not a crime. Her real crime was her decision to seek solidarity with Satan – to make a deal with the Devil – when she first formulated her Theory of Intersectionality. She found common cause with racists like Katherine McKinnon, who promoted lies that Black men rape Black women to establish dominance over them. A Black woman who loves Black people wouldn't publish such dreck let alone find kinship with racists. She claimed during an interview that her parents were active in the

Civil Rights Movement and that she came from a family of "Race Men and Race Women" who actively spoke about politics, racism, and sexism while at the dinner table.[27] I find it hard to believe that a person who grew up in such a conscientious family would not know such thinking is wrong. She gets a 1.5 for Race Pride.

Role Model As far I know, Dr. Crenshaw has lived an exemplary life morally. She reminds me of the scores of Black educators that I came across in my life. I actually like her. But, I don't like how she pushes ideas that she knows to be false to get whatever professional accolades she can. I can't stand careerists! Other Black scholars, both young and old, see what she does and they emulate it. She gets a 2.0 as Role Model.

Impact on the Race What has been the impact of Intersectionality on the Black Race? Further division and enmity among the sexes and even among the sexual orientations. Black male-female relations are all-time low thanks in large part to Intersectionality and the media and pop culture icons who promote it. Black women live in a state of perpetual fear and loathing of Black men because they've been taught by feminists like Kimberle' Williams Crenshaw that we have created a culture of rape and abuse to compensate for not being real men.

And what about Black women? What have they gained from Intersectionality? Did Ms. DeGraffenreid get her job back? Besides Anita Hill, what other Black woman, who has alleged sexual harassment or racial discrimination, has she represented? Has the workplace improved for Black women since the advent of Intersectionalism? I would say, "No." Seems like only one Black woman has been helped by Intersectionality and that woman is Kimberle' Williams Crenshaw. She gets a 1.5 for her Impact on the Race.

Final Score Her overall score is a 1.5. $(2.5 + 1.5 + 2.0 + 1.5)/5 = 7.5/5 = 1.5$)

Richard Pryor

Early Life

Richard Franklin Lennox Thomas Pryor[29] was born on December 1, 1940, in Peoria, Illinois to a mom who was a prostitute and a dad who was a pimp. Both of his parents worked for his paternal grandmother who was a madam of a whorehouse. His being exposed to the sex trade by his family could explain why he was abused as child and why he experimented sexually with men as well as women as an adult.[29] People from all types of life, including politicians, frequented his grandmother's establishment.[30] His grandmother's affluence allowed young Richard to attend private school.[30] The school eventually kicked him out because of his family's underworld ties.[30] He began working at "a packing house," or a fruit packaging and distribution center, shortly, thereafter.[30] He spent two years in the army before being discharged.[29]

Early Career

After leaving the Service in 1960, Pryor began doing standup comedy at nightclubs across the Midwest and Northeast until he wound up in New York. He was the opening act for singer Nina Simone.[29] He became a master of timing, improvisation, and story-telling by working the nightclub circuit. Although he was influenced by White comic Lenny Bruce, it was Bill Cosby who had the single greatest influence on Richard's early comedic style. Cosby was the first Black comic to crossover to White audiences and Pryor coveted Bill's success. As the decade rolled by, he frequently appeared on late-night talk shows and performed at Las Vegas casinos.[29][30] Tired of the bland brand of comedy he had been doing since the early Sixties, Pryor left Las Vegas for Berkeley, California, and immersed himself in the counterculture of sex, drugs, and rock n' roll that emerged towards the end of the decade.[29] He began performing blue comedy, or the variety that is raunchy and filled with profanity. In 1968, he released the self-titled album, Richard Pryor, which featured cursing and the use of the racial slur, Nigger.[29]

Stardom

By the 1970s, Richard Pryor had become a star. He appeared in films and on television shows. He had become a screenwriter for popular shows like Sanford and Son.[29] He released numerous comedy albums including the seminal hit, That Nigger's Crazy in 1974 and Bicentennial Nigger in 1976[29] marking the 200th anniversary of the founding of the United States with a blistering critique of the country's race relations. Pryor also starred in numerous movies including Silver Streak, Car Wash, Which Way Is Up?, Greased Lightning, and Blue Collar. In 1975, he became the first Black person to host Saturday Night Live[29] paving the way for numerous Black comics to either host and/or star on the popular sketch comedy show and go on to be stars like Eddie Murphy, Chris Rock, Tim Meadows, Michael Che', Tracy Morgan, Keenan Thompson, Leslie Jones, and Dave Chappelle.

Going on into the Eighties, Pryor's success continued. He was a household name and even appeared in kids' shows like Sesame Street and movies like The Muppet Movie.[29] He starred in fifteen movies[29] including Stir Crazy, Bustin' Loose, Some Kind of Hero, Richard Pryor: Live on Sunset Strip, The Toy, Superman III, Brewster's Millions, Jo Jo Dancer: Your Life Is Calling, and Harlem Nights. Although his health and fame had declined by the Nineties, he was seen as a revered figure and an elder statesman of the entertainment world. In 1995, he wrote his autobiography Pryor Convictions and Other Life Sentences. He was awarded the first-ever Mark Twain Prize for American Humor by the Kennedy Center in 1998.[29]

His Popularization of the N-Word

During Slavery and Segregation, the word nigger was used as a derogatory term by Whites to demean and dehumanize Blacks. Because many Blacks have internalized racism and developed self-hatred as a result, they also use this awful term to **denigrate** themselves and other Black people. But, in a strange act of "rebellion," they also have embraced it as a term of endearment for their fellow Blacks. Some have argued it's a term of empowerment. Perhaps, this was a defense mechanism used to take some of the sting out of the word. "Yeah, I may be a nigger, but I'm going to be a proud nigger!" or so the thought goes. This might be why Eazy-E, Ice Cube, Dr. Dre, MC Ren, and DJ Yella decided to call themselves NWA, or Niggas Wit Attitude. "If you're gonna be a nigga, you might as well be a kick-ass nigga. A Nigger With an Attitude!" It perversely makes sense.

During and after the Civil Rights and Black Power movements of the 1950s, 60s, and 70s, it became unpopular for both Blacks and Whites to use the terms nigger, nigra, negro, or colored. Negroes, as they were previously called in the 1950s and 1960s, were now calling themselves Black and by the late 70s, Afro-American, in honor of their African ancestry. For a very brief period, the word was banned from the American lexicon. Whites were very careful to avoid using it in the presence of Blacks or else there was the risk of a serious confrontation that could lead to serious bodily injury or death at the hands of a Black person who was either called it or overheard it. Blacks also reduced their use of this odious epithet among themselves and those who did use it strenuously avoided using it in mixed company. Richard Pryor changed all that. When he decided to say that word over and over, again, while entertaining mixed audiences, he made it acceptable for everybody to say it, again. He made the most hateful word in the English language something that everyone could laugh at, again. But, unbeknownst to him and the other "niggers" in the audience, everyone else was laughing at them, not with them.

Richard Pryor is responsible for the ubiquitousness and popular usage of the word Nigger today, especially among youths regardless of their race. Turn on your radio, TV, or computer and you'll see it and hear it. Go anywhere in the public (e.g., a bus, a train, a school, a restaurant, or a mall) and you'll not only hear it from the mouths of uncouth Black youth and adults, but you'll hear it being said by teens and adults of every race, color, and creed. You'll hear it in the rap song blasting from the speakers of the car passing by. Even at the White House, it's being said and I'm not talking about in Trump's White House, but in the Obama White House. At the 2016 White House Correspondents Dinner, comedian Larry Wilmore concluded his speech by telling the outgoing President, "We did it, my nigga!" to the uproarious laughter of the mostly White crowd. And that wasn't the only time the President was publicly referred to as a nigger. When he ran for re-election in 2012, I watched a news story about a White woman in California who printed out anti-Obama bumper stickers that said, "Don't Re-Nig!" Thanks to Richard Pryor there's no safe place where the words nigger, nigga, nicka, nikka, nukka, ninja, or some other version can't invade. Almost every rapper or comedian, especially the Black ones, uses it in his/her performance. All of them were influenced by Pryor. All of them!

It was only after watching two movies about White teens that I realized how universally accepted this word was. Watching the 1995 movie, Kids was the first time that I heard White kids call themselves nigger. In a scene towards the end of the movie, a White male youth boasted, "I'll fuck up a nigga anywhere!" It sounded like a verse in a rap song. While watching the 2004 movie Mean Girls I saw a Vietnamese girl tell another Vietnamese girl "Nigga, please!" in Vietnamese during a school assembly. Watching both scenes was shocking. Black kids say it so much that they call any and everybody a nigga regardless of their race, especially if they're angry. I think of the 2020 viral video of a Black female McDonald's employee fighting a White customer who assaulted her. Every other word she said as she was hitting him was "nigga."

Many Blacks have dubbed non-Black people that they consider cool or view as having a similar bottom caste status as Blacks in America as "honorary niggas." These Blacks have no qualms about these "honorary niggas" using the word in their presence; calling themselves and other non-Blacks niggas; or even calling another Black person a nigga. In December of 2021, I went out for dinner one evening and these young Latino men were sitting in the booth behind me saying, "nigga this and nigga that" like they were Black. It was almost every other word. Earlier in the month, I overheard a Latino man call his son a nigga. He tried to clean it up after he saw me pass by, by calling the boy, a ninja. But, the cat was out of the bag. I now know that he uses the word and I have since heard him say it on another occasion. I wouldn't be surprised if he calls me or other Black people niggers, too. That's the irony of it all. Non-Blacks still reserve the right to use the word in the way that it was originally used. Being called a nigger is the worst insult someone can give you and they know it.

Now, if Pryor were alive today, he would say that he was just telling a story and that's the type of language that the characters in his stories used. That's what he saw and heard growing up and that he was being "authentic" or "keeping it real" in today's vernacular. But, as comedian Dave Chappelle once pointed out during one of his sketches, "keeping it real" can also go very wrong. Black artists, entertainers, and individuals, in general, have been "keeping it real" with their use of the word nigger for so long that it's become socially acceptable for everyone to use it whenever and wherever. Since there's no longer a check on our impulse to use this awful word, our "lips are like an oo-wop (a gun) as (we) start to spray it."[31]

Artists and entertainers, especially if they're Black, have a responsibility to be socially conscious with their work. They have a duty to portray themselves and other Black people in the best possible light. While I love Richard Pryor, I have to admit that he was being very irresponsible when he decided to say the word nigger during his performances. The use of that word became more popular as he became more popular. Soon, other Black comedians began to imitate him in order to become successful. It became okay for actors, athletes, rappers, and singers to use it in their artwork, performances, and workplaces. Then, it became okay for ordinary people to use in their daily discourse. Nigger is just another word until it isn't.

While Nigger's usage has expanded exponentially in our vernacular, other words used to demean other people because of their race, ethnicity, religion, or sexual orientation have greatly diminished or altogether disappeared from it. For instance, the word Honky, which is a slur used against Whites, is never even said today not even when talking about it in a historical sense. Words like redneck, hick, hayseed, and Bubba serve as sanitized substitutes. I doubt many Black youth or young adults have ever heard the word let alone have used it. Older Blacks, who grew up during the horrors of Segregation, have long since refrained from using it. During the 1970s, it was often used as a punchline along with nigger in popular sitcoms such as The Jeffersons, All In The Family, Good Times, and Sanford and Son. Yet, Nigger not only persists, it flourishes. Even the relatively harmless words like honky dory or honky tonk have been banished from everyday speech. And don't you dare say the F-Word when referring to a gay man. The punishment will be swift and severe as it should be. There's no such backlash when a racist says, "Nigger," however. Now, I'm not advocating that we go back to a time when it was okay to use offensive language against other groups, but can Nigger go into the dustbin of history just like those other words? This oversaturation of the public discourse by the word Nigger is sadly as much the legacy of Richard Pryor as anything else.

Score

Leadership Richard Pryor is the undisputed King of Comedy. There's no greater comedic actor before or since. He is the standard by which all comics are judged. He was a superstar. He was a risk-taker. He didn't play it safe. Through his sharp wit and incredible storytelling ability, he was able to show the good, the bad, and the ugly sides of Black Life in America. He humanized poor and working-class Black people. He was a fierce critic of American Racism. He was a businessman who owned commercial real estate and founded his own production company. [29][32] Lastly, he was introspective and willing to humble himself and change. After visiting Africa, he "vowed never to say (Nigger,) again."[33] He gets a 3.0 for his Leadership.

Race Pride Race pride is a mixed bag for Richard Pryor. He was a proud Black man who didn't take any shit off anybody. But, on the other hand, he "was a whore" by his own admission. If the money was right, he was willing, at times, to compromise his values like he did "when he made a conscious decision to splatter his routine with the word" Nigger.[32][33] But, by in large, he portrayed all of the characters he played with dignity. When he played the first Black NASCAR driver Wendell Scott in the film Greased Lightning, it was one of several roles where he demonstrated that he was a Race Man, or someone who upholds his Race. Pryor earns a 2.0 for having an average amount of Race Pride.

Role Model Based on how he conducted his personal life during her early years, no one should pattern themselves after Richard Pryor. However, he was generally a good guy who made people laugh when they wanted to cry. Although his roles were largely comical, he wasn't a modern-day minstrel. He either worked with or employed other Black actors, writers, and producers. He used his fame to bring attention to racism and other societal ills. He gets a 2.5 in the Role Model department.

Impact on the Race Pryor's impact on the race was tremendous. He was part of the first group of new Black stars that emerged after

Integration in the 1970s. If it wasn't for Richard Pryor, there'd be no Eddie Murphy, Chris Rock, Will Smith, Martin Lawrence, Dave Chappelle, Steve Harvey, Bernie Mac, D.L. Hughley, Cedric the Entertainer, Mo'Nique, Sommore, Wanda Sykes, Tiffany Haddish and all the thousands of actors and comedians who have followed him since. Even Bill Cosby, Pryor's one-time role model and mentor, benefitted from there being a Richard Pryor because there was a clear contrast between their two styles which allowed different audiences to choose between the two. While Richard was more of a movie star, Bill was able to find his niche on television. I argue that there would be no Cosby Show if there had been no Richard Pryor.

Like Rudy Ray Moore's Dolemite, Richard Pryor's characters and impersonations gave Black fans a chance to see themselves, their family, friends, and neighbors and have a good hardy laugh. It was like he was holding a mirror in front of these people and showing them a reflection of their lives. Other than the boastful toasting of Jamaican Dancehall DJs and the funky soul music of James Brown, there was no bigger influence on Rap than Richard Pryor's foul-mouthed routines. Even Millennial and Generation Z comics and their audiences, who have never seen or heard of him, have been influenced by him. Pryor gets a 3.0 for his Impact on the Race.

Overall Score Richard Pryor's final score is a 2.1 or a solid C average. (3.0 + 2.5 + 2.0 + 3.0)/5 = 10.5/5 = 2.1)

Jay-Z

Background

Shawn Corey Carter also known as Jay-Z was born on December 4, 1969, in Brooklyn, New York.[34] He lived with his mother and two siblings in the Marcy Projects.[34] Because he expressed an early interest in Rap, his mom bought him a big, portable radio called "a boombox."[34] Later, he went on to high school with future rappers AZ, Busta Rhymes, and the Notorious B.I.G.[34] According to a biography written about him on AllMusic.com by Jason Birchmeier, Shawn was known on the streets as "Jazzy."[34] But, in all likelihood, he got that name from another rapper he was associated with in the late 80s known as JAZ. (In 1989, Jay-Z appeared in the other rapper's video entitled, "Hawaiian Sophie.") Later, he was associated with New York rappers like the Notorious B.I.G., DMX, Big Daddy Kane, Positive K, and Big L.[34]

Rap Career

In 1995, Jay formed Roc-A-Fella Records with Dame Dash and Kareem "Biggs" Burke.[34] It was a bootstrap operation with the trio doing all their marketing and distribution themselves. Like Too Short, an enterprising artist from Oakland, had done almost a decade earlier, they would "sell records out of da trunk." The rapper's first major studio album entitled Reasonable Doubt debuted in 1996.[34] It sold over a million records. From 1996 to 2017, Jay-Z released 13 platinum or multi-platinum albums including Reasonable Doubt, Vol. 2...Hard Knock Life, Vol. 3...The Life and Times of S. Carter, The Blueprint, The Black Album, Magna Carta Holy Grail, and 4:44.[34] In 2003, he collaborated with R&B Superstar, R. Kelly, to release The Best of Both Worlds, and in 2018, he collaborated with his wife, pop star, Beyonce' to release Everything Is Love.[34] In October 2021, he was inducted into the Rock and Roll Hall of Fame along with fellow rapper LL Cool J.

Jay-Z the Superstar

No one can argue that Jay hasn't had a successful career over the last 25 years. He's been extremely successful. He may be the most commercially successful rapper of all time. The business magazine <u>Forbes</u> has him on its billionaire's list. He's either outlived or outshined all of his mentors, peers, and rivals for the throne. But, none of that was by accident. In fact, most of it is not because of the efforts of Jay-Z alone. Corporate America and the rest of the American Establishment had a vested in seeing him rise to the top.

Jay-Z emerged as a star in the wake of the murders of Hip-Hop's greatest rappers and rivals: Tupac and Biggie. These guys were the greatest emcees of all time. Yes, there are/were rappers aka lyricists that were as just as good if not better than those two. Rappers like Rakim, Big Daddy Kane, LL Cool J, the GURU, Eazy-E, The D.O.C., Snoop Doggy Dogg, Kurupt, Nas, Busta Rhymes, Scarface, Bun B, Outkast, Big Pun, Bone Thugs & Harmony, and Twister come to mind. But, no artist before or since has had the impact on Rap music and popular culture worldwide that they did. Nobody!

I argue that Tupac is the greatest rapper of all time not because he rhymed the best. Biggie was a better rapper, or lyricist than Pac hands down. 2Pac was no slouch on the mic, however. His greatness stems from his influence over Rap and Pop culture. All the ladies loved him and all the guys, including Biggie, wanted to be a thug just like him. Pac's influence continues to this day.

So, Jay-Z, Master P, Ludacris, Cash Money, 50 Cent, Nelly, TI, Lil' Jon, Rick Ross, and several other "pretenders to the throne" benefitted because of timing. They were in the right place at the right time. There was a void in Rap, and they filled it. I can't knock them for that.

Two other reasons that accounted for Jay's emergence to the top spot were the musical tastes of fans had changed and the fans themselves had changed. Rap was largely a Black thang in the

1970s and 1980s. But, by the mid to late Nineties, rap audiences had switched from being mostly Black to being mostly White. That's still true today. Also, fans no longer demand that rappers have great and complex rhyming skills. All they care about is listening to easy-to-recite rhymes and choruses over great beats. I believe that the only reason that many fans even care about the beat is because they attend rave parties at dance clubs where they get high on ecstasy and its derivative molly along with marijuana, codeine cough syrup, PCP, embalming fluid, pills, and a whole host of other drugs. You can't really pay attention to what a rapper is saying, nor do you care if you're high. But, you will hop up on the dance floor to a funky beat. All you have to do nowadays to be a successful rapper is produce a track with a great beat. It doesn't matter to these kids if their favorite MCs were reciting "knick, knack, paddy wack" rhymes, or the kind that you would hear in a nursery rhyme. It's so bad, now, that all they do is just mumble hence the term "Mumble Rap" where they sound high and they repeat the same words with the same cadence over and over, again. Everybody just sounds the same.

The biggest reason, in my opinion, for Jay-Z becoming the most successful rapper, not the greatest, of all time is because the music industry engages in shady business practices. One is called payola. Record companies pay bribes to radio station employees to get them to play their artists' songs all day, every day to generate a buzz among fans and thus, generate record sales. It can also come in the form "of cash, trips, appliances, drugs, sex and anything of value for today's marketplace."[35] Record companies also buy thousands or even tens of thousands of their artists' records right after their release to inflate record sales and to end up higher on the <u>Billboard</u> charts. This is "why you keep hearing the same ten songs" on the radio every hour on the hour.[35] New York radio station Hot 97 was once known as "Hov 97" because it promoted Jay-Z so heavily from the mid-1990s through the early 2000s.[36] (Jay-Z is also known as Hov or Hova ((pronounced Hove, or Hove-uh.))

The more records a rapper sells the more likely rap fans will get on the bandwagon and buy a copy of his/her record. This is because in the ultra-materialistic world of Hip-Hop material success is everything and if you're ain't "stuntin'," or showing off your wealth or if the White Media's not talking about you, you ain't nothing. That's why when there was a beef between Jay-Z and Nas back in the early 2000s so many rap fans bought into the lie that Jay-Z must be a better rapper because he sold more records than Nas did. Well, of course, you're going to sell more of your own records if you're buying them.

Enter White Capital: Divide and Conquer

Jay has always been an opportunist. He's always seeking a better opportunity for himself. There's nothing wrong with that. Everybody should want to do better. The problem comes when you seek opportunities at the expense of others, especially that of your family, friends, or race. Jay-Z saw an opportunity to reach another level of fame and fortune when he was approached in 2003 by music executive Doug Morris with an offer to become Def Jam's CEO.[37] All he had to do was agree to cut his original business partners, Dame Dash and Kareem Burke, out of Roc-A-Fella Records, a business the trio had co-founded.[37]

During those secret meetings with Morris, who was the CEO of Universal Records which owned 50% of the Roc-A-Fella record label, Jay discussed not only his new role at Def Jam, but the sale of the other 50% stake in the Label that he, Dame, and "Biggs" Burke co-owned to Universal.[37] But, he didn't bother to tell Dame or Biggs that he was selling their company. Not only did he make $16.6 million from the deal, but Jay-Z also made another $30 million in salary during his three years as Def Jam's chief executive.[37] Additionally, he received complete ownership of the master tapes of all his records that were produced under Roc-A-Fella's distribution deal with Def-Jam.[37] Now, you're talking about hundreds of millions of dollars in royalties over the last 17 years that his partners Damon Dash and Kareem Burke were cheated out of. They have every right to feel robbed because they were.

Jay-Z tried to buy off his former partners the same way he had with Nas. (After Nas demolished him in the 2001 song, Ether, Jay did some major damage control by making peace with Nas by offering the Queens rapper an opportunity to perform with him during Hot 97's Summer Jam concert.) But, his ploy to mollify them failed. Neither Dame nor Biggs would sell their rights to Jay's first album Reasonable Doubt in exchange for the Roc-A-Fella name which Universal gave to him after he sold the company to it up from under his compadres.[37] (Reasonable Doubt is the only album in his catalog of music that he doesn't own outright.)[37] Damon did sell his share in the clothing line Rocawear to Jay for $22 million which the music mogul later sold for $200 million.[37] This duplicitous pattern of behavior, which he has exhibited over and over, again, will be examined in detail throughout this chapter.

Shawn Carter the Businessman

By becoming a record executive; selling Rocawear; inking a huge deal with the concert promoter, Live Nation; and forming a new record label, Roc Nation, Shawn Carter aka Jay-Z has cemented his reputation as a "businessman" in the minds of his adoring fans, especially the Black ones. I know Jay, his handlers and publicists, and the media all say he's a brilliant businessman. But, is he? I am going to examine the following four businesses to see just how good an entrepreneur and businessman he really is: 1.) Rocawear; 2.) Gold by Jay-Z cologne; 3.) Ace of Spades; and 4.) Tidal.

In 2007, rap mogul Jay-Z sold his fashion company, Rocawear, to Iconix for $204 million.[38] Turns out the Hip-Hop clothing line was severely overvalued. So much so, that Iconix sued him for misstating his firm's actual value. It seems that he finessed, or conned them into paying an exorbitant price for his company. They had to write off 99.5% of what they originally paid.[38] They also sued him for violating their licensing agreement when he allowed another clothing manufacturer to sell Roc Nation sports gear.[38] In a settlement agreement with Iconix, Mr. Carter agreed to pay $15 million for intellectual property that he had previously sold the clothier when they bought Rocawear.[38] Apparently, he hadn't dotted all the "i's" and crossed all the "t's" when he entered this deal. But, as usual, everything worked out for Hip-Hop's golden boy. "Both sides agreed to drop all claims against each other, without admitting wrongdoing or unlawful conduct." according to Forbes.[38]

Is Jay-Z a grifter, a con man, or just "a hustla" as he used to rap about? In one Jay-Z song, entitled, "I Just Wanna Love (Give it 2 Me,)" producer/songwriter Pharrell sang, "I'm a hustla, Baby!" In another song, he said, "Can't knock the hustle!" But, maybe, we should. Why does he keep getting sued by his former business partners? On Friday, October 29, 2021, Shawn Carter had to testify in court over a lawsuit brought against him by Parlux Fragrances because of a 2012 deal they struck with him to promote the Gold by Jay Z cologne which they claim that Mr. Carter did not honor.[39] Jay-Z countered that Parlux did "crappy work" because they sold his cologne in pharmacies instead of at luxury retailers.[40] I don't know who's right or who's wrong nor do I care, but I do wonder why such a "successful businessman" and "cultural leader" is often sued for breach of contract and deception. I would argue that Shawn Carter aka Jay-Z is also guilty of deception and breach of contract when it comes to his Black fans and Black people in general.

Like the other mogul named Sean, Sean "Puffy" Combs that is, Shawn Carter decided to dabble in the world of wines and spirits. For years, he'd mention Cristal champagne and Belvedere vodka in multiple songs on his albums. But, in 2006, an executive at Cristal dissed and dismissed Rap fans during an interview by saying, "What can we do? We can't forbid people from buying it. I'm sure Dom Perignon and Krug would be delighted to have their business."[41] Hov became incensed and demanded a boycott. Ironically, LVMH Moet Hennessy, the maker of the brands cited by Cristal's executive when he disparaged Rap fans who bought his swill, would buy a 50% stake in Jay-Z's champagne business 15 years later. Maybe, Jigga, as he is also called, was crying crocodile tears over being dissed and was setting his fans up to purchase his very own champagne. Inquiring minds want to know.

Later that year, Cattier, a French winemaker, introduced Armand de Brignac and began pressing cheap table grapes, you know the kind you buy at the store, into expensive champagne that Jigga sells in restaurants and nightclubs all across the country anywhere from $300-$65,000 a bottle.[41][42] Wine buyer Lyle Fass called it "the biggest rip-off in the history of wine" and a study on how "to sell wine that sucks. Because it's probably the most brilliant marketing in the history of wine."[42] So, once again, Jay-Z is out here scamming people. He nicked named his swill Ace of Spades which he sells in a gold bottle.[41][42]

While the amount of money that Mr. Carter paid Sovereign Brands in 2014 for its share of the Armand de Brignac brand remains undisclosed, Forbes estimated his original stake was worth $50 million by 2006.[42] After selling a 50% stake in the brand in 2021 to LVMH, the firm that owns luxury bagmaker Louis Vuitton as well Moet and Hennessy, his stake ballooned in value to $300 million according to Forbes.[43] I wonder if we'll be reading someday about Jay-Z being sued because LVMH has buyer's remorse over purchasing half of his champagne company. On the other hand, why is he selling such a large stake in a "successful" company and how much of a loss did he take? Maybe, it's because people aren't usually concerned about buying overpriced champagne in a gold bottle during a pandemic and a related recession. Mr. Carter probably had to offload some of that debt he and/or his company hold as well as recoup some of his losses.

Hopefully, LVMH gets "the cool clout and lifestyle marketing savvy of a pace-setting Black cultural leader at a time when the luxury sector's (i.e., Gucci, Prada, & H&M) racism is under particular scrutiny" that it paid for.[41] Jay-Z has never had a problem with White capitalists using his Black face to hide their racism and sell their plans and their products to the masses. Think about his promoting of the building of the Barclay Center as community revitalization and job opportunities for poor Black Brooklynites who were eventually displaced by the gentrification of Brooklyn on behalf of the NBA's Nets basketball team after it moved from New Jersey to New York. Think of his 2019 deal with the NFL to produce the Super Bowl's halftime show after first saying we should boycott the League in solidarity with Colin Kaepernick. Then, he had the audacity to say that his deal was "the next step" in the fight against police brutality. Negro, please!

His modus operandi is to bait and switch. He promotes "Black Capitalism" but only as a vehicle that drives him into the "loving arms" of White capitalists. He'll talk about racism and classism, but only if he can profit off the protests against them like when he created "Occupy Wall Street" t-shirts to piggyback off the "Occupy Wall Street" movement of 2010-2011. The Movement's organizers and supporters immediately saw it for what it was and instantly condemned his crass commercialism.

Thinking he could duplicate the same success that fellow Rap Mogul, Dr. Dre, had when he sold Beats By Dre to Apple for $3 billion, Shawn Carter bought the Norwegian music streaming company TIDAL in 2015 for $46 million.[44] The ever opportunistic, but incurious and unstudious Shawn thought he could easily "flip" the distressed streaming service like a real estate investor buys; "fixes up;" and quickly resells a distressed home to a wealthier sucker. But, he didn't do his homework. He didn't study. He didn't take stock and ask himself, "What do I know about the music streaming business and is it worth the risk?" After he bought the company, it became immediately apparent that he bit off more than he could chew. Tidal was a tidal wave that was going to sink his little entrepreneurial boat and cause him to drown if he didn't hurry up and find someone who could hand him a lifeline. Enter Sprint. Sprint paid $200 million to bail out the Jigga Man for a third of the company in 2017.[45] Both parties issued a vague announcement about their rationale for the deal and per usual,

Shawn made a grandiose, but vacuous statement about the impact on consumers by a deal he made. According to The Verge, Jay-Z issued a press release where he said, "Sprint shares our view of revolutionizing the creative industry to allow artists to connect directly with their fans and reach their fullest, shared potential. Marcelo understood our goal right away, and together we are excited to bring Sprint's 45 million customers an unmatched entertainment experience."

Four years later, Tidal was still taking on water and Sprint, now owned by T-Mobile, had been suffering from a bad case of buyer's remorse when it finally demanded that Jay-Z find a suitable buyer to help it offload this junk stock that it bought from him. Who did Shawn call to get him out of this tight jam? It was none other than his old buddy Jack Dorsey, CEO of Twitter and SQUARE. Mr. Carter was forced to hold a fire sale to get Sprint its money back and wound up selling "his company" for $300 million to Jack Dorsey's SQUARE for half of what it was worth in 2017 when Sprint invested $200 million into it.[44] Not only did Tidal lose half its value from 2017 to 2021, but Jay-Z also faced lawsuits from many of the artists who bought shares of his company to get it off the ground like Kanye West. Mr. West claimed that he was owed $3 million for his marketing efforts and for bringing in his targeted amount of new subscribers.[46]

For over 25 years, Shawn "Jay-Z" Carter has been a master at getting people to buy into his brand. The biggest selling point of his brand is that he's a successful businessman. But, he isn't really. None of the businesses that he's been involved in have been substantial or sustainable. He doesn't design, manufacture, or distribute his clothing line, his cologne, his alcoholic beverages, or even his music. Most of his so-called enterprises have been based on licensing agreements. After he acquired TIDAL, which required real business acumen and tons of capital, he nearly ran it into the ground. Even when he was CEO of Def Jam, he didn't last long despite having a successful music career. This is probably because he lacks the education, experience, and emotional IQ aka temperament to be a business executive. If he had an MBA; had worked as an executive for 10-15 years; and had the patience, dexterity, and the sense of duty and integrity to be willing and able to answer to a variety of stakeholders like senior executives, a board of directors, government regulators, suppliers/vendors, and most importantly, shareholders, maybe he would've been successful as Def Jam's chief executive.

So, in summary, Jay-Z ain't no brilliant businessman. He's just a hustler who knows how to sell "the sizzle without the steak" which is mostly what American business is about. Symbolism over substance. The idea that Shawn Carter aka Jay-Z is a successful entrepreneur and businessman mostly has been a shell game where the sucker (e.g., Iconix and Parlux) is fooled into betting a large sum of money on the premise that he/she can find the ball among the three shells being moved around by the hustler (e.g., Jay-Z) running the game and still win big. Jay has been running a shell game on his fans, his business partners, and the Black Community for decades, now. If he's pulling a con on the real billionaires who own LVMH or SQUARE, he might find himself in a prison jumpsuit real soon like the young lady who founded Theranos, Elizabeth Holmes.

Is He Really a Billionaire?

In the Summer of 2019, it was announced by Forbes that Jay-Z had become the first billionaire rapper. According to the June 3, 2019 article written by Zack O'Malley Greenberg, the Jigga Man derived his humongous fortune from the following assets: 1.) Armand de Brignac valued at $310 million; 2.) $220 million in cash and investments including $70 million of Uber stock; 3.) D'Usse' brand cognac produced by rum maker Bacardi which Forbes valued at $100 million; 4.) $100 million from his streaming service, Tidal; 5.) $75 million from Roc Nation, a joint venture with concert promoter Live Nation; 6.) a $75 million music catalog; 7.) an art collection worth $70 million; and 8.) $50 million in real estate. [47] Now, someone reading this article from a cursory view would think, "Wow, Jay-Z's a billionaire!" The numbers published do add up to $1 billion. But, those published numbers don't tell the whole story. What's unpublished, or private more likely tells a very different story. It probably shows that Jay-Z's not really a billionaire and more likely he's just another one of Corporate America's rags-to-riches poster boys. This story was less about the truth and more about <u>Forbes</u> selling more magazines and getting more views online as well as convincing America and the rest of the world that African Americans have arrived.

There are two reasons why I don't believe Jay-Z's a billionaire. First, so much of his net worth is either not publicly traded like stocks and bonds and <u>Forbes</u> provided no public records like real estate appraisals that we can scrutinize. Thus, there's no real way to value the star's net worth. You just have to take <u>Forbes'</u> word for it and of course, Jay-Z will never tell. He's just happy to be mentioned. Secondly, his path to becoming a billionaire doesn't square with the pattern and practice of other so-called self-made billionaires, or those who didn't inherit their billions. According to Martin S. Fridson, the author of <u>HOW TO BE A BILLIONAIRE</u>, the few self-made billionaires that do exist have achieved their status primarily for the following three reasons: 1.) They grew up middle-class; 2.) Their fathers were either businessmen or professionals; and 3.) They derived their wealth from owning their own businesses not from owning stocks in other people's businesses.[48]

Jay-Z grew up in poverty. His father bailed on his family because he couldn't provide for them. Growing up poor has instilled ambition in a lot of young people. But, according to Fridson, having ambition is simply not enough. One's education and upbringing are the key drivers for achieving success and they are necessary to accumulate extreme wealth.[48] On top of that, race and racism are the chief determinants of who's rich and who's poor in America. So, this is no knock on Jay-Z. He can't help the family he was born into. However, the odds of someone like him ever being worth six or seven figures are daunting. But, for someone like him to generate a net worth of ten figures, the odds are astronomical.

64

According to Forbes, over 60% of his 2019 net worth came from three sources; Armand de Brignac, TIDAL, and cash and investments.[47] The first two assets have become failed businesses which he had to sell at fire-sale prices less than 2 years later. The value of cash and investments fluctuates daily. His shares of Uber stock at the time were worth $70 million.[47] But, Uber has yet to turn a profit and probably never will. Its stock price is down in value which also means his stake in the company is worth less than it was in 2019. I argue that his net worth is considerably less than a billion, now, if it ever was that much.

The same Forbes article touting his billionaire status also mentioned how Warren Buffet was a mentor of sorts to Mr. Carter.[47] But, Mr. Buffett did not accumulate "a billion dollars purely by investing in stocks for his personal portfolio…No doubt, small investors can benefit from adopting Warren Buffett's uncompromisingly rational investment philosophy. Anyone who hopes to reach the Forbes 400 list, however, will be better off studying how Buffet built a vast industrial and financial empire on the foundation of a struggling textile company."[48] Other billionaires associated with the stock market include George Soros, Julian Robertson, Ned and Abigail Johnson of Fidelity Investments, and Fayez Sarofim.[49] These Wall Street titans made their billions by owning investment firms not by buying and selling individual stocks.[49]

Unlike Shawn Carter, Warren Buffett, known as "The Oracle of Omaha," reached millionaire and later billionaire status by taking over companies and making them more profitable. (Jay-Z doesn't own enough stock in Uber to take over the company and when he tried to buy more shares, the rideshare company's founder, Travis Kalanick, rejected his offer.)[47] The secret to Warren's success is using his holding company, Berkshire Hathaway, as an investment vehicle to acquire both profitable and distressed companies across a broad swath of industries like insurance, retail, and fast food.[48] Jay-Z created a holding company, Project Panther Bidco, to purchase Aspiro, the parent company of TIDAL,[50] but he lacked the knowledge, expertise, and most importantly, the money to turn the flailing Norwegian company around. That's why he went to Samsung, Sprint, and SQUARE, hat in hand, looking for a bailout. He also lacked the good sense to avoid purchasing this dud in the first place. Having "street smarts" and naked ambition can't make up for not having a father in the home and an ivy league education. Two things that Warren Buffet had.

Jay-Z Nets Brooklyn

Despite owning less than 1% of the team, Jay-Z was the public face of the Brooklyn Nets for over a decade. From 2003 to 2013, he touted the benefits of bringing the New Jersey Nets to Brooklyn. Even today, he's still the face of the Nets despite having sold his measly share and the team having changed hands twice: first, from a racist, greedy real estate developer to an arms dealing, money laundering Russian, and now, to billionaire tied to the Chinese Communist Party. For years, Brooklyn's native son held press conferences; gave interviews; and rapped about how the Barclays Center was going to bring jobs to "thousands and thousands of people." It created only a few hundred and those were mostly low-wage service and security jobs at the arena. (You know the kind of jobs that keep you living in the Marcy Projects not moving out of them.) On top of that, the City of New York will lose over $40 million in taxes plus suffer another $180 million in lost economic opportunities over the next 30 years.[51][52] Eminent domain was used to seize poor Black Brooklynites' property and give it over to a rich White developer.

Jigga recruited players and helped design the corporate suites.[51] He even took pictures with local Black youth knowing full well that they would be plastered everywhere to promote the new arena while engendering community support.[51] The Reverend Al Sharpton, whose National Action Network was supported by the Nets' original owner Bruce Ratner, tugged on Black folks' heartstrings even further when he shamelessly said, "we've gone from Jackie [Robinson who integrated baseball as a Brooklyn

Dodger] to Jay-Z, where we can not only play the game but we can own a piece of the game."[51] Black Brooklynites, who walked by these images or heard the Reverend Al's words repeated over the local news, felt proud that a local boy from the projects did well for himself and was giving back to the Community. But, in reality, Shawn Corey Carter was just the smiling Black face of a capitalist venture owned and subsidized by powerful White and Honorary White men like Bruce Ratner, Mikhail Prokhorov, Michael Bloomberg, George Pataki, and Joseph Tsai.[51][53]

The Jigga Man purchased his original 1.5% share of the Nets for $1,000,000 in 2003. That percentage eventually went down to less than half a percent, or 0.5%, because Jay couldn't or wouldn't pay the cash calls which are "requests to cover the team's losses."[54] Plus, when Mikhail Prokhorov bought the team in 2015, the rapper's stake got even smaller.[54] Eventually, he sold his stake to former Nets star Jason Kidd and another individual in 2013 for $350,000 after he decided to go into the Sports agency business.[54] That's a 65% loss! Do y'all still think that the Jigga Man is "a business, Man?"

After this hoax was exposed, the NBA created the "Jay-Z" rule which states that no owner or partner in a team can own less than 1% and there can't be more than 25 partners at a given time.[54] How can a guy be considered the "owner of the team" when he owns less than 1% of it? He can when you need a Black celebrity to put a happy face on urban renewal as Negro removal. That's how! That's how "the decadent veil" works.[55] You use Black celebrities, politicians, and preachers to mask Black poverty and displacement while you celebrate Black materialistic consumption fueled by debt and White gentrification of Black neighborhoods as progress and success. That's all the Black (mis)leadership class has ever been good for: using Black people's struggles and aspirations to promote the White elite's interests at the expense of their own people while securing a few crumbs for themselves. Jay-Z and other Black celebrities are just the latest iterations of an old con established long ago by Black preachers and politicians going back to Reconstruction. The Congressional Black Caucus are masters of this scam and now, they're trying to shakedown Washington lobbyists.[56] Barack Hussein Obama adroitly used this ruse to get elected to the White House and Vice President Kamala Harris and former Georgia House Minority Leader and 2018 and 2022 gubernatorial candidate Stacey Abrams are in on the act, too, as well as many, many others.

This incessant, almost craven, desire by many Blacks and Whites alike to see Black professional athletes and entertainers as successful, wealthy business people and leaders on par with the White businessmen who own the studios, record companies, and sports teams that their Black talent works for has been assiduously played upon by Corporate America and the rest of the White elite to confuse the masses. The images of wealthy Black celebrities are used to justify the cutting of welfare, education, and Affirmative Action. They've been used by politicians who balk at paying Reparations. Racists loving point to the handful of Blacks who have been allowed to make it when they shame and blame the Black masses for their failure to access the American Dream. An American Dream that they've been locked out of by these same racists. Jay-Z is just another in a long line of Black celebrities who have over the last 30 years who have agreed to be a willing pawn of White capitalists and their puppet politicians. After all, how can anyone justify the need for massive investment in Black America by the Government and Big Business if there are tons of Jay-Z's, Master P's, Jordan's, Oprah's, and LeBron's?

It also allows for fanciful notions to spring up in the minds of millions of aspiring Blacks who are desperate for the hope that "a role model" like Jay-Z provides. "If he's a billionaire and can own a sports team, then I can, too!" or so the *illogic* goes. In 2021, there were stories about Jay-Z teaming up with Jeff Bezos to buy the Washington Football Team or the Denver Broncos.[57][58] This is pure fantasy. Even if he were a billionaire, which he is not, he's nowhere in the category of a Jeff Bezos, a Warren Buffett, or a Michael Bloomberg. Mentioning Jay-Z in the same breath as Jeff

Bezos or Warren Buffett is the same sleight of hand that the editors at Forbes pulled when they had Oprah on its January 2012 cover standing between Bill Gates and Warren Buffet. Single-digit billionaires don't compare to those who are worth tens of billions and certainly not those who are worth hundreds of billions. In 2021, none of the single-digit billions including Jay-Z made the 400 Richest Persons' List. Because of the Pandemic, only the Super, Duper-rich are getting richer. Anybody below that ain't part of the 0.1%. They're in the 99.9%, who are employees, not bosses, just like the rest of us.

A Strange Investment

In late May of 2019, about a week before he was added to the billionaire's list, it was reported that Jay-Z had invested in a company that tracks people out on bail, probation, or parole for local, state, and federal offenses. The company is called "The Promise" and creates a smartphone app that allows law enforcement to track a person who's on supervised release movements and also to inform them when they are supposed to take a drug test or to report to court.[59][60] This is supposedly a cheaper alternative to the ankle monitoring devices that are widely in use today.[59][60] Of course, Jay-Z tried to spin it and make it seem like he was helping people under court supervision rather than just making a fast buck off them. He said, "$9 billion is wasted incarcerating people who have not been convicted of crimes. We are increasingly alarmed by the injustice in our criminal justice system. Money, time, and lives are wasted with the current policies. It's time for an innovative and progressive technology that offers sustainable solutions to tough problems."[59][60] Think about the sophistry, or the slick-sounding argument he's trying to make here for a second. He's trying to say that his firm's app will improve the lives of the million Black men and women under supervised release. This man has no shame.

His constant justification of his wanton greed as being beneficial to those he exploits is beyond reprehensible. He always likes to paint his brands and business ventures as something other than what they are: money-making machines solely for his benefit. He's not being benevolent or altruistic. His organizations are not nonprofits or civic organizations like churches, schools, museums, food pantries, or nongovernmental agencies that exist to help improve society. Jay-Z is no "cultural icon," civic leader, or philanthropist. He's just another hustler out here trying to get paid. That's fine as long as you're being honest about it. Jay-Z is not. If you're just some greedy rich guy trying to make even more money for yourself, just say that and keep it pushin'. Own that shit! Trump does. Gordon Gecko did. Your idols Bezos, Buffett, and Gates do. Why don't you? Jigga, you ain't no messiah or people's champ. So, stop frontin' like you are one!

"My Presence is Charity"

Jay-Z has made some very strange, even contradictory statements over the years. Let's examine a few. During a concert, he performed a freestyle in tribute to rapper Nipsey Hussle who was slain about a month earlier. After his death, the LA rapper was lauded for his entrepreneurship and community redevelopment efforts. So, in that same spirit, Jay spoke the following words, "…Gentrify your own hood before these people do it. Playing eminent domain and have your people moving. That's a small glimpse into what Nipsey was doing…"[61] Now, that's interesting that he'd recognized that gentrification and eminent domain are twin evils plaguing Black communities all over the country that are the result of White real estate developers influencing politicians to give them tax breaks and subsidies and to use the Government's power of eminent domain to seize the private property of citizens in order to build condos, coffee shops, and luxury stores. However, the previous residents couldn't get loans to purchase or remodel homes or start businesses. They live surrounded by blight and crime because city, county, state, and federal officials don't care enough about their Black constituents to provide them with government services and make capital improvements in their communities like they do in White ones. (I guess we're supposed

70

to gentrify our hoods by laundering drug money. At least, that's what he suggested in "The Story of OJ." Well, why didn't he do it?) It's funny how he abhorred gentrification and eminent domain in 2019, but from 2003 to 2013, he didn't care anything about eminent domain when it was used to gentrify Black neighborhoods in Brooklyn to make way for the Nets coming to town. But, we're supposed to just clap and cheer and not notice his hypocrisy, right?

At a concert in Cleveland, Hov stopped his show briefly after he spotted a little Black girl in the audience to give her a pep talk by saying, "At this very moment, America is way more sexist than they are racist, but young lady you got the potential to be the next president of the United States, you believe that."[62] Now, that's a nice thing to say to inspire a precious little girl. The only problem is it's not true. America has always been more racist than it has ever been sexist even today. Black Women catch more hell than White, East Asian, Latino, Middle-Eastern, South Asian, and Native American women because they are Black. The same is true for any other combination of Black and some other demographic (e.g., male, female, gay, straight, rich, poor, young, or old.) If you're Black and suffering in this country, it's mostly because you're Black. No other reason comes close.

Despite what feminists, the media, social media, academics, and so-called liberal Democrats tell you, there's NO BLACK MALE PATRIARCHY in existence in the United States. There's no systematic oppression of women, children, or members of the LGBT+ community by straight Black men. The overwhelming majority of Black men are not batterers. Black men are neither the biggest purveyors nor the biggest consumers of porn. Despite what's being portrayed in movies and music, we are not the biggest pimps or sex traffickers nor are we the most prolific sexual offenders. That title, according to FBI statistics, belongs to White men.[63] (They lead in many other crime categories as well.) It's high time that Black men and women defend Black men's honor, integrity, and reputation and stop letting other races and the misguided or traitorous among us malign and defame our characters. You demonize first whom you wish to destroy. Because they have destroyed and continue to destroy Black men, Black women and children are left unprotected. If they remain unprotected at the rates that they are for much longer, there won't be any Black people left in this country in the next 50-100 years. So, in today's small Black children's lifetimes, Black people will be so marginalized that they might as well be extinct.

Perhaps, the most arrogantly ignorant remark that he has publicly made is "It might sound arrogant, but my presence is my charity. Just who I am just like Obama's is. Obama provides hope. Whether he does anything, the hope that he provides for a nation and outside of America is enough."[64][65] So, all Black folk have to do is bask in the glow of Hov and Barack Obama and everything will be alright? Like prosperity is spread through osmosis. Like if we see or spend time around you, we'll absorb it. Negro, if you don't get the fuck out of here! His comments where he compares himself to Obama remind me of similar comments made by another narcissist. During an episode of The Boondocks, Robert "Grandad" Freeman also compared himself to the First Black President.[66] After it was announced that Obama had won, Robert declared, "Well, it's been a long, Black Struggle and I felt me and Barack deserved a party."[66] Like, it was just those two Negroes who did it? As if, they were the only ones who struggled and thus, deserved to be celebrated? Talk about narcissistic. But, that was Robert Freeman. That is Barack Obama and that certainly is Jay-Z.

Friends with the Obamas

The election of Barack Obama to the Presidency also led to the ascension of Jay-Z to the status of a Black leader. Both, Jay-Z and his wife, Beyonce', endorsed Obama's election and re-election in 2008 and 2012. Because of their friendship with the Obamas, Jay and Bey became the Barack and Michelle of Hip-Hop. They were, then, and still are today the President and First Lady of Hip-Hop. But, even before the election of the First Black President, Jay-Z was being groomed by Corporate America to be a Black Leader.

Because Jay and Bey were presidential pals, I'm sure this friendship yielded some votes for the two-term President. In 2008, Barack Obama, then a US Senator and presidential candidate, expressed his appreciation for Jay-Z's music when he brushed off his shoulder during a speech alluding to the MC's popular song, "Dirt Off Your Shoulder." The rapper campaigned for the presidential hopeful during that same year. His wife, Beyonce', sang the national anthem at the 2009 inauguration and later sang at an inaugural ball while the President and First Lady danced. This symbiotic relationship between these two "power couples" continued throughout Obamas eight years in the White House. When First Lady Michelle Obama launched a healthy school lunch initiative, Beyonce' created a music video called "Get Me Bodied." Jay told the press that he and Barack were so tight that they texted each other.[67] The President, however, denied those claims.[67] Jay even helped the President raise $4,000,000 by hosting a fundraiser for his re-election bid at his nightclub in 2012.[68] The Carters and the Obamas have remained close even after the First Black President's two terms in office. The former President and First Lady have, either separately or together, attended parties with the President and First Lady of Hip-Hop or have gone to their concerts.[67] The former President even inducted the Jigga Man into the Rock and Roll Hall of Fame in 2021.[69]

"What's the Next Step?"

Two months after Forbes declared Jay-Z a billionaire, he was back in the news announcing with the NFL's commissioner, Roger Goodell, that he had entered an agreement to produce the halftime shows for the Superbowl. Everybody was shocked because the NFL boycott was going full steam ahead; former San Francisco 49ers quarterback Colin Kaepernick, who had just participated in tryouts weeks earlier, was still out of a job; and Jay-Z, Forbes' newly minted billionaire, was still not independent enough to walk away from the NFL's crumbs. The rapper gave all kinds of lame excuses as to why he decided to walk away from the movement that Colin had started and embrace the NFL. First, he tried to claim

73

that his deal with the league was "the next thing," or step in the fight against police brutality.[70] He explained that protests work by outsiders (i.e., Black Activists) making a bunch of demands.[70] Then, the insiders (i.e., the White Establishment) take notice of their demands and offer to negotiate.[70] When that explanation didn't fly with the reporters gathered at Roc Nation's headquarters, he said that we shouldn't make it about one guy's job, meaning Colin's, when the welfare of millions was at stake.[70] But, he never did explain how his contract with the NFL helps "millions and millions of people" or addresses police brutality.[70] For his part, Roger Goodell tried unconvincingly to claim that this move represented what the NFL's players wanted.[70] He said that the league was instituting an initiative that focused on "the concerns of the players" and that it attempted to move the conversation about racism and police brutality from "protest to progress."[70]

The whole sorry affair was a charade orchestrated by Jay-Z to justify his avarice by making it seem like he was doing this for his people. That presser was more of the same "I do this for my culture…industry shady, you need to be taking over" bullshit that we've been hearing from Jay for years.[71] He ain't helping nobody but himself, Roger Goodell, and the NFL's owners. Interestingly, it was New England Patriots owner Robert Kraft, a close personal friend of Jay's, who orchestrated this deal.[72][73] This is the same Bob Kraft who contributed millions to the campaign of Kaepernick's chief nemesis, President Donald J. Trump. So, once again, Jay-Z like Barack Obama is the Black face of White interests.

As I've said before, you've had several subsequent stories about Jay-Z becoming an NFL owner or him partnering with a mega-billionaire like Jeff Bezos, whose net worth is $195.7 billion, to buy the Washington Football Team or the Denver Broncos.[57][58] All of which is pure fantasy ginned up by the master manipulators in the media to get Black people all excited about one billionaire Negro instead of worrying about their own troubles and fighting for a better future. Jay-Z, with a supposed net worth of $1 billion, doesn't have the cash nor the financing to buy an NFL franchise. The last team that was up for sale was the Carolina Panthers which sold for over $2 billion. That's over twice as much as Jay's individual net worth and $500 million more if you add in his wife's net worth at $500 million. You'd have to have a net worth in the tens of billions of dollars like the current Panthers' owner David Tepper, whose net worth is $15.8 billion according to Forbes,[74] to even be a serious contender to purchase an NFL team. And why would a man like Jeff Bezos, who's worth is almost 200 times Jay-Z's supposed net worth, even think about partnering with him to buy a team? He could buy 9 or 10 teams easily in his sleep.

This episode also put a spotlight on Jay-Z's ignorance and hypocrisy. Previously, he supported Kaepernick's "stance;" wore the embattled quarterback's jersey in solidarity with him; and said he would never do a halftime show. Not only did he stab Colin Kaepernick in the back by making a deal with the NFL to produce the Super Bowl halftime show, but he also blamed Black Americans for police brutality. He said it was the absence of fathers in Black homes that caused Black youth to not respect authority and when these wayward, fatherless youths and adults encounter the police, they mouthed off and get shot as a result.[75] This is patently false and another reason why EXPERTS like sociologists and psychologists should be talking about what causes society's ills and offering possible solutions to them and not high school dropouts who just happen to be rich and famous.

Racism not only infects the minds of Whites and other non-Blacks, but it also infects the minds of Black people. We're all indoctrinated with anti-Black propaganda from early childhood and Jay-Z's no different. But, the profit motive also has Hova singing a new tune. He can't jeopardize his new deal with the NFL by criticizing racist police. So instead, he criticizes their victims.[75] But, I think it goes deeper than that. Jay-Z has always been in solidarity with the White Establishment and has always seen their interests as his. Could it be that he was one of those dealers who bribed the cops and snitched on rival dealers and even associates in exchange for staying out of jail and acquiring more territory? I don't know, but that seems like something the Jigga Man would do given his track record.

The Story of Hov, Jay

During an interview in 2021, Jay-Z admitted to experiencing racism at his level. The interviewer asked, "Are there incidents even at this stage in your life – so you're famous – you're rich – you own stuff – where you run into racism that's evident to you? That's easy to recognize at this stage of your life?"[76] Hov Jay replied, "Yeah. Yes! Yeah, but it mostly comes when you try to challenge the status quo. (If) I'm being quiet and entertaining, everyone's cool. Uh, man, it's great. You don't feel racism. But, when you try to challenge the club (the good ol' boy network,) it's like right. Oh no, we should have a seat at – to use the Solange album title. We should have a seat at this table! And, uh, then, it gets into a space where it's like 'Wait, you guys are mad at me about the same thing you guys are doing?' And it's just – it gets into a weird space."[76] What, Jay-Z, the billionaire, experiences resistance when he challenges the status quo? Welcome to Black life in America where your success – hell, your very presence challenges the status quo of a supposed White superiority and a supposed Black inferiority. The interviewer probes further by asking, "Are you in meetings, now, in your business life where you're the only Black man in the room?"[76] To which Jay-Z replies, "Well, when I was doing the Nets I was definitely the only Black guy in the room." [76] Finally, the interviewer asked, "Well, what was that like?"[76] Jay-Z gave an OJ-esque reply by saying during his time with the Brooklyn Nets, his celebrity allowed him to transcend his race.[76] Well, I guess he's not Black. He's Hov, Jay. Ok.

Perhaps, his most salient commentary on racism was his song, "The Story of OJ."[77] This song and the critical acclaim that he received in the press solidified Jay-Z's status in the minds of many that he was a Black leader. This is my favorite Jay-Z song because he admits that no matter what else a Black person is or what he/she achieves, he/she is still a nigger in the eyes of most White Americans. There's an old racist joke that goes like this: "What do you call a Black man in a suit? A Nigger. What do you call a Black Man with a Ph.D.? A Smart Nigger. What do you call a Black millionaire? A Rich Nigger." And what do you call a Black man who steps out of line and demands freedom, justice, and equality? A Dead Nigger!"

When he ends the song's refrain with "Still Nigga"[77] and repeats it over and over, it's not so much a lament, but simply an acknowledgment that while I as a Black person in America have been dealt a lousy hand, I still have to play it and play it to win. My question for him is why aren't you taking the NEXT STEP and using some of your resources to help other Black People avoid the obstacles and pitfalls that you and many others before you have faced so that they, too, can be winners at this game called Life? Tony Delerme, the creator of the YouTube channel TD Hip-Hop Media, attempted to shed some light on why famous, successful, wealthy, and "powerful" Blacks like Jay-Z, Diddy, Tyler Perry, Michael Jordan, Oprah Winfrey, Obama, and others don't take the next step and shepherd the Black masses, who slavishly follow them, to freedom and prosperity when he said the following:

> *"Like I've said before, these 'billionaire' celebrities like Jay-Z and Diddy are scared of power. They talk that "boss talk," but when it comes to actually being one and challenging the system of Racism-White Supremacy, they fold and opt to collaborate with them every time. And I can hear someone in the comments section say, 'Why does Jay-Z and Diddy have to do something for Black people? Well, then stop pretending to be for Black people. Then, you can do whatever you want. You don't see me talking about Lil' Uzi Vert. Do you? Exactly."*[78]

Black celebrities, businesspeople, preachers, and politicians, like so many of the Black people who follow them, only want the trappings of success (i.e., nice homes, cars, and clothes) not real success (i.e., sustainable businesses, institutions, and communities.) They only want the appearance of power (i.e., prestige or clout) not real power (i.e., making policies; writing laws; balancing budgets; and employing large numbers of people) which comes with risk and responsibility which they feverishly try to avoid. It's this mentality, held by both the leaders and the followers, that keeps Blacks stuck in the morass they're in around the globe.

Jay-Z is not a Black Leader

Before I explain why I believe Jay-Z is not a Black leader, I want to first define what a leader is and more, specifically, what a Black leader is or should be. A leader is someone who has followers, or people he/she guides in a certain direction. It's as simple as that. It matters not if he/she is rich, poor, well-known, unknown, attractive, unattractive, popular, unpopular, elected, unelected, religious, secular, a politician, or a celebrity. As long as he/she has a following, he/she is a leader of some sort. On that basis, Jay-Z is a leader. He is a leader because of his influence and his influence derives from his celebrity. But, does that make him a Black leader? I argue it doesn't. A person can be Black and be a leader without being a Black leader.

A Black leader, a true one, is not just a Black person who is wealthy or prominent. He/she is also principled and those principles are rooted in liberating Black People. Liberation doesn't just have to come in the form of revolution, activism, protests, or politics. It can also come in the form of art that represents the culture and values of a people and depicts us in our best possible light, not our worst. Jay-Z's art, if you can call it art, is tragedy porn made by a poor, uneducated Black kid who sold his soul to White racists so he could escape the ghetto. It glorifies crime, drugs, guns, and violence. It makes Black nihilism, or self-destructiveness cool and is mass-marketed to the global masses as authentic Black Culture and as something we as Blacks, especially

78

our youth should be proud of. Jay-Z is NO cultural icon. He's just a hustler and a huckster still running a con game and selling cheap wares like he was when he was on the streets of Brooklyn. Now, he's just running a much bigger game playing for much bigger stakes on a much bigger stage with many, many more marks to fool.

Liberation can also come in the form of business and business practices. Wealthy people are the ones who can most afford to form and own a business. They have the money to risk. Poor and middle-class much less so. Jay-Z became wealthy because of his successful rap career. He has a right to do whatever he wants to do with his money. If he wants to sell cheap clothes and bottom-shelf liquor at luxury prices, that's his right. If he wants to be a shark, a gobble up every opportunity that comes his way, that's his right. Finally, if he wants to be a ruthless cutthroat who cheats his business partners and defrauds his investors, that's also his right. But, he does not have the right to call himself a Black leader while not taking on any of the responsibilities that come with the title. He casts himself as a Black businessman without first understanding and respecting what that means for an economically exploited people starved of businesses and employment opportunities created by their own people.

A Black business leader would sell and market his/her goods and services to Black people to meet an underserved need. He/she would also hire Black people and constantly look to the Black community as a pool from which to recruit and develop talent. This does not mean he/she would exclude others. It just means that he/she would include members of his/her community when considering candidates for hiring and promotion and if you can't find any Black talent, create it by offering scholarships and career training.

When Jay-Z acquired and then, revamped TIDAL, its staff remained lily-white.[79] Now, in fairness, it was a Norwegian company, and ain't too many Black people in Norway. However, there are more than a few Black people in the music business and the streaming music business and he could have hired some of those people to work for his company. He also would see other Black-owned businesses (e.g., the B.E. 100s) as investment opportunities. A Black businessman has to take these things into account. A businessman, who just happens to be Black, does not.

A Black leader wouldn't dare use the racist term, "boy" to demean another Black man he disagreed with as he did with world-renowned singer, dancer, actor, and activist Harry Belafonte.[80] A Black philanthropist would support Black causes first before supporting more general ones just like other philanthropists from other racial and ethnic groups do. They already have a vision and mission. They don't need their agents, business managers, attorneys, or others telling them how, when, and where to invest, spend, and donate their money. Why did Jay, a homeboy from Da 'Hood with a criminal record, have to partner with two non-Black billionaires, Bob Kraft and Clara Wu Tsai before he started addressing the need for criminal justice reform?[72][81] Wouldn't that be something he'd naturally be concerned about given his background? Why did Jay-Z and Beyonce need to partner with the blood diamond distributor Tiffany's before they could ever think about offering $2 million in scholarships to HBCU students? To billionaires, $2 million is pocket change. So, what's the problem? Donating a couple million in scholarships to Black colleges should be an afterthought for them. I know donating to yeshivas, or Jewish institutions of higher learning is to Jewish businessmen, both large and small.

Lastly, a Black billionaire businessman would use his wealth to invest in political influence not only for himself like getting a tax credit or a contract with the government, but also to get laws passed and policies instituted that help African Americans and perhaps, even, Black People globally. The late Jewish billionaire Sheldon Adelson was a major proponent of positive US-Israeli relations and donated millions and millions of dollars to politicians in both countries to ensure that the relationship remained cooperative and friendly. Not only has Jay-Z been rich for a long time, but he was also friends with a President. He helped Obama get elected and re-elected. But, what does he have to show for it? What policy initiatives that would have benefitted Black people did he push before the President or Congress? How many lobbyists on K Street has he hired? You're a billionaire, but you're not doing what billionaires do? Buy politicians! Maybe, he tried, but things got weird when the White – I mean the real billionaires told him to "Stay in your lane, boy!"

Score

Leadership: Jay-Z is a celebrity. He's rich. He's famous. He's influential. But, he's not a leader. He's not a politician or a Fortune 500 CEO. For a so-called billionaire, he doesn't spend much, if any, of his money on campaigns, lobbyists, trade associations, think tanks, Political Action Committees (PACs,) Super PACs, universities, churches, hospitals, scholarships, endowments, or on any other significant endeavors or institutions. These are things that most 50-something-year-old executive-level businessmen do. Because he lacks real power, political influence, or moral authority, he's not a leader in any serious sense. He gets a 2.0 in the Leadership category.

Race Pride Jay-Z will only demonstrate race pride if it's profitable for him. As long as it was cool, he was down with Kaepernick, and both, he and his wife wrote and performed songs that were about police brutality and injustice.[75] But, as soon as a Super Bowl halftime show contract came available, Jay-Z was singing a different tune.[75] Outside of the "Story of OJ," he's never produced any socially conscious song or record nor associated himself with any social movement. He gets a 1.0 in the category of Race Pride.

Role Model Jay-Z's a terrible role model. He dropped out of school; bragged about selling drugs; glorified gangsterism; betrayed his friends; sold out his old neighborhood to gentrifiers; made it cool for millions of White kids and others to sing, "Nigga" with the song "Jigga My Nigga;" and preached to millions of

Black kids that "getting by and getting over however you can" is the way to go. He gets a 1.0 as a Role Model.

Impact on the Race One of the biggest impacts on the Race, he had was his decision to deliberately lower the quality of Hip-Hop music. He openly admitted that he records mediocre rhymes because it's more profitable to do so and compared himself to General Motors because the automaker offers consumers average to below-average quality vehicles because it pays more for them to do so. As a rap fan, that's my biggest beef with him. If you expect me to give you my hard-earned money which is my best, then, I expect you to give your best by recording dope rhymes to a funky beat on the CD/MP3 you're selling. The quality of Rap has seriously diminished since Jay-Z ascended to the throne. Over those 26 years, rappers don't even rap anymore. They mumble. His Impact on the Race has been negligible if not negative. He gets a 1.0 in this category.

Total Score His final score is a 1.0 or (2.0 + 1.0 + 1.0 + 1.0 = 5.0/5 = 1.0.)

Al Sharpton

Early Life and Career

Alfred Charles Sharpton, Jr., was born October 3, 1954, to Alfred Charles, Sr., and Ada Richards Sharpton in Brooklyn, New York.[82] His family prospered for a time and moved to the middle-class neighborhood of Hollis in Queens. After his parents split over his father having an affair, Young Alfred and his mother moved into a low-income neighborhood in Brooklyn.

Alfred grew up in the Church. He was a small child when he began preaching and touring with world-renown Gospel singer Mahalia Jackson.[82] He graduated from high school in 1975 but dropped out of college two years later.[82] Al was both a youth minister and a student activist.[82] In 1969, he served as the youth director of Jesse Jackson's Operation Breadbasket's New York chapter.[82] Two years later, he founded his own nonprofit entitled, National Youth Movement.[82] He worked for Shirley Chisholm during her 1972 presidential campaign.[82]

For much of the 1970s, Al Sharpton worked as a tour manager for the legendary Soul singer, James Brown. Not having a father in his life, Al saw Brown as a surrogate father and his son, Teddy as his brother. "I learned manhood from James Brown," said Sharpton. Sharpton eventually married a background singer in Brown's band named Kathy Jordan.[82] They have two daughters. Although Sharpton was raised Pentecostal and was originally an ordained minister in that denomination, he later became a Baptist.

Early Activism

During the 1980s, New York City was a racial powder keg. White politicians like Democrat Ed Koch and Republican Rudy Giuliani stoked White fears over Blacks committing crimes; moving into their neighborhoods; and marrying their daughters. Inspired by this demagoguery, Whites began attacking and killing Blacks. Notable incidents include the shooting of four Black Men by Bernhard Goetz; a White mob attacking three Black Men in Howard Beach; and the murder of Yusef Hawkins in Bensonhurst. Al Sharpton either spoke out against or protested over these incidents and more, but none brought the "Good Reverend" more fame or infamy than the rape of Tawana Brawley. Tawana was a Black teenager who claimed in 1987 that six White Men raped and abused her. Afterward, they smeared feces on her and dumped her in the trash. She alleged that the men behind this dastardly deed were police officers and a prosecutor. The case was thrown out of court because the grand jury and the prosecutors blamed the victim. Sharpton, for his efforts, was sued by the six men accused, one of whom was Steven Pagones, the District Attorney for Duchess County.

Confidential Informant # 7

Like any good "Jack of All Trades," Sharpton has had a multitude of jobs: preacher, roadie, activist, candidate, "advisor," and pundit. But, there's one job that "Big Al," as he used to be called, doesn't like to talk about and that was the role of Government Snitch. Al Sharpton admitted in 1988 that he was a police informant claiming that he was trying to keep drugs out of the Black Community. According to NYPD and the FBI, he was supplied "a bugged briefcase" to record Italian mobsters and Latin dealers.[82]

There is also a videotape of him meeting with a drug dealer. It was first aired on HBO's Real Sports with Bryant Gumbel in 2002[83] which I watched at the time. On the tape, Sharpton was dressed in a sequenced purple cowboy outfit listening and nodding his head while an unknown man, an alleged dealer, is talking. Sharpton acknowledged that it was him on tape, but that he wasn't there to buy or sell drugs or act as an informant, but he was only there for legitimate business reasons. He said he listened quietly and nodded his head and played along while the guy was talking about drugs because he was in fear of his life and just wanted to get out of there. Whether Al was telling the truth or not, who knows, but it wasn't a good look for the "refined agitator."[85] But, like most of the unflattering news about him, it didn't stick.

Many Black activists are skeptical about Sharpton's claim about being a Mafia informant. First, snitching on the Mob is hazardous to one's health and they will not rest until they have killed you. Second, Italian gangs are extremely racist. They would never do business with Blacks on a high or even a mid-level. So, it's highly unlikely that an Al Sharpton, who has no history as a drug dealer or gangster and thus, no street credibility, would be associated with mobsters or be allowed to get close enough to approach let alone talk to a Mafia captain like Michael Franzese.[82][84][85] These activists believe it was more likely he served as a stool pigeon against his people. So, do I.

Larceny and Fraud Trial

On March 19, 1990, Al Sharpton went on trial for 67 charges alleged against him by the State of New York.[86] The New York Attorney General accused Mr. Sharpton of larceny and fraud and alleged that he stole $250,000 from a defunct nonprofit that he started in 1969 called the National Youth Movement.[86] The Reverend and his legal team countered that these are retaliatory charges brought against him by Attorney General Robert Abrams who was angry at Sharpton over the Tawana Brawley case.[86] Mr. Abrams denied it.[86] Four months later, the Reverend Al Sharpton was acquitted of all charges thanks to the brilliance of Attorney Alton Maddox, Jr.[86]

Sadly, Rev. Al quickly abandoned his savior; showed him no support; and would not testify on his behalf when Mr. Maddox faced disciplinary proceedings that led to his law license being suspended for over 30 years over his role in the Brawley case. The fact that he would turn his back on a man that got him up from under 67 charges speaks to Al Sharpton's lack of character. He's a user and a snake. If he can't be trusted and depended upon to return a favor for a man who kept him out of jail, how can Black Americans trust him to represent us in the White House and in corporate boardrooms? The answer is we can't, and you'll see why after I examine his misdeeds during the Obama years.

In the Wilderness

Twelve years after he came to national prominence over the Brawley case, Al Sharpton was seen as a joke, a Jesse Jackson wannabe, and a buffoon with a pompadour dressed in sweatsuits and gold chains. As the 80s turned into the 90s and the 90s progressed into the 2000s, he pared down his flamboyancy; cut his hair; trimmed his mustache; lost some weight; wore buttoned-down suits; and appeared on cable news and national talk shows. He became a Baptist preacher. He shadowed, his mentor, Jesse Jackson and founded the so-called National Action Network (NAN) which is much like Jackson's Rainbow/Push Coalition, an organization completely beholden to him. He copied Jackson even further with his own Madison Avenue Initiative which was styled after Rev. Jackson's Wall Street Project in that it was touted as a means to get Corporate America and the US Government to do business with Black businesses and hire Black people. He protested and spent months in jail over the US military using Vieques, Puerto Rico, an island populated almost exclusively by Blacks, as a testing ground for its bombs. He ran for Mayor of New York, the US Senate, and even for President in 2004. But, it was to no avail. Nobody was listening. If anything, they were laughing at and besmirching him. But, then, from 2007 to 2008, a little-known, young, and handsome Senator from Illinois ran for President and won, and Al Sharpton hitched his cart to Obama's bandwagon and the rest is as they say, "is History."

In the Halls of Powers (Al's in the Big House)

During Obama's Presidency, Al Sharpton became the premiere civil rights leader in the country. He was the HNIC, or the Head Negro in Charge. I knew he had "arrived" when I saw him on C-SPAN arrive at the 2010 White House Correspondents Dinner. Obama used the Reverend as his pit bull against attacks from critics, especially those who were Black and/or left-leaning. For his efforts, he got a TV show on MSNBC called <u>Politics Nation</u>. Although I'm sure they were shocked and amazed that a man who just a few short years earlier had been seen as a joke had become a presidential advisor, many a Black careerist followed his footsteps hoping they could get some of the Democrats' and the mainstream media's largesse.

The <u>60 Minutes</u> segment entitled, "The Refined Agitator," which quotes Sharpton's description of himself, best encapsulates this supposed "New Al Sharpton."[85] Leslie Stahl, his interviewer, said his "change from confrontational to accommodating"[85] was because he decided he would never criticize the President. As a result, Sharpton became the Obama Administration's liaison to Black America; his attack dog against critics; and a cheerleader for many of Obama's pet projects like school privatization. He even toured the country with the racist former House Speaker Newt Gingrinch,[85] the man whom it would later be revealed plotted to take down Mr. Obama even before he was sworn in. But, politics does make strange bedfellows.

For being a staunch Obama loyalist, Rev. Al, as he is affectionately called by his fellow pundits at MSNBC, was rewarded with a nightly show because at that time the network's owners, General Electric and Comcast, thought it would be profitable for the channel to be the Obama News Network (ONN.) Ms. Stahl seemed to marvel, as did Mr. Sharpton himself, at his transcendence beyond "Civil Rights" into areas like immigration policy, gay marriage, education reform, and other "non-Black issues."[85] Mr. Sharpton claimed that he had changed with the times and that accounted for his growth.[85] He has also changed his style, appearance, and haunts. No longer wearing tracksuits and medallions and hanging with the Brothers and Sisters in Brooklyn and Harlem, these days the Good Reverend can be seen smoking cigars and sipping on the finest spirits with New York's White elite at "the Havana Room"[85] and flying on private jets.

Watching this interview 10 years later reminded me of a PBS show about Vernon Jordan that came out in 2020 where his friends marveled at how well he, too, had made the transition from Civil Rights to Corporate America. They gushed about Vernon in the same way that Leslie did when she talked about how Sharpton had become a mainstream political figure which is what he wanted all along. He admitted as much during the interview when he said that he was always looking for acceptance and that he wanted to get back all that he had lost after his father left him.[85] Al Sharpton's political journey was always more about his personal redemption than it ever was about Black people's freedom.

But, what did Al Sharpton do with his newfound legitimacy and gravitas after he eclipsed Jesse Jackson as the premier civil rights leader? How did he use his access to power during the eight years of Obama to benefit Black People? Well, let's take a look.

First, he spent eight years on MSNBC and anywhere else he could be seen or heard building a Big, Black Wall around Obama to safely protect him from any criticism from Blacks or the Left. He created a climate where it was almost treasonous for any Black person to ever question the First Black President about his policies. He told Leslie Stahl to do so would be giving aid and comfort to Mr. Obama's enemies on the Right and that the President never promised to have a Black Agenda when he was a candidate.[85] Like most Black misleaders, Mr. Sharpton is deliberately being misleading, disingenuous, and derelict in his duty to represent the interests of Black Americans to those in power like Dr. King did and to a lesser extent Jesse Jackson did. Sharpton instead decided it was his job to represent the President's interests to Black America and force us to swallow them. So, Obama could go on about his business ignoring and even harming us while doing his level best to help every non-Black constituent group he could. While it is true that he didn't run on a Black Agenda, he was the first presidential candidate to talk about the Black-White Wealth Gap and by doing so impregnated the minds of African American voters with expectations that he was going to do something significant to close that gap. Therefore, they should support him. Al Sharpton gave Barack Obama and future Presidents like Joe Biden cover to do absolutely nothing for Black America while claiming to have our backs.

Perhaps, Sharpton's greatest betrayal of Black people, is when he, along with the Urban League's Marc Morial, and the NAACP's Ben Jealous signed a Memorandum of Understanding (MOU) with Comcast in 2010. They passed it off as a golden opportunity for Black-owned networks to partner with the cable giant to have access to its millions of subscribers and for Black vendors to win contracts with the multibillion-dollar company. But, none of it came to fruition. It was all a mirage. Black-owned cable channels like Diddy's Revolt, Magic Johnson's Aspire, and The Africa Channel are not shown in all of Comcast's markets, particularly in those that have a large Black subscriber base in cities like Atlanta and Philly where they would benefit the most.[88] Despite Blacks making over 40% of the company's subscribership, Comcast had only contracted $3 million worth of business with Black-owned companies in 2014. This is despite it having an advertising and programming budget of over $15 Billion.[87]

Worst of all, the Memorandum of Understanding agreed to by Sharpton & Co. led to the Supreme Court striking down the granddaddy of all civil rights laws, the Civil Rights Act of 1866 in 2020. Five years earlier, Byron Allen, founder of Entertainment Studios, sued Comcast, Time Warner Cable, Al Sharpton, the Urban League, and the NAACP for $20 Billion, alleging racial discrimination.[87] After five years of legal wrangling, the case made its way to the High Court where the Justices ruled against Mr. Allen and more importantly, the 1866 Civil Rights Act saying that he and all future plaintiffs like him who allege discrimination must prove, but for discrimination that they were harmed. Now, it's virtually impossible for Blacks, other racial and ethnic minorities, women, and LGBT+ persons to sue over discrimination in the workplace and in the awarding of business and government contracts because of the extremely high bar of proving an organization's decision was based solely on discrimination and not if it was just a motivating factor. This is known as the "But For" standard.[88] But for racism, you would have gotten that house, that car, that job, or that contract. (I say if any part of a decision is based on bias and discrimination, then, the entire decision is tainted, and you have to rule in favor of the plaintiff.) Essentially, this KKKangaroo Court said that you can get away with racial discrimination as long as you can find an additional reason for your decision.

So here, you have a so-called civil rights leader fighting against civil and economic rights instead of fighting for them. Economic rights are among the most important because without them you don't truly get the benefit of being an American. Whereas voting rights, which are supposed to secure all the other rights, today are just manipulated and regulated by the Two Parties for their sole benefit. Rev. Sharpton is nothing more than a vote herder for the Democratic Party. This man, like so many in the Black Misleadership Class, has sold Black voters and consumers into captivity to the Democratic Party and Corporate America for crumbs. From 2004 to 2021, $140,000 from Comcast went to his so-called National Action Network, alone, while the NAACP received a measly $30,000 over the same 8-year period.[87] At least, the Urban League got close to a million dollars at $835,000.[87]

Although Comcast was the defendant, in this case, the Trump Administration also argued in front of the Court in support of Comcast's position and that's even though Comcast's cable news network MSNBC slams Donald Trump day and night. (Ironically, the family that owns Comcast are Republicans, yet they pander to Democrats. Profits trump principles all day, every day.) Because Byron Allen's basis for filing the lawsuit was the Civil Rights Act of 1866 and Chief Justice John Robert's naked hostility towards anything dealing with civil rights for Black Folks, the Court only ruled on the Civil Rights Act and not on any of the other merits of his case. That was sent back to the 9th Circuit Court of Appeals before Mr. Allen and Comcast eventually came to a settlement agreement. So, while Mr. Allen got his channels on Comcast, the rest of Black America is in an even more precarious position than it was before this decision thanks in no small part to one Alfred Charles Sharpton.

Back on the Outside Looking In (Back in the Fields)

Now that Obama no longer needs him, the so-called Reverend Al Sharpton has been busy trying to maintain his HNIC status. (Although his show has been relegated to weekends on MSNBC, he's still herding votes and making excuses for the Democrats and begging for money for his National Inaction Network.) The problem is he's not the "it guy" anymore. He's having to compete with the Steve Harvey's, the Marc Lamont Hill's, the Charlamagne Tha God's, the D.L. Hughley's, the Van Jones', the Joy-Ann Reid's, the Jemele Hill's, the Amanda Seales', the Jamilah Lemieux's and all the other talking heads, politicians, and celebrities who supposedly know a thing or two about politics and who have anointed themselves leaders in the Black Community. In fact, there isn't really an HNIC anymore. There isn't a need for one because there are just too many Black influencers for Team White Supremacy to choose from. They don't need a singular Kneegrow for all the other kneegrows to look to for leadership and guidance. There are hundreds – no thousands of Pick Me Kneegrows. Pick Me! Pick Me! Pick Me! Plus, with the advent of Social Media, Black Sheeple are now more than ever easily swayed to act against their own interests. Any halfway decent-looking fool with a smartphone, the gift of gab, and a (social media) following can anoint him/herself a Black leader.

Score

Leadership Despite his fame or infamy, depending on how you look it at, Al Sharpton is not a leader. He's not a pastor despite being a preacher. But, that's ok. Jesus didn't have his own church, either. And just like the people in Jesus' day, Al's not very fond of paying his taxes. The IRS and both the State and City of New York have had to hound him over his failure to pay taxes on time, in full, or at all.[82] You and I, the taxpayers, have to subsidize Big Al or should I say Little Al now that he's rail-thin.

His organization, the National Action Network, is just a shell corporation with a big ol' slush fund just for him. There's nothing "national" about it. There's a headquarters in New York and a lot of local chapters with P.O. boxes for addresses. The Rainbow/Push Coalition doesn't have any or many branches, either, but Jesse Jackson is certainly a national leader. Having a TV show and a radio show doesn't make you a leader, either. However, none of these things add to or take away from Sharpton. There are no formal qualifications for becoming a Black Leader. There's no screening process internally on the part of Blacks. All you have to do is be prominent enough that enough Negroes know who you are and/or have White Folks vouch for you. (Like it or not, what White folks say matters to us.) Sharpton's two for two because he's in both of those categories. His "power" is through his ability to influence millions of people both Black and White to work together. Sadly, he uses his influence in the interests of the people who are paying him namely the Democratic Party, Comcast, other corporations, and wealthy donors who finance his organization. Unlike Dr. King or Rev. Jackson, he preaches from his pulpit on behalf of the powerful instead of the powerless. Even at the height of his power and influence, he chose to lend his voice to support a lying, ass-covering politician in the White House instead of using his clout to influence that politician to create policies that help Black people or even the American people as a whole. Squandering such an opportunity is unforgivable. Al Sharpton gets a 0.9 in the Leadership category.

Race Pride The man wears a perm. Need I say more? That in and of itself suggest he has self-image and self-esteem issues related to being Black. I don't care what he says about being loyal to James Brown. But, my biggest knocks against him are his decision not to hold Barack Obama accountable and his negotiation of numerous Memorandums of Understanding (MOUs) with Comcast and other corporations in exchange for his support and silence over their racism. He gets a 1.5 for Race Pride.

Role Model Al Sharpton's story of overcoming poverty and adversity and reaching respectability is admirable. However, a lot of people have done that. What would've been more impressive would have been his demonstrating moral character and integrity while reaching prosperity. When I think of him, I think of a Pharisee or a Sadducee. His rhetoric has been mostly right, but his actions have often been wrong. So, when it comes to him and other so-called preachers, I do what Jesus admonished us to do and that is to do what they say, but not what they do. As a Role Model, he scored a 2.0.

Impact on the Race Al Sharpton's Impact on the Race has largely been negligible if not downright negative and as the decades go on, that becomes more and more apparent. He's only helped himself and it's been at the expense of the very people he says he's here to protect. Almost none of the cases where he has been asked to be a part of have brought justice for the victims and their families in the form of convictions of the perpetrators no matter if it's been Michael Griffith, Yusef Hawkins, Tawana Brawley, Amadou Diallo, Sean Bell, Trayvon Martin, Michael Brown, and Eric Garner to name a few.

I hate to beat a dead horse, but his failure to be Black America's advocate when he had the ear of the President is inexcusable and unforgivable. Every prominent African-American leader, who had an audience with a President, from Frederick Douglass to Harriet Tubman to Booker T. Washington to A. Phillip Randolph to Martin Luther King to Barbara Jordan to Vernon Jordan to Jesse Jackson, all advocated on behalf of Black people for relief and redress from the federal government except Al Sharpton. This was a complete abdication of his responsibility and a total dereliction of duty and for that, he should be "court-martialed" and banned from the Black Community. He should not be able to hang his hat or show his face anywhere in Da 'Hood and he can forget about coming to the Cookout. He scores a 0.9 in this category.

His total score is a 1.06, or a D-minus. $(0.9 + 1.5 + 2.0 + 0.9 = 5.3.$ $5.3/5 = 1.06.)$

Vernon Jordan

"The lesson here my friends is that members of the White Business power structure are bad politicians. They fail to understand that Blacks *will no longer be junior partners in the old alliance.*"[89] – Vernon Jordan

"The best way to get close to White folks is to use Black folks and get the attention of White folks and then, get their crumbs later on. So, that's always the game. A Brother that's down with the Community today is with Whitey tomorrow because his interest all along was to be with Whitey. We just didn't figure it out, you know, because we were taking him seriously."[90] – Alton Maddox on Black leaders' bait and switch tactics against the Black masses.

"Wherever White people are, there's opportunity. The system sees to that!"[91][92] – Vernon Jordan

The previous three quotes best sum up Vernon Eulion Jordan, Jr. who was born in Atlanta, Georgia on August 15, 1935, and died on March 1, 2021, in Washington, DC. His parents were Vernon, Sr., and his wife, Mary Belle Griggs Jordan.[93] He grew up in segregated housing projects with his parents and brother, Windsor.[93] He graduated from the same high school as the future Mayor of Atlanta, Maynard Jackson, did: David T. Howard High.[93] As a youth, he worked for his mother's catering business that serviced a lot of wealthy Whites and he worked as a waiter and caddy at a local country club. During his summer breaks from college, he worked as a driver for the former Mayor of Atlanta, Robert Maddox.[93]

Education and Early Career

After high school, Vernon attended DePauw University in Indiana.[93] He graduated in 1957 as the only Black in a class of 400.[93] He went on to Howard Law School in D.C. and graduated with a law degree in 1960. After law school, Mr. Jordan became a civil rights attorney. The firm he worked for sued the University of Georgia over its segregation policy in 1961.[89] The plaintiffs, Hamilton Holmes and Charlayne Hunter, won admission to the all-white institution.[89] Jordan, himself, walked Ms. Holmes past an angry White mob so that she could safely enroll.[89] Throughout the Sixties, Vernon would work for several civil rights organizations such as the NAACP, the Southern Regional Council, and the Voter Education Project.[93] In 1970, he became the United Negro College Fund's executive director and president of the National Urban League (NUL) in 1971.[93]

The Urban League

For ten years, Vernon Jordan led the Urban League as president. (Founded in 1910 to help rural Blacks migrating to cities adjust to urban life, the League is more moderate than the NAACP and certainly more conservative than Dr. King's Southern Christian Leadership Conference ((SCLC)) and the Student Nonviolent Coordinating Committee, or SNCC ((Snick.)) The Urban League "looked to corporations and the federal government for support."[94] During his tenure, he served as a gadfly to Presidents Richard Nixon, Gerald Ford, Jimmy Carter, and Ronald Reagan. He sincerely believed his antagonistic approach was the only way for the White Establishment to take HIM seriously and ostensibly the cause of Black people seriously.[89]

According to his daughter, Vickee Jordan Adams, other people took his words seriously, too.[89] White Supremacist, Joseph Paul Franklin, admitted to shooting Vernon Jordan after he was convicted in 1996 for another killing.[93] Previously, he had been acquitted of attempting to murder Mr. Jordan in 1980.[93]

Known for his fiery rhetoric and his fundraising skills, Jordan became "the preeminent Black spokesman" of the 1970s.[95] The HNIC!!! (Jesse Jackson and Al Sharpton would later go on to hold that title in the decades that followed.) He was a keynote speaker at the first and only National Black Political Convention which was held in Gary, Indiana in 1972. Vernon Jordan was handsomely compensated for his fundraising efforts on behalf of the Urban League. His office, staffed by three assistants, was three times the size of the one he would later have as a corporate lawyer in Washington.[96] He had a chauffeur-driven car and his own restroom.[96] Clearly, Vernon, had moved a long way from the West Atlanta projects of his childhood.

Although he was a civil rights leader, Mr. Jordan was not afraid to wade into the waters of national politics and economics like "jobs, poverty, health, and welfare" and face the ire of pseudo-intellectuals like Bill Buckley, Jr.[95] One person whose anger he could not ignore was Jimmy Carter's. During the 1977 National Urban League Convention, Mr. Jordan had the temerity to criticize the President and claim that he hadn't done enough for Black people,[97][98] who were the only group to give the Georgia Democrat 90% of their vote. (Interestingly, Blacks are making this same complaint today 44 years later about Joe Biden and the Democratic Presidents before him: Barack Obama and Bill Clinton.)

He accused the Carter Administration of having "…no full employment policy. We have no welfare reform policy. We have no national health policy. We have no urban revitalization policy. We have no aggressive affirmative action policy. We have no national solutions to the grinding problems of poverty and discrimination."[97][98] Those remarks sent Carter through the roof and he took Vernon behind the woodshed.

He did have a conservative streak, though, which caused him to take some odd positions and make some questionable remarks. He endorsed President Carter's pick for an FBI director calling the man nominated to be the Nation's Top Cop "a civil libertarian."[99] Huh? He told the Elks, a fraternal organization, that because Blacks like them, himself included, had "achieved in our society, (they) are often accused of being middle class, as if that were some kind of crime. We make no apologies for seizing the responsibilities thrust upon us by our education and our skills, for we are using what we have to help others make it, too."[100] Who have you all helped besides yourselves?

After, the rabid racist and government informant, Ronald Reagan was elected in 1980, Mr. Jordan inexplicably announced that he would give the new President the benefit of the doubt and was going to "wait and see" if "equality could be achieved by conservative means."[101] Now, this is the same Ronald Reagan, who courted racist voters by announcing the start of his campaign from Philadelphia, Mississippi, the town infamous for the murders of civil rights workers, Goodman, Schwerner, and Chaney. Four years later, he endorsed Jimmy Carter's Vice-President, Walter Mondale, who went on to suffer the worst drubbing by a presidential candidate in history by losing 49 out of 50 states in the General Election.[102]

Like many of today's Black leaders, his only message to Black voters was to beware of the Big, Bad Republikkkan Wolf who only wants to devour all the little Black Sheep and like many Black leaders of today, he seemed to believe in the mystical power of the vote.[102][103] If Black Folks would only just vote (for the Democrats,) all their problems would go away. It's the exact opposite of Frederick Douglass' assertion that "the Republican Party is the ship and all else the sea around us." Single-party voting has been a ruinous strategy for Blacks over the last 150 years. Since the end of the Civil War, both Parties have taken turns writing us off or taking us for granted and will immediately dump us overboard in favor of whiter and lighter voters as soon as the opportunity presents itself. Today, the Republicans are mostly a White Party and the Democrats, who are also racist, are desperately trying to replace Black Voters, their base, with Asians, Middle-Easterners, Latinos, and Native Americans – you know the whole People of Color (POC) coalition. (What the Democrats don't seem to understand is that as soon as those groups become assimilated they will vote Republican just like White ethnics ((e.g., Jews, Poles, Irish, Germans, and Italians)) did before them.) Bloc voting only works if you have an agenda and we have no agenda because Black leaders like Vernon Jordan refuse to create one and Black people refuse to demand one. Despite his reputation as a firebrand, he never once made real demands of elected officials or candidates for office before persuading his followers to vote for them. This is tantamount to political malpractice.

Post-Civil Rights Career

A year after nearly getting killed, Vernon became a lawyer and a lobbyist for Akin Gump Strauss Hauer and Feld,[96] a high-powered law firm, and never looked back. After all, he wasn't "no civil rights leader anymore!"[91] Perhaps, after getting shot in the back and lying in that hospital bed for 98 days, Vernon decided it was better to join the "Evil Empire" than to rebel against it. But, unlike Darth Vader, he never turned on his Master. Or perhaps, like any apprentice, he was being groomed by a master. I believe he was being groomed during his tenure at the Urban League and his becoming a corporate fixer was the desired outcome. Heading such a "prestigious" civil rights organization shouldn't be seen as boot camp, but rather as special forces training for such an elite African American leader because of all the political, corporate, and philanthropic connections he would make from a decade of fundraising and "activism."

Despite his rhetoric, Vernon Jordan had never been a radical. He had always been a Racial Moderate having "worked for several moderate civil rights groups during the 1960s choosing the mainstream even as a young man and staying with it when many of his colleagues took a more confrontational approach."[94] So, he had always been an accommodationist seeking a higher spot on the plantation not seeking to flee it or even burn it down.[94] Todd Gitlin, a sociology professor at NYU had this to say, "Jordan was part of the civil rights movement that wanted to integrate existing institutions, to change nothing but their coloration. So, it's perfectly logical that the way you integrate the power structure is by joining it and once you've joined it you conduct yourself accordingly, you advance yourself."[94] That's exactly what he did, too. During the Carter Administration, Vernon used to ask for a phone booth outside the White House just so he could call people and tell them he was calling them from the White House.[104] What a character – no what a clown!

During his eighteen years as a D.C. attorney, Vernon Jordan became a senior partner; supervised dozens of lawyer-lobbyists; earned over a million dollars a year; and was the favorite attendee of all the exclusive parties in town. But, what did his law firm, its clients, and the Washington elite get in exchange? They got a friend with "political judgment, advice, wide-ranging connections, together with an ability, unusual and therefore highly prized in Washington, to keep his mouth shut."[104] President Clinton said fondly of Jordan that he would never "betray a friendship."[104] Since Vernon was not a legal heavyweight, his value came from his interpersonal skills such as affability, obsequiousness, charm, humor, wit, networking, and the ability to put others at ease.[105][106] These are the things he learned as a young man while waiting tables and chauffeuring cars. While talent and technical expertise are important traits to have when working on a job or completing a task, it's your interpersonal skills that determine your success in work, business, and life in general. That certainly was the key to Vernon's success.

White People just loved Vernon Jordan. They invited him to all their parties and black-tie affairs. The New York Times, the Washington Post, CNN, MSNBC, and elite liberal publications like Vanity Fair just gushed all over him. During the Lewinsky Scandal, prominent D.C. reporters like Al Hunt came to his defense.[104] Just look at how fondly they talked about him. Louis Gerstner credits Jordan with his decision to leave his job as the CEO of the cigarette and junk food maker, RJR Nabisco, to become the CEO of IBM. "Vernon has this way with words, with insights, to sum up a point of view. He was an important influence on my decision," said the executive.[94] A former Washington Post reporter named Ms. Quinn said the following during the Lewinsky

Scandal, "Vernon has a place in the community. He knows where he's going to be for the rest of his life."[106] Incredible! This was an extremely rare case of White people favoring a Black man (Vernon Jordan) over a White man (Bill Clinton.) But, that's just how much they loved their Vernon.

He's most famously known as the "First Friend" because of his very close relationship with the 42nd President, Bill Clinton. Jordan and the Clintons became acquainted with each other during the Seventies and from that time until his death Vernon played the role of mentor, confidant, and facilitator for the former Governor of Arkansas. He lifted Clinton's spirits when he lost his re-election bid for Governor and when his best friend, former law partner, and Deputy White House Counsel, Vince Foster, committed suicide. After he was elected President in '92, Bill Clinton appointed Mr. Jordan to the chair of the transition team, a role that elevated him to national prominence. It was Jordan who helped the President mend fences with Zoe Baird, the woman who would've been the first female Attorney General until Clinton pulled her nomination because it was discovered that she had hired undocumented workers to be her nannies and hadn't paid their social security taxes for them.[104][107] He was the President's golfing buddy. Vernon Jordan would constantly be seen playing golf with Bill Clinton and chauffeuring him around on a golf cart during his Presidency.

He was often the President's emissary and functionary delivering messages to and from the White House to Cabinet members, politicians in both parties, campaign donors, business executives, and the media. If you were Black, he was often the bearer of bad news like he when told Mike Espy, the first and only Black Agriculture Secretary, that he was fired[104] or when he lied to Lani Guinier when he told her that both he and the President would have her back during the confirmation process for Assistant Attorney General for Civil Rights, but they didn't.[108] Republicans called her a "Quota Queen" because she supported Affirmative Action and they attacked her stances on voting rights and gerrymandering.

Neither Clinton nor Jordan nor the Black Misleadership Class (i.e., the Congressional Black Caucus and the Civil Rights establishment) had her back and her nomination wound up being withdrawn and she was all alone.

He was also the inspiration behind President Clinton's "Mend It; Don't End It" approach to Affirmative Action according to Chris Edley, a former White House aide.[94] Sixteen years earlier during a speech to Black executives, Louis Farrakhan had described precisely how Washington policymakers had gutted Affirmative Action by 1980 when he said they, "redefined it and redefined it and redefined it until you couldn't find it, anymore."[109] It was because of the "First Friend" that Affirmative Action was "redefined" out of existence. Gee, thanks, Vernon!

His advice and service to the President weren't limited to domestic matters, either. Vernon Jordan convinced Bill Clinton to support the passage of the North American Free Trade Agreement (NAFTA) shortly after he took office to the delight of his corporate clients and the dismay of labor unions. Most troublingly, he supported the Clinton Administration's deportation and repatriation of tens of thousands of Haitian refugees back to Haiti where they faced persecution and death.[110][111]

But, his single biggest contribution to the rise of William Jefferson Clinton, was taking him to the infamous Bilderberg Conference in 1991 and introducing him to businessmen and politicians from around the world.[104] That single move led to Bill Clinton's Presidency.[104] Finally, Vernon used his legendary networking skills to get the President's mistress a job at Revlon and testified on his behalf during his Impeachment Trial. When it came to his pal Bill Clinton, Jordan was a boule' in every sense of the word. He truly was an adviser and servant to the king.

He received a king's ransom for his "distinguished" service. Jordan, who had been serving on corporate boards since his days at the Urban League, had occupied a seat on 11 corporate boards, or 5% of board seats held by Blacks in 1996. That's an astonishing feat considering that at the time only 222 Blacks were sitting on corporate boards out of 9,592 seats.[91] It also paid him a pretty penny. In 1996, he earned tens of thousands of dollars yearly from every board that he served on including RJR Nabisco where he earned an annual salary of $50,000.[91] In addition to RJR Nabisco, he was a director for American Express, Xerox, Sara Lee, Revlon, Ryder Systems, Dow Jones, and Union Carbide. It was also a family affair. Jordan's daughter, Vickee Jordan Adams had bestowed upon her a high paying public relations job at Dow Jones, the former owner of the Wall Street Journal and publisher of stock reports and indexes like the Dow Jones Industrial, thanks in no small part to her dad, Vernon, serving on that company's board.[112] He was a member of two golf clubs in Washington, D.C., and even regularly vacationed in Jackson Hole, Wyoming.[113] He was even elected President of the Economic Club of Washington.[93] Vernon certainly came a long, long way from his days as a caddy.

After 18 years of carrying water for White politicians and businessmen in Washington, Vernon Jordan moved back to New York and entered the world of Wall Street by taking a job with the investment bank, Lazard Freres in 1999. The following year he had been made a Senior Managing Director for the bank.[93] In 2008 and 2009, he earned $3.04 million and $3.7 million, respectively, and almost $2 million a year in 2006 and 2007.[114]

Legacy

Most Black politicians and "activists" are just brokers or middlemen between Whites and Blacks. They offer nothing of value to either group, especially to Blacks. They give Blacks empty symbolism and false hope while they overtly or covertly serve as shields for Whites against accusations of racism. I first heard the term broker being used to describe a character who was a politician in a play I saw in the 1990s at the Fox Theatre in Atlanta. He was played by Taurean Blaque of Hill Street Blues fame. He played a shady state legislator in the South who just traded his Civil Rights legitimacy (Blackness) in exchange for favors from White politicians and businesspeople. The fictional state senator from Baltimore, Clay Davis, who was featured in <u>The Wire</u>, comes to mind when I think of a useless Black politician who trades on his Blackness to curry favor for himself at the expense of his constituents. Vernon Jordan certainly fits the mold.

Perhaps, the most damaging legacy of Vernon Jordan is the election of William Jefferson Clinton. It was Jordan who paved the way for Bill Clinton to become President and Hillary Clinton to be a First Lady, Senator, Secretary of State, and Presidential Candidate. It was his embrace of the Clintons, especially Bill, in the 1970s that made the political climate more favorable for a conservative, Southern Democrat rather than a liberal Democrat from the West Coast or the Northeast to become President. If you don't believe me, ask Mickey Kantor, Clinton's Campaign Manager and Commerce Secretary, who said without hesitation or qualification, "Vernon Jordan anointed this governor!"[94] Because he picked this young, "still wet behind the ears" politician back up after he lost his first re-election campaign for Arkansas Governor and because he introduced him to the billionaires at the Bilderberg Conference[94] that we got millions of Black men incarcerated under the 1994 Crime Bill written by Joe Biden and signed into law by Bill Clinton. It's because of Vernon Jordan's buddy that Welfare was cut and hunger and poverty increased among the Black poor. It's because of Vernon's homie that Affirmative Action is virtually nonexistent. We also got almost three decades of job losses in the millions because Vernon's Bud signed NAFTA. How many hundreds of thousands or even millions of Blacks were shut out economically because of this disastrous trade deal? Thanks to the Presidential Pal we got detrimental and deleterious US foreign policies towards Africa and the Caribbean, particularly in Rwanda and Haiti.

We also got a bellicose and resurgent China that's replaced the United States as the world's number one economy in the last decade and will replace the US as the world's policeman in the next decade due to its extensive military buildup. Bill Clinton facilitated the rise of China by giving the communist dictatorship "Most Favored Nation" trading status year after year during his Presidency. Now, America's in a cold war with Communist China and someday soon it will be a hot one. The draft-dodging Bill Clinton also normalized relations Vietnam, a country where 58,000 of our brave troops died at the hands of communists all so American business can find another cheap trading partner with whom to do "bidness" with. Shortly after that 1997 agreement, Americans were buying shirts that said, "Made in Vietnam."

Lastly, it's because of Mr. Jordan's "ace boon coon's" hijinks and shenanigans with Ms. Lewinsky and the lies he told to cover them up that we got George W. Bush, a man who had absolutely no business being in the White House. Subsequently, the American People suffered 8 years of mismanagement, malfeasance, and war. Perhaps, Alton Maddox was right when he said that "Vernon Jordan is the most dangerous Negro in America!"[90] Imagine the damage he could've done had he accepted Bill Clinton's offer to be his Attorney General. He would've had real power instead of just being a "power broker."

The following quote was said about the rapper Jay-Z but it is equally applicable to Vernon Jordan: *"All that money all that influence and all the resources that he has access to (have) simply gone to waste."*[78] The reason those resources have gone to waste is because Vernon Jordan suffers from Vernon Jordan disease. What is Vernon Jordan disease, you say? Vernon Jordan disease is:

"...a degenerate condition among Blacks in privilege that results in a loss of any memory of what they came to Privilege to accomplish and further, any memory of the millions camped outside the gate with Louis Farrakhan...[I]t afflicts only those Blacks who both wish feverishly and after careful screening are allowed to be close to the President socially. Inasmuch as the mere mention of Vernon Jordan disease violates a Privilege city ordinance, I am likely to be fined heavily by the foundations and

105

corporations charged with the responsibility of enforcing this little-known ordinance."[115][116]

Vernon Jordan was once a waiter and caddy at a country club in Atlanta. These roles are similar to that of being a butler. They're all servile and that's all Jordan ever did was be a servant of rich White people instead of a leader of the poor Black people from whence he came. Despite his law degree, his activism, and his work as an executive at the highest levels of Corporate America, Vernon chose not to be much more than a high-priced butler, or servant of White interests.

Score

Leadership Vernon Jordan had this uncanny ability to find himself in spaces where Black people aren't typically found and are certainly not welcomed. Being the only Black in his class in college is an example. Other examples include being invited to the White House; becoming a partner at a major law firm; serving on numerous corporate boards; vacationing on Martha's Vineyard; being a member of global secret societies like the Bilderberg Conference and the Council on Foreign Relations; and serving as a trusted advisor to Presidents. He was blessed with an abundance of people skills that gave him a high enough emotional IQ that allowed him to make fast friends and to rise up the ranks of both civil rights organizations and corporations. This allowed him to reinvent himself and prosper twenty years after he started his career.

Vernon Jordan, Johnnie Cochran, Douglas Wilder, and Maynard Jackson were among the few Black attorneys of their generation to make big money although they did so relatively late in life compared to their White counterparts because of Segregation. Vernon Jordan's professional career spanned 60 years. He receives a 3.0 in Leadership for the level of prominence he achieved. That's the only reason he was still considered a Black leader during the 2nd half of his life. Black people, especially the Black Professional

Class, are obsessed with seeing Black Faces in High Places. Theirs is a politics of Black Firsts not of Black Power.

Race Pride I don't have a problem with anyone wanting to make lots of money and pursue happiness. (I would like to do the same myself. I mean who wouldn't?) I have no problem with anyone wanting to reinvent him/herself in order to achieve their goals. If he wanted to be a lawyer in private practice that's fine with me, but don't continue to claim to be Mr. Civil Rights when by your own admission you're "no civil rights leader anymore!" (This is my same criticism of John Lewis.)

Vernon's sin was not that he wanted to pursue wealth and "power." His sin was that he diminished his previous life as a civil rights attorney and made it his business to please rich White people and put them at ease. I remember seeing him at a Christmas event videotaped by C-SPAN. The audience was singing carols. I believe he read a poem and gave some additional remarks as well as made some jokes. The whole time he was smiling and "putting on a show for White folks" and they just ate that mess up. It was disgusting. That's why he served on so many boards and received so many awards.[117] It's because he made Whites feel like they'd been fair with Blacks because after all, Vernon Jordan was their friend. (The phrase "some of my best friends are Black" comes to mind.) Former American Express Chair and CEO Ken Chennault solidified this idea of Vernon being a confidant, or "trusted advisor" to White executives when he shared a story about him telling Mr. Jordan that he knew that he "had arrived was when White CEOs would ask you to introduce them to other White CEOs." He gets a 1.5 for Race Pride for spending the last 40 years of his life being a sophisticated entertainer, mascot, cheerleader, shill, and shield for the White elite.

Role Model Words have consequences and when he announced to the world that he was no longer "a civil rights leader," the world took notice and began to emulate him. Soon after a young Ron Brown left the Urban League for a job in Corporate America stating he was done being an expert "on all things Black." What's wrong with being an expert "on all things Black?" What's wrong with being a Black lawyer, doctor, scientist, businessperson, or actor? Why do so many Black people wrongly believe they have to eschew, or forsake their Blackness in order to be successful? Vernon Jordan convinced himself and others that there was something wrong with being president of the National Urban League or other Black-led organizations. It's like they can only be affirmed and validated if they are part of something White-owned and operated. For them, "the White man's ice is colder."

Vernon Jordan went along to get along. When the RJR Nabisco began targeting Blacks, particularly Black youth, to increase its sales of cigarettes, Jordan said nothing while serving on their board. This kind of "go with the flow, make no waves" careerism on the part of too many Black professionals has been detrimental to Blacks as a group and in the long run harmful to the very individuals who practiced it. He mentored many young Black executives to adopt his way of thinking. Again, Chennault said, "Vernon, I think, is the person most responsible not just opening up the door for Blacks in business, but guiding them on the pathway of success."[89] Guiding them onto his pathway to success. A pathway that is racially moderate and accommodating to White racism. This mentality is what produced the likes of Colin Powell, Jeh Johnson, Tim Scott, Larry Elder, Candace Owen, Stephen A. Smith, Jason Whitlock, Michael Jordan, Charles Barkley, Shaquille O'Neal, Cedric Richmond, Valerie Jarett, Kamala Harris, and Barack and Michelle Obama among many, many others. He gets a 1.5 as a role model.

Impact on the Race Skip Gates cringeworthily described Vernon Jordan as the Rosa Parks of Wall Street. He thought his genius lied in his vision of "top-down integration." Of Jordan, he said, "Vernon Jordan was the first person to realize that a devastatingly effective form of 'Black Power' would be top-down integration at the heart of American Capitalism: Wall Street. Vernon Jordan has done more to integrate the corridors of financial power than any

African American in history. Vernon Jordan is the Rosa Parks of Wall Street."[89][118] How so, Professor Gates? By serving on more corporate boards than any other Black person in history? Even by Mr. Jordan's own estimate "the Street has a long way to go." When Rosa Parks refused to give her seat at the back of the bus, she helped all Black people move to the front of the bus. Hers was a Bottom-Up Integration. Top-Down Integration only helps those who are already at the top like you "Skippy Boy."

Equally ridiculous to Prof. Gates' assertion was Chennault's description of Jordan as "the first crossover artist."[89][118] For the record, he was not. Rosa Parks went to jail fighting for freedom. Vernon Jordan did not. Rosa Parks was impoverished for her efforts. Vernon Jordan became rich. White folks ran Rosa Parks out of Montgomery! They loved Vernon, however. He was also not an artist. But, just like most crossover artists, once he won acceptance by a White audience, Vernon never returned to his original Black audience. He forgot about the very people who made him successful.

Chennault said he was transformative. But, I don't see how. He didn't open many doors for Blacks while he was in Corporate America. He was often the only Black face in the room and almost none replaced him after he left. The few that he did "mentor" were molded into his image and likeness to be acceptable to White America. The former AMEX executive called Jordan a crossover artist because "he was able to move from civil rights to business."[89] I don't know why people think that's such a great leap. Many civil rights activists are businesspeople or aspiring business people who were denied an opportunity in business, so they became activists in order to demand redress. Since he was a lawyer, it would make sense that he would continue to practice the business of law once he left the nonprofit sector.

In the final analysis, Vernon Jordan's positive impact on his race was marginal if not negligible. During the ten years that he was at the helm of the Urban League, no major nor minor legislation on behalf of Blacks was passed in Congress due to his agitation or lack thereof. After he became a corporate executive in the early 1980s, the flood gates didn't open for young Blacks to become law partners and managing directors of investment banks. If anything, opportunities for Blacks have receded in the 40 years since his ascent into the executive ranks. He receives a 1.0 for his Impact on the Race. His overall score was a 1.4 or a D (Poor.) (3.0 + 1.5 + 1.5 + 1.0 = 7. 7/5 = 1.4.)

Maynard Jackson

My favorite politician is Maynard Jackson, the first Black Mayor of Atlanta. He was brash and arrogant, yet kind and intelligent. He was the kind of Black Man who didn't let anyone intimidate him. It was through his efforts that Atlanta became an international hub of transportation and commerce and he was instrumental in his City winning the bid for the Summer Olympics in 1996. It was his bold, unflinching vision for the future that secured Atlanta's place as the Black Mecca.

Early Life

Maynard Holbrooke Jackson, Jr., was born in Dallas, Texas on March 23, 1938, to the Reverend Maynard H. Jackson, Sr., and Dr. Irene Dobbs Jackson.[119] He was the only male child out of six children.[119] Both his parents were educated professionals with his father being a Baptist minister and his mother being a French Professor.[121] The Jacksons lived in Dallas for several years after Maynard was born before moving to and settling in Atlanta in 1945.[119] Maynard, Sr., had become the Pastor of Friendship Baptist Church while his mother, Irene, was hired at Spelman College.[119] His maternal grandfather, John Wesley Dobbs, played a prominent role model in young Maynard's life, especially after Maynard Sr., died. Dobbs was a prominent figure in Black Atlanta and he was known as "the Mayor of Sweet Auburn," a middle-class Black neighborhood where the Reverend Martin Luther King, Jr., also grew up. A fifth-generation Georgian on his mother's side, Jackson's maternal great grandfather founded a church and his aunt was the famous opera singer Mattiwilda Dobbs.[119][120]

Maynard graduated from David T. Howard High School at the age of 14.[121] Like Martin Luther King, he went to Morehouse College, an all-male liberal arts college established in 1867 exclusively for Black Men. He graduated in 1956 at 18. He briefly attended law school at Boston University before dropping out.[119][121] He worked as a salesman for a few years before resuming his legal studies at North Carolina Central University, an HBCU in Durham, where he earned his Juris Doctor in 1964.[121] While at North Carolina Central, he met and fell in love with Burnella "Bunnie" Hayes and the young couple married soon after in Danforth Chapel on Morehouse's campus.[119] Both, the College's President, Dr. Ben E. Mays, and Rev. Dr. Sam Williams, Pastor of Friendship Baptist Church, officiated their ceremony.[119] Jackson briefly practiced law early in his career: first, with the National Labor Relations Board and later with the law firm of Jackson, Paterson, Parks, & Franklin.[119][122]

Senate Race

After a few years of practicing law, 30-year-old Maynard Jackson ran for the US Senate in Georgia against arch-segregationist, Herman Talmadge in the 1968 Primary.[123] Jackson said he had been inspired to run after hearing that presidential candidate Sen. Robert Kennedy had been assassinated.[124] He was also inspired to rid Georgia of an entrenched racist politician. Maynard told reporters after he made his announcement that he remembered growing up seeing a sign with the initials L.S.M.F.T., or "Lord Save, Me From Talmadge!"[120] The unemployed lawyer borrowed $3,000 on June 5, 1968, the same day that Bobby Kennedy was killed in order to file his candidacy in time for the election.[119][123]

He ran on a platform that focused on "urban affairs, Federal aid to education, and the anti-poverty and welfare programs" as a way to target Black voters and voters who lived in the state's cities.[124] Jackson was soundly defeated in the September 12th Democratic Primary with Talmadge winning both urban and rural counties.[124] However, there were allegations of voter suppression where Black voters in rural areas, many of them illiterate, were told "to put an 'X' by Talmadge's name and that would cross him out." But, what they were really doing was voting for Sen. Talmadge.[119] Despite losing the race, Jackson won statewide and nationwide appeal which set him up to ultimately win the Atlanta Mayor's Race in 1973.[119]

Atlanta City Council

Following his Senate race, Jackson ran for Atlanta City Council in 1969 and was elected Vice Mayor.[119][125] In January of 1970, Maynard was sworn in by the newly inaugurated Sam Massell, who was the first Jewish Mayor of Atlanta and who only four short years later would be his rival.[119][125] Ironically, had the City's Kneegrow leadership not been divided, they could've had elected one of their own in Horace B. Tate in 1969.[125] Joining Maynard Jackson on the Council were four other Blacks including Joel C. Stokes, a young banker, who was appointed by Mayor Massell as Chair of the Finance Committee.[126]

According to his first wife, Bunny, the Board of Alderman as the City Council was known at the time wasn't exactly welcoming to Mr. Jackson.[119] Whenever the Mayor wasn't able to attend a committee meeting, the Vice Mayor could attend instead and his vote would count the same as if the Mayor was there himself. Well, the White aldermen no longer wanted to follow that tradition after Maynard Jackson became the Vice Mayor and they tried to change the rules. But, Black Atlantans rallied around Jackson and the racists who opposed him backed down. Maynard's use of this power also bothered Mayor Massell because he would vote in the manner that he thought was best rather than vote in the way the Mayor thought he should. This often shifted the City's policies in a direction that was contrary to what Mayor Massell would have wanted had he been present to vote. The Mayor and the Vice Mayor were often at loggerheads as a result. This constant friction between the two men set up a scenario where they would be running against each other for the Mayor's chair in 1973.[119]

Run for Mayor

When Jackson ran for Mayor of Atlanta in 1973, not everybody Black was enthusiastic. Many in the Black Establishment felt he should fall in line and wait his turn. Some of them including construction magnate H.J. Russell and politician Jesse Hill thought they could draft his agenda for him and dictate what positions he should take.[119] But, Maynard wasn't having it. He flat out told them that he would run on his own agenda. Eventually, they backed down and supported him.[119]

Perhaps, no one took more umbrage at Jackson's run for Mayor than the incumbent, Sam Massell. He had such a sense of entitlement to the Mayor's chair that he couldn't think straight. After having won four years earlier largely off the Black vote, he felt like the Black Community owed him something and how dare a Black man run against him. Instead of touting his accomplishments during his tenure and his relationship with his constituents, he ran a campaign of fear and division[127] similar to that of the Dixiecrats of Old and to that of the Republikkkans in the decades that followed. During the last two weeks of the race, he ran ads that exclaimed that "Atlanta's Too Young to Die!"[127] He made a racial appeal to White people suggesting that the City would go to hell and a handbasket if a Black man became Mayor.[127] Not only that, he went around telling Black People that they had to "think white" and that "Atlanta's greatest Black leader doesn't happen to be Black."[119] All this racial antagonism by Massell did was make Black voters even more determined to put Jackson in office.[119][127]

On October 17, 1973, Atlanta elected Maynard Jackson its first Black Mayor. When he was inaugurated in the Atlanta Civic Center roughly three months later, over 5,000 people attended from all walks of life.[119] There was a tremendous sense of optimism floating throughout the City. Not only was this a huge moment in Maynard Jackson's life, but it was a huge moment for local politics. The 18-member City Council was evenly divided between Blacks and Whites and Blacks had also taken over the school board.[119][128]

First Term

Since there wasn't much of a honeymoon after he was inaugurated, the new Mayor got right to work. The first thing he did was a review of where the City held its bank accounts.[119] He discovered that none of the banks holding City funds had any Black board members.[119] When he asked the banks' executives to change that, they balked and one CEO even told him he couldn't find any Blacks qualified to serve on his board.[119] When Mayor Jackson threatened to pull the City's funds from their banks and put them in New York, San Francisco, or Chicago banks, they hurried up and found some Blacks to serve on their boards.[119]

The next thing he had to do was to find a new police chief because the current one, John Inman, was a rabid racist. The final straw for this redneck came in 1974, ten years after the height Civil Rights Movement, when he elected to sic police and police dogs on peaceful protesters holding a rally.[119] Ironically, it was Sam Massell, the City's first Jewish Mayor and its "greatest Black leader," who hired and then, extended the contract of this White Supremacist.[119] Jackson's predecessor tried to gum up the works for the new mayor by giving the rabid racist a seven-year contract which would've extended beyond the incoming Mayor's first term.[119] This was unprecedented.

Being the proud and shrewd Morehouse Man that he was, Maynard Jackson wasn't going to sit and take that and he immediately thought up ways to fire the Police Chief. After three months of trying and a Georgia Superior Court's ruling in Chief Inman's favor, the Mayor came up with the brilliant idea of creating a Department of Public Safety and hiring his old Morehouse classmate, Reginald Eaves, to be its new director. All of the City's public safety agencies fell under this department's umbrella and the Police Chief reported directly to the Public Safety Commissioner.[119] This move incensed White Atlantans everywhere from the Chief, himself, to the rank-and-file officers to business leaders to city councilpersons to the average, ordinary White citizen.[129]

Eaves' tenure as Public Safety Commissioner was fraught with controversy at the outset, however. He was accused of nepotism and cronyism when he helped his nephew get a city job; a Black advertising firm a contract; and hired a secretary with a criminal record.[129] It was nothing that Whites in power haven't done and continue to do. It's called patronage aka the good ol' boy network. But, the thing that got him in the most trouble were allegations of cheating on the Sergeant's test by Black officers to get promoted.[119] Council President Wyche Fowler, a so-called White liberal who often sought to undermine Atlanta's First Black Mayor, called for the Commissioner's firing.[119] The Mayor feeling betrayed said, "I shall never forget what Wyche Fowler did!"[119]

Jackson's biggest accomplishments during his first term were initiating and completing several construction projects including the expansion and renovation of Atlanta's Airport.[119] He developed an Affirmative Action program that eliminated White businesses' monopoly over city contracts.[119] It was thanks to this program that scores of millionaires were created from among the many thousands of Black entrepreneurs who were no longer shut out of opportunity because of racism. Black construction companies were able to build roads and runways and Black restauranteurs and retailers were able to get airport concessions contracts and serve millions of patrons a year who came through the world's busiest airport. He also believed that Urban Renewal need not be Negro Removal aka gentrification. He did this by ensuring that Interstate 85 was built around Black neighborhoods instead of through them.[119][121] In addition to expanding the Airport's capacity to handle international flights, he also sought investment and trade opportunities between local and foreign firms and governments starting in 1975 with a tour of the Middle East.[130] The Jackson Administration cut crime while lowering complaints of police brutality; built parks; supported fine arts; opened the budget-making process to the public; and improved the economy.[131]

Mayor Jackson also performed a lot of symbolic gestures to demonstrate that he cared about Atlantans and would create a climate that would foster civic pride and unity. He continually tried to improve race relations despite the White Community rebuffing him. When Martin Luther King, Jr.'s mother, Alberta Williams King, was assassinated while playing the organ in Ebenezer Baptist Church, the same church that her husband and both her sons pastored, he ordered that the flags over City Hall be flown at half-staff until she was buried.[132] He also spent a weekend in one of the City's housing projects to better understand the plight of the residents and as a result worked to improve their living conditions of those residents and of others in low-income housing around the city.[133]

Besides, having to deal with rising crime and the ongoing police officers' cheating scandal, during the last year of his first term, the Mayor had to deal with a strike held by 1,000 Black garbagemen and other municipal employees. During the previous year, they had taken a "holiday" and called out after he refused to give them a $500 annual raise.[134] In 1977, garbagemen and other City workers made an average of $7,500 a year[135] or less than $34,000 in today's money. Those are poverty wages. They asked for a $1,000 a year raise[135] which would only increase their salaries to $38,000 annually in today's money. But, the Mayor cried poverty and refused to budge. He managed to break the strike by hiring over 700 replacement workers and rehiring over 400 who wanted their jobs back.[136]

It had been only nine short years earlier that Dr. King lost his life supporting a similar strike in Memphis, Tennessee. Ironically, it was Black People's pain and outrage caused by that murder along with Bobby Kennedy's three months later that led Jackson to consider a career in politics. Jackson had previously been a labor lawyer and he was elected largely by Black poor and working-class voters. He was endorsed by labor unions during his elections for Vice Mayor and Mayor in 1969 and 1973. Yet, he along with "Daddy King" [137] and other Black leaders tied their fortunes to White business interests over their own people. Sadly, over the last 50 years, members of the Negro Petite Bourgeoisie, or the Black Middle Class also known as the Black Misleadership Class have too often favored their "class" interests over racial solidarity with the very Black masses that helped them get to where they wanted to go.

Maynard and Burnella "Bunny" Jackson divorced sometime near the end of his first term.[119] They had three children: 2 girls and a boy. The former couple remained friends for life. On August 26, 1976, Maynard Jackson met his second wife, Valerie Richardson, at a friend's house.[119] The two married a year later[119] and they had two girls.

Second Term

Near the start of his second term, Jackson fired his Public Safety Commissioner, Reginald Eaves.[138] Mr. Eaves was not only in charge of the Police Department, but he was also the head of the Fire Department and other City departments and agencies that dealt with public safety. The Mayor said his reasoning for removing Mr. Eaves was because of "serious errors in judgment" after allegations of cheating on the part of Black officers during testing took place and "he should have known, if he did not know, that cheating was taking place."[138] While many Whites immediately condemned the Commissioner as guilty and demanded that Mr. Jackson fire him, many Blacks praised him for reducing both crime and police brutality.[138]

In a move that showed solidarity with freedom fighters in Rhodesia (later Zimbabwe,) Mayor Jackson held a fundraiser for Joshua Nkomo, leader of the Patriotic Front. The money raised would be given personally to the resistance leader. Mr. Nkomo, who spoke that weekend at Morehouse College's commencement,[139] fought alongside Robert Mugabe against the racist apartheid government of the Republic of Rhodesia.

Like most cities, Atlanta has its fair share of crime and throughout the 70s and 80s, when there was this explosion of crime committed largely by Baby Boomers, the "Capital of the South" had multiple crime waves. From 1974 to 1978, when Reginald Eaves was Commissioner, crime and interestingly complaints of police brutality went down.[138] After 1978, crime began to pick up despite an expanding local economy. As reported by the New York Times, crime, in general, was up by 29% with rapes going up by 53%.[140] By August of 1979, murders had exceeded by six the number of all the reported homicides in 1978 for a total of 149.[140][141]

The business community fearing the loss of conventions demanded the Mayor do something.[140] The daily news coverage, especially from the local press, put even more pressure on the Jackson Administration. Despite being under tremendous scrutiny by both political and corporate interests, Mayor Jackson adroitly convinced trade associations and professional organizations like the Radiological Society of North America to keep their conventions in Atlanta and corporations like Georgia Pacific to move their headquarters there.[140] Governor George Busbee took it upon himself to send in state troopers to patrol the city and embarrass Atlanta's First Black Mayor.[140][141] Jackson took additional steps to fight crime such as hiring the former Sheriff of Multnomah County, Oregon, Lee P. Brown, as his new Public Safety Commissioner in 1978;[142] appointing former US Attorney General, Griffin Bell, as an advisor on crime;[143] signing into law an ordinance that required a 60 day waiting period to buy a handgun;[144] installing a new police communications system which included erecting police booths downtown.[145]

As if things couldn't get any worse, a serial killer spent the next two years preying on the City's youth and children. The media dubbed the crisis, which took place from 1979 to 1981, the Atlanta

Child Murders. During this time, both the City and the Nation were terrorized. (It wasn't like it is today. During the Eighties, stories of missing and exploited children from all over the country were reported nightly. You'd see pictures of missing children and women on the backs of milk cartons and on mailers. It was a scary time to be a kid or a parent. The combination of the hysteria over missing children, rising crime, rising teen pregnancy rates, new drugs like crack and meth exploding on the scene, and the emergence of a little-understood virus that attacked the immune system and that would eventually lead to the AIDS pandemic caused Americans to feel under siege.) Mayor Jackson and the Atlanta City Council did all they could to handle the situation: imposing a curfew; police conducting door-to-door searches; hiring a psychic; asking for assistance from both the state police and the FBI; and even offering a $100,000 reward. Neighborhood residents conducted armed patrols and volunteers formed search parties. But, for two years, there were no leads.

All of the victims were Black and many of them were poor. Activists and community organizers began demanding more from the Mayor and many thought that he, the Black Bourgeoisie, the police, and the White Establishment weren't doing enough or not as much as would have been if these had been White kids who had been missing or murdered. Some even speculated that these crimes were racially motivated.[146] The Mayor discounted this theory and told Black residents to "lower their voices."[147] Now, these attacks may or may not have been racially motivated, but it was rather insensitive and condescending for him to tell adults, who are at their wits' end over their kids being kidnapped and murdered, to "lower their voices." People have a right to express themselves and shouldn't be treated like kids. The only people who get talked to like this are Black People and sadly, it's often by other Black People worried about offending White People.

On June 21, 1981, a 23-year-old Black man, named Wayne Williams was arrested for murder.[148] Although the two victims were adults, Public Safety Commissioner Lee Brown was convinced that he had the right man. Some in the Black Community saw this arrest as a public diversion and speculated that Williams was being used as a patsy to deflect attention from a possible racial motive for these killings of Black children and the true perpetrators of these crimes could be White Supremacists like the Klan. I remember watching Lee Brown tell CNN's Soledad O'Brien that the disappearances and murders stopped once Mr. Williams was captured.[150] I also remember watching her interview Wayne Williams from prison and he didn't seem to do or say anything that supported his innocence. He was very cryptic and defensive instead of vociferously defending himself.[148][150] So, I don't know whether he's innocent or not. I also don't know if it's true that the disappearances and the killings of Black children stopped just because he had been arrested. But, the case was closed and both Atlanta and the rest of the world were ready to move on.

One of the last things Mayor Jackson did during his second term, was to fight for a fair and accurate count of Atlanta's population during the 1980 Census to ensure that the City got its fair share of revenue and resources from the federal government as well as representatives in the Congress and the Georgia Legislature after redistricting. He wrote an Op-Ed in the New York Times in response to an editorial it had published condemning US mayors who testified in front of Congress about the problems that came about during the Census.[151] The Jackson Administration eventually sued the federal government over the Census Bureau's miscounting of Atlanta's residents.[152] Civil rights leader, former Congressman, and former UN Ambassador Andrew Young succeeded Maynard Jackson as Atlanta's Mayor in 1982.

Post-Mayoral Career

After Maynard left office in 1982, he had to leave his beloved city for Chicago because local corporate law firms, banks, and major corporations shunned him in retaliation for his insistence that they be fair with Blacks.[119] So much for his "support" in the White business community. He joined the law firm of Chapman and

Cutler as a managing partner in 1982.[119] He opened their Atlanta office and used his charm, political acumen, and contacts to secure contracts with "Black-Run cities."[153] During this time, he also established the National Association of Securities Professionals (NASP,) a trade association for Black and Hispanic professionals in the securities industry.[119]

Third Term

After a successful law practice, Maynard Jackson decided to run for a third term as Mayor in 1989. By this time, Atlanta was prosperous and growing and there had been 16 years of "Black Rule." So, while it appeared that White Atlantans had gotten used to and had accepted the idea of their fair city having a Black mayor, it didn't mean they weren't up to their old tricks. They found a Black they could back or maybe he just volunteered his services. His name was Michael Lomax. He, like Jackson, was a lawyer and a Morehouse Alum. He taught at Spelman College, Morehouse's sister school, and was the Chair of the Fulton County Commission. Mr. Lomax's strategy was to attack Mr. Jackson's record as Mayor and tag him as out of touch and out of date and try to convince voters that he was the face of a new generation of Black leaders in Atlanta. He ran ads to address White fears about Black crime.[154] Ironically, you have a Black man trying to Willie Horton another Black man. I guess I shouldn't be surprised, though, because, for the past 18 years, Mr. Lomax has been the head of the United Negro College and he has turned that once-proud, venerable fundraising arm for private Black colleges and universities into a shell corporation and tax shelter for White billionaires like Bill and Melinda Gates and the Koch brothers all so he can make a seven-figure salary. So, it should not be surprising that he made racist appeals to Atlanta's White elite just so he could be its next mayor.

Jackson, for his part, ran a more subdued race in '89 than he did in '73 and '77 when White racism was more overt. He made overtures to Corporate Atlanta to show that he'd be more of a

122

"team player" this time around.[153] He also tried to reassure the Black poor that he would do more to make sure they weren't left out.[153] It was a delicate balancing act.

Michael Lomax's strategy backfired. I don't know if his polling numbers were too low or some backroom deal was made, but Michael Lomax ultimately dropped out of the race two months before the election.[153] Former King apostle, the Rev. Hosea Williams decided to run after Lomax bowed out.[153] Maynard Jackson easily won for the third time.[153]

Mayor Jackson hit the ground running during his third term. He hired a new police chief, Eldrin Bell, to tackle Atlanta's pesky crime problem.[155] He wanted to address poverty, drug addiction, police brutality, homelessness, and AIDS.[119][156] However, he found limited success during his last four years as Mayor because of the intractability of the problems of race, class, and special interest politics. He also suffered from health problems and he wanted to leave a financial legacy for his family.[119][157] His biggest accomplishment during his final four years as an elected official was securing the winning bid from the International Olympic Committee (ICOG) for Atlanta to host the Summer Olympics in 1996.

Later Years

After he left elected office for good, Maynard Jackson was bit by the entrepreneurial bug and started opening businesses for himself. He expanded the reach of his firm, Jackson Securities, which he founded in 1987. It was an investment bank that specialized in municipal finance. Another venture he founded was called Jackmont Hospitality, an airport concessions company. It had operations throughout the South.[158]

While he remained active in the Democratic Party, he was also critical of the Party and served as an advocate for Black interests within it. He ran unsuccessfully against multimillionaire businessman, Clinton fundraiser, and future Virginia Governor,

Terry McAuliffe, for the Chair of the DNC in 2001. Mr. Jackson and his chief supporter, Congresswoman Maxine Waters, founded a Jackson campaign for the Chairmanship because the Democrats were once again taking their most loyal constituency, African Americans, for granted and always passing over Black candidates in favor of White candidates.[121][159] (This complaint, although needed, has become rather tiresome.) At the time, I remember watching Ms. Waters on C-SPAN recount to an audience at a DNC meeting that Terry McAuliffe just casually and cavalierly told her and a group of Black delegates, "I know I got y'all in the bag!" It was like he just expecting them to fall in line without question like good little girls and boys. Maynard Jackson also spoke at this gathering and aired his grievances. Although he did not win the post, he did gain influence. He became the DNC's National Development Chair and the Chair of its Voting Rights Institute.[121]

Death

Maynard Jackson suffered a heart attack while waiting for a flight to Atlanta at Reagan National Airport in Washington, D.C. on June 24, 2003.[119] He later died of cardiac arrest at a Virginia hospital.[121] He was 65. He was survived by his wife, Valerie, ex-wife, Burnella, his five children, and three grandchildren.

Score

Leadership Maynard was part of the small group of first Black Mayors that emerged in the late 60s and early 70s. He was elected three times. It was his drive, ambition, and vision that inspired millions of Black people across the country and around the world; lifted hundreds of thousands of Black Atlantans out of poverty; solidified Atlanta's position as the capital of the "New South;" and made Georgia's capitol a Mecca to millions. He was a transformative leader. Although he never fulfilled his ambitions for higher office, he gets high marks for trying. He receives a 3.7 in Leadership.

Race Pride Maynard Jackson was a member of the Black Bourgeoisie that arose during Segregation, a largely light-skinned elite who often embraced White high society's social norms and prejudices. His upbringing largely shaped his life and worldview. He was color struck. He favored the lighter-skinned Bill Campbell over the darker-skinned Marvin Arrington to be his successor in the 1997 Mayoral Race and exhorted Black voters to support Campbell on that same basis.[160][161] However, he was a very proud Black man whose efforts opened the doors of opportunity to millions of Blacks, of all shades, in Atlanta and worldwide. His was a politics that combined the best elements of Black Militancy and Black Respectability. He receives a 3.7 in Race Pride.

Role Model Maynard Jackson was a highly articulate, intelligent, and educated man. He was supremely self-confident. He was a risk-taker and unafraid of any challenge or criticism. He was unbought and unbossed. He was the Chief Advocate of Black Power in the form of Politics. He is my role model. He gets a 3.9 in this category.

Impact on the Race Maynard's legacy has long outlived him. Blacks around the world are still making the pilgrimage to Atlanta and making opportunities for themselves. He was never patient and never accepted that Blacks had to patiently wait before they could receive freedom, justice, equality, opportunity, and the American Dream. Nobody else did. Black politicians, at all levels of Government, walk in his footsteps. Barack Obama stands on his shoulders. Even today 50 years after his historic victory, young Black men and women are inspired by his example.

However laudable his accomplishments were, we must talk about his failures. Black Atlantans, the poor and working-class, did not integrate as well as they could have under his and his successors' leadership. Poverty and its associated ills continue to plague them. They have largely been left behind. He also conceded too much to the White Establishment, particularly during his third term. Lastly, he didn't keep a tighter leash on his appointees and associates who took advantage of the public trough for themselves when the Mayor was not looking. Therefore, he gets a 3.7 for Impact on the Race. His final score is a 3.0 or B average (Good.) (3.7 + 3.9 + 3.7 + 3.7 = 15.0/5 = 3.0)

Doug Wilder

Lawrence Douglas Wilder was born the seventh of eight children on January 17, 1931, in Richmond, Virginia.[162] His grandparents were slaves.[162] His father, Robert, sold insurance and his mother, Beulah Olive, was a maid.[162] He was named after songwriter and author, Paul Laurence Dunbar, and ex-slave turned abolitionist, Frederick Douglass.[162] He's most famously known for becoming Virginia's first and only Black Governor in 1989 and the first Black Governor since P.B.S. Pinchback became Louisiana's during Reconstruction.[162] New York's David Paterson, Massachusetts' Duval Patrick, and Maryland's Wes Moore are the only three Blacks who have served as a state's governor in the 34 years since Wilder was elected.

Early Life

He described his growing up in segregated Richmond during the Great Depression as "gentle poverty."[162] This probably means his parents, despite being Black and poor in the South, shielded their children from the deprivation and abuse they experienced as adults. Wilder attended Virgin Union University, an HBCU, which he paid for by working as a waiter and a shoeshine boy.[162] He graduated with a Bachelor's in Chemistry in 1951.[162]

After college, he was drafted into the US Army and fought in Korea where he earned a medal for valor.[162] He was later promoted to Sergeant.[162] During his service, Douglas Wilder fought for the rights of Black soldiers in the newly "desegregated" military.[163] Because of his efforts, many Black veterans of the Korean War received opportunities and promotions they otherwise wouldn't have received because of racism.[163]

Despite being a college graduate and a war hero, Wilder couldn't find a steady job in 1950s America where achievements such as his didn't guarantee employment for a Black man.[163] So, in 1956, he went to Howard Law School.[163] After finishing law school, Doug went on to have a successful career in private practice.[163] Wilder married Eunice Montgomery in 1958.[162] They had three children.[162] They divorced in 1978.[162]

Political Career

Douglas Wilder got his start in politics serving in the Virginia state legislature known as the General Assembly. He was elected to the state senate in 1969 "with a plurality of the vote in a three-way race against two White candidates,"[164] and he was the first Black since Reconstruction to do so.[162][163] Early in his legislative career, Wilder fought for Black voting rights and fought to rid the state of the last vestiges of Slavery and Segregation. He got the racist words "darkie" and "massah" removed from the state's anthem "Carry Me Back to Old Virginny."[163]

After he spent 16 years in the legislature, Doug set his sights on the executive branch. In 1985, he ran for Lieutenant Governor. During that race, former US Senator, Harry F. Byrd, Jr, cautioned Virginians to consider that "The next Lieutenant Governor will only be a 'heartbeat' away from the Governor's office."[165] In other words, he was saying, "Don't y'all let that nigger git in there! We might end up with a nigger governor!" It must've rankled the former Senator that a Black had the gall to stand in front of a portrait of his father, Harry F. Byrd, Sr., an arch-segregationist, while announcing that he was running for Lt. Governor. Other Republikkkans tried to brand him as a "liberal" which is another code word for nigger. Thanks, in large part, to the popularity of the outgoing Democratic governor, Chuck Robb, Wilder's skillfulness as a politician, and the Black Vote, he was elected.[163][164][165]

Four years later, Wilder sought to make history for a third time by becoming the first Black to be elected Governor of any state in the United States. Long gone were the big Afro, the raised fist, and the demands for radical change that he came in with when he was first elected.[163] His politics had become as conservative as his appearance.[163] Just like he did four years earlier, Wilder crisscrossed the state going into both its Whitest and its Blackest parts and all areas in between promising voters of all stripes that he would balance the budget; pave new roads; grow the economy; be tough on crime; and keep abortion "safe, rare, and legal."[166] He avoided talking about Race, his Race, and Racism, however.[166] It was a strategy that worked because on November 8, 1989, he became the 66th Governor of the Commonwealth of Virginia. No small feat since no Black person had become governor of any state for almost 100 years.

Doug Wilder spent his four years in the Governor's Mansion doing exactly what he promised by cutting costs; fighting crime; executing death row inmates; expanding highways; and petitioning the federal government for more infrastructure dollars.[162][164] During his Governorship, he was often embroiled in conflicts with his fellow Virginia Democrats.[164] There was also a recession in 1991 and Republicans won many seats in the General Assembly that year.[164] Governor Wilder was scapegoated by the White members of his Party for these losses.[164]

While he ran and mostly governed as a Racial Moderate, Gov. Wilder did do a few positive things on the racial front. He showed solidarity with the global anti-Apartheid movement when he divested state funds from South African firms.[162] He took an intellectually disabled Black man named Earl Washington, Jr., off death row after it was revealed that DNA evidence may prove his innocence.[162] That thoughtful action by the Governor later led to Mr. Washington's complete exoneration after further DNA tests proved his innocence years later.[162] His most celebrated and most controversial act was his granting clemency to high school basketball star, Allen Iverson. Iverson had been convicted and sentenced as an adult to five years in prison after a brawl broke out between Black and White teens at a bowling alley in Hampton, Va.[167][168] After the star athlete, who was 17 at the time, was released from prison, he went on to finish high school; attend Georgetown University on a scholarship; and have a successful NBA career.

While Wilder made noises about running for higher office like President and US Senator, the only other position he held after Virginia's Governor was Mayor of Richmond. He was elected to the post in 2004 after spending the previous two years working to have the City's charter changed so that Mayor can be directly elected by the voters rather than appointed by City Council.[162][164] Even before taking office, Wilder was embroiled in controversy when he demanded that the Police Chief be fired and went on a crusade against corruption in City Hall and on the School Board.[164] During his one term, he improved the economy; lowered crime; and got the City's fiscal house in order.[164] He did not run for re-election in 2008.[162][164]

A Racial Moderate

Douglas Wilder's political career is best summed up by a single phrase used to describe his political philosophy: "Calculated Compromise."[163] He can also be described as a **Racial Diplomat**, or a Black person who believes it's his job to make White people feel comfortable with him.[169] I prefer to use my own term of "Racial Moderate" to describe him and other Black leaders like him. A **Racial Moderate** is any Black person, in this case, a leader who feels he/she must always downplay racism in order to get anything done and/or to advance his/her career. Douglas Wilder certainly fits the bill. He believed and still believes that for a Black person to get ahead in life he/she must eschew their Blackness. These Blacks believe if make their Blackness "disappear," White folks will embrace and reward them.

Unfortunately, he is largely right. There's no way he would've become Governor in 1989 if he hadn't. The sad thing is that Black leaders like him, who grew up under Segregation, have already **paid that price**. Why do today's and tomorrow's generations of Black People have to still **carry that cross**? Today's Black

130

aspirants fervently believe they have to do the same thing, but to an even greater degree than those of the past. Many feel like they have to forget about other Blacks altogether and do whatever it takes to reach success. However, they hypocritically continue to use their people to get ahead. It seems like most of us are just a bridge for them to cross to get next to White people, whom they slavishly believe will grant them the acceptance they crave. Vernon Jordan, a Racial Moderate himself, once gleefully exclaimed, "Wherever White people are, there's opportunity..."[91] Famed New York civil rights attorney, Alton Maddox, once joked during a speech that Black leaders are "double agents."[90] I won't go that far, but their role in stymieing Black Progress is certainly long and troubling.

Black people often face the dilemma of being square pegs trying to fit in round holes. Many, if not most, feel they have to "cut off their corners" in order to fit in the round hole of White society. KPFT host, Dr. Abdul Haleem Muhammad, brilliantly summed up this conundrum when he asked his radio audience a rhetorical question about the two candidates running for Houston's Mayor in 2009. He said, "I have no problem with Annise Parker being openly gay, but can Gene Locke **be openly Black**?" If he'd have asked Doug Wilder, the answer would be, "No!" And that's what troubles me about Racial Moderates like Doug Wilder, Edward Brooke, Colin Powell, Barack Obama, and many, many others. They think the only way to success is through eschewing Blackness and embracing Whiteness.

Score

In the area of <u>Leadership</u>, Douglas Wilder receives a 3.85 for becoming the first Black Governor since Reconstruction and the first Black Governor elected in any state. For <u>Race Pride</u>, he receives a 2.5 because he downplayed his race for the sake of pleasing Whites and he teaches other Blacks to do this despite all the racism he's faced in the past and continues to face to this very day. As a <u>Role Model</u>, he receives a 2.5 for the same reason he did under Race Pride. While it's great that he was another Black First, we need leaders who put their people first rather than their own career advancement. Wilder's Impact on the Race yields him a 2.0 because his ascension to the highest office of his state largely helped him and a few lucky thousand Black college graduates and professionals who either worked for the state; received degrees from state colleges and universities; had contracts with the state; or worked for a private business that benefitted from his policies. For the millions of other Black Virginians, there was no significant improvement in their daily lives during his four years as Governor. The same was true for Black Americans as a whole under the eight years of Obama. The politics of Black Firsts is symbolism over substance and we're famished over here because we have had no sustenance since the Sixties. His Total Score is a 2.17, or a solid C. (3.85 + 2.5 + 2.5 + 2 = 10.85/2 = 2.17)

John Lewis

John Robert Lewis was born on a farm outside Troy, Alabama to Eddie and Willie Mae Lewis on February 21, 1940.[170] His parents were sharecroppers.[170] They had 10 children.[170]

Early Life

John knew he wanted to be a minister when he was 5 years old.[170] He would practice his oratory skills by giving sermons to his family's chickens.[170] John and his family lived in majority-black Pike County, Alabama.[170] The rural area was so deeply segregated that he had only seen just 2 White people by the time he was 6 years old.[170] He had few books to read at home and he received both his primary and secondary education in a one-room school.[170] Whenever the Lewises went into Troy, the White residents there were hostile towards them.[170] As a teenager, he was once denied entrance to the library because he was Black. Once during his youth, he visited Buffalo, NY. He saw for the first time the difference between the way Blacks and Whites interacted in the North versus how they did in the South.[170][171] There was less segregation and some integration between the two races unlike in Alabama and other Southern states.

As a youth, John was inspired by Dr. Martin Luther King, Jr., and the successful bus boycott he led in Montgomery, the state's capitol.[170] In 1958, he met Dr. King and discussed filing a lawsuit against Troy State University for denying him admission.[170] King told him that such a suit would put his family in jeopardy and advised him to attend a Historically Black College or University, instead.[170] John studied to become a minister at American Baptist Theological Seminary and after he finished there, he went on to Fisk University where he earned a Bachelor's in Religion and Philosophy.[170][171]

Activism

It was at Fisk University where John began his activism. From 1959 to 1960, he belonged to the Nashville Student Movement where he and other students held sit-ins at downtown businesses and other public accommodations to desegregate them.[170][171] In 1961, he took a break from school and became a Freedom Rider. The Freedom Riders were 13 young people, 7 Black and 6 White, who traversed the South on buses from Washington, D.C. to New Orleans to desegregate interstate buses.[170][171] (A year earlier, the Supreme Court had declared segregating passengers by race on buses that traveled on the interstate highway system was unconstitutional.)[170] For two years, Lewis participated in Freedom Rides throughout the South where he suffered numerous beatings and arrests.[170]

He became Chairman of the Student Nonviolent Coordinating Committee (SNCC,) or Snick, in 1963.[170][171] After being elevated to this post, John became more prominent in the Civil Rights Movement and was invited to speak at the March on Washington later that year.[170] He was the youngest member of the "Big Six" civil rights leaders who spearheaded the march and rally.[170] As SNCC's Chair, he set up Freedom Schools, where activists studied the tactics of nonviolent resistance and held Freedom Summer, a voter registration drive in 1964.[170] Both, he and Hosea Williams led over 600 protesters to the Edmund Pettis Bridge on Sunday, March 7, 1965[170] in an attempt to march from Selma to Montgomery to petition Alabama's Governor and lawmakers to give Black Alabamians the right to vote. Local and state police were waiting at the other end of the bridge for the marchers and as soon as they approached them, the "lawmen" and their dogs viciously attacked the peaceful protesters. Women and the elderly were brutalized. No one was spared. Many were killed. John Lewis was beaten by a cop within an inch of his life. His head was permanently scarred,[170] and he suffered brain damage as a result.

Lewis, a once-great speaker, was reduced to stammering and stuttering for the rest of his life.

Life After the Civil Rights Movement

John was ousted from SNCC in favor of Stokely Carmichael in 1966[170] probably because the organization's members felt he wasn't militant enough to lead it from a focus on Integration to one on Black Power. (Lewis' militant Integrationism and his opposition to Black Nationalism or even Black self-interest would appear over and over, again, throughout his political career.) Later that year, he accepted a job with the Field Foundation.[170][171] In 1967, he went onto the Southern Regional Council.[170][171] From 1970 to 1977, he worked as the Director of the Voter Education Project (VEP) where he registered over 4 million minority voters.[170][171] After an unsuccessful run for Congress, Lewis joined the Carter Administration as an Associate Director of ACTION, a federal agency that sponsored volunteerism.[170][171] He left that post in 1980 and the following year got himself elected to Atlanta's city council.[170][171]

In 1986, he ran, again for the 5th Congressional District of Georgia and won. The race pitted him against an old friend from SNCC, Julian Bond, and exposed schisms in Black Atlanta[170][172] based on class and color. Bond was tall, light, and handsome while Lewis was short, brown, and bald. Bond, who was from Atlanta, was more popular with the City's Black Bourgeoisie while Lewis was more popular with the Black poor and White suburbanites. Bond was Hollywood while Lewis was Down Home. It was a real-life Tortoise vs. the Hare race with Julian Bond winning a plurality of votes in the initial primary race while John Lewis won the runoff and the nomination thanks to his mudslinging and popularity among White voters. Although the primary left Black Atlanta badly divided and cost him a dear friend, John won his prize. He beat his Republican opponent by a margin of 3-to-1 that November.[170][172]

John Lewis served in Congress from 1987 until he died in 2020. He was popular among Democrats and Republicans, alike. Despite having spent 33 years in the House of Representatives, he didn't write many bills and his most significant piece of legislation was a bill that authorized and funded the Smithsonian's National Museum of African American History and Culture.[170] Most of his bills never even got out of committee let alone passed. When they did, they were largely ceremonial ones like the Gold Medal Technical Corrections Act which posthumously awarded gold medals to Dr. and Mrs. King from Congress[173] and the Martin Luther King, Jr., Historic National Park Act of 2017 which made the King Center in Atlanta a national park.[174] My analysis of Propublica's data from the 102nd Congress to the 116th Congress, shows the Congressman proposed 317 bills or an average of less than 3 in a two-year term and only three of his bills became law during these 29 years. By any objective standard, his legislative record is abysmal. This man drew a six-figure salary for decades and yet, had very little to show for it. Perhaps, the words of one of his former colleagues, the late New York Congressman Major Owens, may explain why the Congressman couldn't get the job done, " 'However, I'm not a "successful" politician, if by successful you mean that I've been able to deliver. I've never been able to deliver large numbers of patronage jobs…That's not to say that I haven't been able to produce – I have. I've produced programs for the poor and the oppressed – but not jobs for my supporters."[175] Seems like Ol' John couldn't even "produce."

Lewis, like many Black politicians, saw himself as a moral crusader rather than a policy wonk or dealmaker.[172][176] But, fighting moral crusades aren't why people are sent to Congress. They're sent there by voters to "bring home the bacon" also known as "pork," or money dedicated to their Congressional district or state. "As Theodore Cross bluntly pointed out, 'the politically powerful are able to – and do – vote themselves government jobs, subsidies, franchises, protective contracts, and at times, wonderful Christmas trees of economic benefits.' "[177] White politicians understand this. Black ones don't. Very little of the legislation that John Lewis wrote translated into economic benefits for the Blacks of Georgia's 5th District or Black America at large.

Lewis did achieve rank while he was in the House. He was appointed Chief Deputy Whip in 1991 and Senior Chief Deputy Whip in 2003.[170] These were largely ceremonial posts with no real power or influence. He didn't get these promotions because of his legislative or fundraising prowess, however. No, John got them because he was willing to be the Democrats' pit bull against Republicans like Newt Gingrinch and George W. Bush. While no one is saying that the odious Gingrinch and Bush didn't deserve to be attacked for their dreadful positions and policies, but was this the best way to serve his mostly Black constituents who desperately needed jobs, contracts, tax breaks, and other government assistance? Let White Democrats and liberals bash President Bush and Speaker Gingrinch. Members of the Congressional Black Caucus (CBC) need to understand that they often are going to have to cross the aisle and work with Republicans to have money sent their Districts' way. Sent Black People's way. What's in the interest of the Democratic Party is often not in the interest of Black Folks.

John Lewis was one of Congress' staunchest liberals. Like the Congressional Black Caucus, he was a member of, he was known as "the conscience of the Congress."[170] His voting record is full of examples of him voting for liberal causes and policies. He was anti-war until he wasn't. On four separate occasions, John Lewis either sided with the President or voted in favor of war or military intervention. He "supported the troops" after President Clinton invaded Haiti in 1994.[170] He also backed Clinton's airstrikes against Iraq in 1998.[170] He voted in favor of invading Afghanistan in 2001 after the September 11th attacks.[170] Lastly, he voted against ending President Obama's seven-month-long bombing campaign and invasion of Libya in 2011.[170] Because the US and its allies felt a "Responsibility to Protect," hundreds of thousands of Libyans if not millions were killed or displaced particularly the native Black population in the southern part of the country. Thousands of Black immigrants from West Africa were sold and are still being sold into slavery throughout the Middle East and North Africa from Libya. This tragedy might have been averted if John Lewis had decided to vote his conscience.

It's no secret that Congress is captured by "Big Bidness" and its lobbyists meaning that the majority of Representatives and Senators are willing to sell themselves to the highest bidder. The Congressional Black Caucus, the so-called "Conscience of the Congress," is no different and they bend over for cheap. Wall Street, Big Pharma, military contractors, Native American tribes, and law enforcement associations are just a few of their numerous corporate sugar daddies.[178][179][180] John Lewis had a few sugar daddies of his own, too. One of them was Chief Chad Smith of the Cherokee Nation.[180] It was Smith who led the push to banish Black Cherokee Freedmen, who are the descendants of slaves owned by the tribe, from the Cherokee Nation of Oklahoma.[180] During a visit to the Indian nation, Lewis spoke fondly of Chief Smith and promised to do all he could to assist them in any way he could.[180] If he didn't know about the vote to strip Black Cherokees of their citizenship, he should've and if he did and still rewarded them for their treachery, it was a betrayal of Blacks everywhere.

Perhaps, the greatest paradox of his Congressional career was when he gave cops even more immunity to kill with impunity by voting for the so-called "Protect and Serve" Act of 2018.[179] Not only was it a betrayal of Blacks, specifically, and of oppressed people in general, but it was a betrayal of himself. Lewis, who during the Civil Rights Movement had been arrested 40 times and beaten four times by police, of all people, should have known better than to support such a racist and oppressive measure. But, he did it anyway.

Originally, Congressman Lewis endorsed Hillary Clinton for President in 2007. But, after Barack Obama's victory in the Iowa Caucuses the following year and the groundswell of support that followed, he changed his mind and endorsed Obama, instead. He reacted to Obama's winning the Democratic nomination by saying, "If someone had told me this would be happening now, I would have told them they were crazy, out of their mind, they didn't know what they were talking about...I just wish the others were around to see this day...To the people who were beaten, put in jail, were asked questions they could never answer to register to vote, it's amazing."[170] Of course, Congressman Lewis failed to demand that Obama do something about the rollback of those rights, by KKKonservatives on the Supreme Court and elsewhere, that those valiant Black people fought and died for.

While reflecting on the 50th Anniversary of the March on Washington in 2013 and the election of the First Black President, John Lewis told a reporter for theGrio the following: "If you ask me whether the election of Barack Obama is the fulfillment of Dr. King's dream, I say, 'No, it's just a down payment.' There's still too many people 50 years later, there's still too many people that are being left out and left behind."[170][181] But, you were sent to Congress, John, so they wouldn't be left out and left behind. What happened?

Maybe, John was having too much fun "reliving Selma" every year with his Congressional colleagues and corporate pals? Every year for 22 years, John Lewis would take a delegation of politicians and lobbyists to "a retreat" in Alabama hosted by the Faith and Politics Institute.[182] For $25,000 a pop, a corporate executive or lobbyist would get access to top politicians.[182] "...Lobbyists representing tobacco, telecommunications, automobile, home mortgage and other companies" frequented this event.[182] Lobbyists for Wal-Mart have also made the trip and the retail giant is a major sponsor of the Faith and Politics Institute and the Congressional Black Caucus (CBC.)[182]

Shamelessly, John Lewis sold his Civil Rights legitimacy to racists, exploiters, and polluters. He even bragged about it. "We don't deliberately set out to win votes, but it's very helpful," Lewis said when asked about the junket.[170] Would a Jewish, Latino, or Asian congressman trade on his people's pain just to rub shoulders and hobnob with the rich and powerful? I don't think so. It's time for a new type of Black Politics and a new type of Black Politician.

The Faith and Politics Institute's page dedicated to his memory says, "Beginning in 1998, as Board Co-Chair of the Faith & Politics Institute, Congressman John Lewis led his Congressional colleagues to Birmingham, Montgomery, and Selma, Alabama on annual Pilgrimages to *walk in his shoes*, *retracing his footsteps* in the Civil Rights Movement. Over the past two decades, the Institute and Congressman Lewis brought US Senators and Representatives, US Presidents, and other national and international leaders on a transformational journey that begins by deepening participants' understanding of the history of racial injustice and ends with their broad and profound desire to work toward racial reconciliation and healing."[183] Interestingly, the Institute described the experience that one of these "pilgrims" would have when going to Selma as a "walk in his shoes" and a "retracing (of) his footsteps" as if he were the only one in Selma on that "Bloody Sunday" in March of 1965. There were 600 other people there with Mr. Lewis and they suffered the same brutality that he did at the hands of the police. Many of them were killed. Attending a "retreat;" going on guided tours; eating sumptuous feasts; and being pampered while cutting deals can't begin to compare to marching for freedom and racial justice. It's insulting to even make the comparison. Hell, some of these same racist legislators and lobbyists that the Congressman palled around with, whine about having to wear a mask during a pandemic and bemoan their "loss of freedom." Oh boohoo!

Why Is John Lewis Being Criticized?

Some will ask, why go after John Lewis, he was a great man who suffered mightily fighting for his people's freedom? My reply is I'm not going after him. I'm critiquing him and no one is above critique and criticism not even good or great people or people that we like. Secondly, for over 50 years he reaped the rewards of seven years of struggle, abuse, and strife. Nothing is wrong with a man reaping the benefits of his hard work and sacrifice. He's supposed to, but he wasn't the only one. Thousands of nameless, faceless Black people suffered and died while fighting for their freedom, and very few of them were as handsomely rewarded for their efforts as the late Congressman John Robert Lewis. Most notably among them was the Rev. Dr. Martin Luther King, Jr. He protested; marched; was jailed; was beaten; and was ultimately killed while striking with garbage workers in 1968. John Lewis, on the other hand, got cushy jobs in the nonprofit sector and the White House; became a city councilman; and spent the last 33 years of his life in the US Congress. He got to see his son grow up. He died at age 80. Martin Luther King died age at 39. His wife was a widow. His kids grew up without their father. They had to depend on the kindness of strangers like Harry Belafonte to get by.

So, when you you're so handsomely blessed you have to pay it back even if you had to suffer to get it. He should've prevented others from going through the same traumas and injustices that he went through. If he had been more strident and forward-looking while he was in Congress as he had been when he was a young activist, perhaps, we wouldn't have suffered and continue to suffer the rollbacks in civil and voting rights that we have since the 1970s. Unfortunately, John Lewis came to believe, "I am Selma and Selma is I" as, political scientist and SiriusXM radio host, Dr. Wilmer Leon once said about him. After being anointed a Civil Rights "icon" and a "legend," by the media, he became the living embodiment of the Civil Rights Movement and he never let anybody forget it. You don't get to take those types of liberties and indulgences just because you've suffered previously, nor do you get to escape from criticism. If you want to get paid, write a book. Get a job in the private sector. But, if you're going to take a job serving the public, then serve the public. Congressman Lewis spent decades resting on his laurels when he should have still been in the race. My critique focuses primarily on his Congressional career because although it's not where he gained his claim to fame, it is where he spent most of his public life.

Score

John Lewis earned a 3.85 in <u>Leadership</u> for having spent 6 decades in public life and having reached the rank of Senior Chief Deputy Whip in the House. During the Civil Rights Movement, he risked his life, time and time, again, for his people's freedom. For decades, he was a living link between that movement and successive generations. He has always remained proud to be Black and he was a genuinely nice guy. I know because I met him. He earned a 4.0 for <u>Race Pride</u>. As an activist, Lewis is the perfect role model. While he could've done more during his four decades as an elected official, his heart was always in the right place. He got a 3.5 as a <u>Role Model</u>. As a member of the "Big Six," his <u>Impact on the Race</u> is vast. We're still feeling the effects of his and other civil rights activists' efforts. I just wish he would've taken some of that fiery brilliance into Congress with him. Even if he hadn't got many bills passed, he would've stood as a bright red line demarcating the boundaries between politician and statesman. His gets a 3.9 for his <u>Impact on the Race</u>. His final score is a 3.05 (3.85 + 4 + 3.5 + 3.9/5 = 3.05)

Colin Powell

Colin Luther Powell was born on April 5, 1937, in New York, New York, and died on October 18, 2021. He was the son of Jamaican immigrants, Luther and Maud Powell.[184] Powell's claim to fame was becoming the first Black Chair of the Joint Chiefs of Staff in 1989 and the first Black Secretary of State in 2001. "Prior to the election of Barack Obama as president in 2008, Powell and his successor, Condoleezza Rice, were the highest-ranking African Americans in the history of the federal executive branch (by virtue of the Secretary of State standing fourth in the presidential line of succession.)"[184] He also wrote a best-selling book entitled My American Journey in 1995 and flirted with running for President in 1996 and 2000. The popular former general had earned numerous military and civilian awards and had served on the boards of many for-profit and not-for-profit organizations.

Early Life and Education

Colin Powell was born in the Black community of Harlem, New York, and raised in a largely Jewish neighborhood in the South Bronx.[184] His father was a shipping clerk and his mother was a seamstress.[184] As a boy, he worked in a baby furniture store.[184] He also worked as a Shabbos Goy, or a non-Jewish servant who performed tasks for Jews who are prevented from doing work on the Sabbath.[184] As a result of living by and working among Jews, young Colin learned to speak Yiddish.[184] He graduated from Morris High School in 1954 and attended the City College of New York (CCNY) where he earned a bachelor's degree in Geology in 1958.[184] He received a Master's in Business Administration in 1971 from George Washington University.[184]

A Black Man in the White Man's Army

While in college, Colin became a member of the Reserve Officer Training Corps (ROTC.) The ROTC was something he excelled at while attending college and he became a member of the Pershing Rifles, an ROTC fraternity and drill team.[184] Upon graduating, he received the rank of 2nd Lieutenant and went to Fort Benning for basic training and afterward, became a platoon leader for the 48th Infantry in West Germany.[184]

Powell served two tours in Vietnam. From 1962 to 1963, the Captain was sent there to be an "advisor" to the South Vietnamese Army.[184] After being wounded, he received a Purple Heart medal and was given a non-combat assignment.[184][187] In 1968, Major Powell began his 2nd Tour of Vietnam where he was tasked with investigating the infamous My Lai Massacre where American troops led by Lt. William Calley raped, tortured, or murdered at least 347 civilians from the Village of My Lai on March 16, 1968[185] Instead of taking these charges seriously, Powell proceeded to cover up the whole sad, sorry affair. He determined that the allegations were untrue and reported to his superiors that "relations between American soldiers and the Vietnamese were excellent."[184] In those "few" cases where they weren't, Powell pointed the finger at the Vietnamese. He later told reporter Charles Lane, "I don't mean to be ethnically or politically unconscious, but it was awful. There was nothing but V.C. [Viet Cong] in there. When you went in there, you were fighting everybody."[185]

Colin Luther Powell professes a deep respect for Martin Luther King, but King was against the war in Vietnam. Powell, however, thought fighting there would advance his career. He justified his decision to go by stating, "If people in the South insisted on living by crazy rules, then I would play the hand dealt me for now...*I was not looking for trouble. I was not marching, demonstrating, or taking part in sit-ins. My eye was on an Army career for myself and a good life for my family.* For me, the real world began on the post."[186] Now, he made this statement knowing full well that his own family back home along with millions of other Black people faced racist terror daily while he was away waging war on other People of Color on behalf of White Supremacy.

Powell, now a Colonel, really earned his stripes when he served as a battalion commander in South Korea from 1973 to 1974.[187] Black soldiers in the Second Infantry Division had become so fed up with the racism of their White officers and fellow soldiers that they revolted and formed their own unit.[187][188] At one point, things got so bad that a White officer almost got killed by these Black troops.[187] Colin Powell, ever the fixer, was the man sent in to clean up this mess. He went along with the assessment of his White boss, General Hank Emerson, that the Blacks were the ones causing the problem and proceeded to drum their leaders like "Private Odom" and "Corporal Biggs" out of the Service for holding meetings and advocating self-defense.[187][188] Then, with the help of three White officers, he suppressed any further dissent by having the infantrymen practice drills day and night so that they'd be "too tired to fight with one another."[187]

Finally, he made them all watch numerous times <u>Brian's Song</u>,[187][188] a movie about the friendship between two football players, one White and one Black. It would have been nice in this case if he had followed his own rule and not "let adverse facts stand in the way of a good decision."[184] A fair-minded man would have found a way to improve race relations, and thus, unit cohesion, by not favoring one side over the other. But, that was not Colin Powell. He wanted the Black soldiers of the 2nd Infantry Division to either become well-adjusted to racism like he had or face a court-martial and a dishonorable discharge. The ex-General, who spent 35 years in the Army, looked back fondly on his year in South Korea.[187] It's probably because it was on the backs of those Black GI's under his command that he was able to climb up the ladder of success.[184][187][188] Despicable!

From December 20, 1989 to January 31, 1990, Colin Powell led the American invasion of Panama and the toppling of Manuel

Noriega.[184] The first to die from this military operation were the 7,000 Black residents of the El Chorrillo neighborhood that was blown to smithereens all because President George H.W. Bush wanted one man captured or killed.[189] General Powell thought such carnage was justified because President Noriega wouldn't follow "democratic principles."[189] It was the first of 28 such interventions that Powell led while he was Chair of the Joint Chiefs of Staff including 1991's Gulf War and the Battle of Mogadishu, Somalia in 1993.[184] Lastly, he supported the Clinton Administration's deportation of Haitian refugees back to Haiti knowing full well they'd be killed.[190][191] Long before Barack Hussein Obama II stepped into the role, it was Colin Luther Powell, who was "the Black face of White imperialism."[192]

Life After the Service

It was the humiliating defeat of US forces by Somalia insurgents at the Battle of Mogadishu, where two Black Hawk helicopters were shot down, 19 soldiers were killed, and one helicopter pilot was captured, that led General Powell to retire.[184] He spent the remainder of the 1990s making millions giving speeches; writing books; joining corporate boards; chairing nonprofits; and promoting the Republican Party. In 1995, he authored his autobiography, My American Journey, which was a New York Times bestseller. There was a lot of talk about him running for President in 1996 and 2000, but ultimately he declined.

The First Black Secretary of State

In January of 2001, Colin Powell became Secretary of State for the George W. Bush Administration. He was the first Black to do so. Infamously, he spoke before the United Nations Security Council in an attempt to gain international support for the US Invasion of Iraq and the toppling of its President, Saddam Hussein. He gave the speech to appease Chicken Hawks like President Bush and Vice President Dick Cheney who were just itching to invade Iraq and who promoted the lie that Saddam Hussein had ties to Al-

Qaeda, the terrorist group based in Afghanistan who orchestrated the September 11th attacks in 2001.

During his speech to the UN Security Council, Secretary Powell alleged that Iraq had weapons of mass destruction (i.e., nuclear and chemical weapons,) but he relied on faulty information including an outdated British intelligence report to bolster his claims.[184] Nevertheless, the US didn't get the yes vote from the UN Security Council it desired. However, it did secure allied support from Britain, France, Spain, Australia, and other Western nations to assist it with its invasion. From 2003 to 2011, it was estimated between 100,000 and 1,000,000 Iraqis had died because of the War. Saddam and his Cabinet were tried and executed. Iraq became a bastion of sectarian violence and Islamic extremism. Several new terrorist groups were formed like ISIS, or the Islamic State of Iraq and Syria and they have since spread to Afghanistan, Libya, Somalia, Mali, and Nigeria. Despite all the blood spilled and all the money spent, no weapons of mass destruction were ever found and US troops are still fighting and dying there. This is the legacy of Colin Luther Powell, the so-called "reluctant warrior."[184]

In September 2001, the United Nations held the World Conference on Racism in Durban, South Africa.[193][194] Secretary Powell refused to attend because he objected to Zionism being equated to Racism in the Conference's draft declaration.[193] He sent junior staff members, instead.[193] So, instead of being a powerful voice to address the scourge of White Supremacy and its legacy of slavery, colonialism, segregation, apartheid, and ongoing racism, Mr. Powell decided it was much more important to appease a very tiny minority of racists.[194] Shameful!

Why Colin Powell Is So Dangerous

Colin Powell is dangerous not because he achieved despite racism, but because he went along with racism to advance his career. This is not to say that he was not smart or that he didn't work hard. He was and he did. But, the problem is he used his gifts and efforts to advance the aims of racists and thus, gain their approval. They promoted him. This is called Meritorious Manumission, or the emancipation of a slave by his master for meritorious service. Some will say, "What choice did he have as a Black man in the White man's Army?" My response is you always have a choice and as the General once said, "don't let adverse facts stand in the way of a good decision."[184][195] Yes, he's a Black man in a racist society, but that doesn't mean he can't make good choices for himself and his race. To say that because he's Black he could only choose between what's good for him or what's good for his people, Black people, is a false dichotomy. A false choice. It's not "either or," but "and" and "both." He did not have to "go along to get along." Those who say he did are giving him a copout.

You can both strive for success and be loyal to your race at the same time. Whites and other non-Blacks do it all the time. Why can't we? Yes, you have to compete as an individual. But, you also have to compete as a member of a group or a team. There will often come a time when you as a Black individual will have to compete against another Black individual within a largely White organization or society. However, you can compete and win a bonus or a promotion without abandoning some level of solidarity with your fellow Black person. You can be competitive, but civil. And when it comes to competing with racists you just have to do what our parents and grandparents have always told us: work harder and smarter. You have to outwork and outsmart racists. You have to beat them at their own game and avoid the traps they set for you.

Powell was a C-student who wanted the accolades reserved for A-students. But, instead of studying hard; experimenting with ideas; and developing his creativity during his youth, he decided in adulthood that "copying pays better than innovating"[196] and he would parrot whatever talking points his White superiors gave him. The so-called "Powell Doctrine," where the military uses overwhelming force to maximize success and minimize losses, is one such example of his lack of innovation and simple-mindedness.[184] I mean "Duh!" What's original about that line of

148

thought? Because Colin Powell never developed his own original thoughts and worldview, he viewed "the White man's enterprise as though it were his own."[197] To him, adopting White people's views of himself and other Blacks was his ticket to success.

Sadly, Colin Powell was so myopically focused on his quest for success that he became too craven to care about destroying the lives and livelihoods of others, particularly those of other Blacks. He wanted to be somebody so bad that he was willing to accept indignities and limitations placed upon himself that no White man in his position ever would. The following quotes from Randall Robinson, founder of TransAfrica, best sum up Colin Powell and other Black careerists like him:

"As a group, African-Americans have virtually no power or influence. Those like Colin Powell, who appear to have mainstream power, enjoy the appearance of power only as long as their circumscribed influence is not directed toward fundamentally altering social and economic conditions for a black community from whence they sprang, at home or abroad. To make the point more broadly, blacks at rarefied levels can maintain altitude only as long as they accept, without unseemly exception, a national policy agenda to which they have made no real shaping contribution."[191][198]

Colin Powell may or may not have become a general had he decided not to cover up the My Lai Massacre in Vietnam or crackdown on Black troops in Korea. We'll never know. But, what we do know is he felt it necessary to do these dastardly deeds to advance himself. "Powell is regarded by those who have worked with him as…one who never ruffles feathers, even when they desperately deserve to be ruffled."[187] We also know that it was a Black man named Clifford Alexander, who served as Secretary of the Army during the Carter Administration, who convinced the President to expand the pool of colonels in line to be promoted to general.[199][200][201] That list of would-be generals included Colin Powell.[199][200][201] Now, if you're Black, which Black face in a high place would you want to serve under: Clifford Alexander or Colin Powell?

Score

Leadership: Powell had a very distinguished military career having served in the Army for 35 years.[184] He became a General officer in less than 20 years. He served as Deputy National Security Advisor, National Security Advisor, Chair of the Joint Chiefs of Staff, and Secretary of State under four presidents.[184] Having reached the highest levels of our country's military and civilian government, Colin Powell receives a 3.5 in the Leadership category.

Race Pride: Powell gets a 0.7 for Race Pride because he made it his business to become well-adjusted to racism. What he did to those Black soldiers in the 2nd Infantry Division was unconscionable.

Role Model: Since he emerged to prominence in the 1990s, Powell has been the template of the Post-Racial Black leader that many young, ambitious Blacks aspire to be. His ascent made it possible for Barack Obama and Kamala Harris to become President and Vice-President, respectively. Barack Obama has already begun to follow in the General's footsteps since he left office: becoming a highly sought-after public speaker and "strategic partner" for NBA Africa.[202] His rise to wealth and fame is certainly inspiring and there have never been any negative stories about his private life. For a White man, that might be enough. But, Colin Powell was Black, and he had a duty to the Black Community. Since he made a career eschewing his Blackness, unless it was beneficial, and stepping on other Blacks to get ahead, when it was not, he gets a 0.8 in the Role Model category.

Impact on the Race: His Impact on the Race has been both negligible and negative since he spent most of his life trying to avoid addressing racism. Therefore, he gets a 0.8. His overall score is a 1.0, or a D average. (3.5+0.7+0.8+0.8 = 5. 5/5 = 1.0)

Jim Clyburn

Born James Enos Clyburn on July 21, 1940, in Sumter, South Carolina, Congressman Jim Clyburn represents the 6th Congressional District in South Carolina.[203] He's been in the United States House of Representatives for 28 years where he's currently the Majority Whip. Clyburn got involved in politics after Black workers at Charleston Hospital led a strike from 1968 to 1969.[203] As the executive director of the South Carolina Commission of Farm Workers, he "helped monitor the strike settlement."[204]

In 1969, he became a volunteer for St. Julian Devine's successful campaign to become the first Black Charleston city councilperson.[203] He went on to be an advisor to Governor John C. West two years later.[203] In 1972, Governor West created the South Carolina Human Affairs Commission in response to the murder of three Black student protesters from South Carolina State University, an HBCU, by state police in 1968.[203] Clyburn was made head of the Commission in 1972 where he served until he was elected to Congress in 1992.[203] His district was drawn to contain almost all the Blacks in South Carolina and he been elected 15 times with minimal opposition.[203]

Despite having a political career based on the sacrifices of civil rights activists and having the overwhelming support of Black voters in a highly gerrymandered district, James Clyburn sees no need to pay it back or pay it forward (for the next generation.) He stakes no positions outside of those embraced by the Democratic Establishment. He's in the pocket of the pharmaceutical companies.[205] Even when he does challenge the existing order, he quickly falls back into line like when he accepted the made-up position of "Assistant Minority Leader" instead of continuing to challenge the outgoing Majority Leader, Steny Hoyer, for House

Minority Whip after the Democrats lost the 2010 Midterms. In another instance, he was forced to apologize to Speaker Nancy Pelosi and Majority Leader Steny Hoyer for complaining about there not being enough Blacks on their staffs in 2019. His district is the poorest in the state and his signature legislation, the 10-20-30 Plan, which he is now trying to rebrand as Reparations, doesn't even help Blacks in Charleston and Columbia because it's written to only help rural areas which are overwhelmingly White and Republican.[206][207] Now, why would a Black Democrat help White Republicans to the exclusion of Black Democrats? Is it because he doesn't really care about Blacks, Democratic or not, outside of his immediate circle? For instance, he helped his daughter, Mignon, get appointed to the Federal Communications Commission, other government agencies, and corporate boards.

Congressman Clyburn likes to paint himself as one who is carrying on the legacy of those brave Black men and women who fought and died for freedom during Slavery, Reconstruction, and Segregation, but his true colors have really been on display during these last four years. Other than having a Southern drawl, he is nothing like our heroes and heroines. He's nothing like the 14 Black men who served in Congress during Reconstruction, eight of whom were from South Carolina, including his ancestor, George W. Murray.[203][208] None of them would've voted for the racist 1994 Crime Bill, authored by Joe Biden, but James Clyburn did."[209][210]

During a 2019 interview with The Washington Post, the Congressman claimed he voted for the 1994 Crime Bill because it was better than the Crime Bills of 1986 and 1988 because it eliminated mandatory minimum sentences for first-time drug offenders; provided $3 billion for drug treatment programs; banned assault weapons; and contained the Violence Against Women's Act.[210] He denied that he was protecting his good buddy, Joe Biden, from criticism.[210] Finally, he complained about not getting any credit for improving the previous two Federal drug laws and stated emphatically that the '94 Crime Bill did not lead to mass incarceration. [210] He described these charges as "foolishness."[210]

Instead of remaining neutral and letting the best candidate for President emerge from within the Democratic Primary, Jim Clyburn put his thumb on the scale and endorsed Joe Biden as his candidate in the South Carolina primary. This led to the former Vice President's victory in the Palmetto state; his endorsement by moderates Pete Buttigieg and Amy Klobuchar, and a landslide win on Super Tuesday. So, those Democrats who wanted to vote for a progressive like Bernie Sanders or Elizabeth Warren to be the Party's nominee had their opportunity stolen from them because Jim Clyburn was willing to trade away the Black vote to the Democratic establishment for absolutely nothing. He traded away the hard-fought, hard-won currency earned by **Blacks Struggling in Amerikkka** to an arch-Segregationist named Joe Biden. Unforgivable!

He even said that he didn't want anything in return after Joe Biden was elected in November 2020. When ABC's George Stephanopoulos asked him, "How do you want Joe Biden to pay you back?," Clyburn replied, "Pay me back? No! I don't want anything out of this! All I want is a country that my children and grandchildren can be able to develop in and be able to pursue their dreams and aspirations. I've been around. I'm four scores (80 years old.) I'm beyond the promise. So, I'm not looking for anything. No, it's not about me at all."[211] It's never been about you or your family, Congressman. You guys are fine. It's about your constituents and your people – Black people. What are you going to do for them? How are you going to use your clout and your voice in the halls of power to create a leveled playing field for them? I guess Ol' Jim has embraced the mentality of, "I got mine! Now, you get yours!" The sad thing is he was sent to Washington to help us get ours.

Since Biden's taken office, the House Whip has barely spoken to the President and thus, has had no influence on shaping the Biden-

Harris agenda. When asked about it he told a reporter, "I don't see myself as having any kind of a role in this Administration."[212] What? Why the hell not? I can't imagine a White, Hispanic, Asian, Native American, or any other non-Black politician saying and doing this kind of foolishness, particularly when he singlehandedly got a President elected. Black people have no representation because Black politicians are both spineless and senseless.

He balks at the notion of Blacks receiving what he calls "pure reparations," or cash payments for Slavery, Segregation, and ongoing Racism. Anytime a constituent asks him at a town hall if he supports Reparations or any policy specifically for Black people, he becomes indignant, sarcastic, or simply refuses to answer.[213][214][215] In the wake of the murder of George Floyd by four Minneapolis policemen, he still supports giving cops qualified immunity, or the protection from being sued for wrongdoing even when they kill somebody.

He became the sponsor of a bill curiously named H.R. 1619, the Catawba Indian Nation Lands Act, on March 8, 2021. (Clyburn even laughed about the name when he introduced it. Did he find humor in the fact that he was proposing a bill to help slavecatching Indians while naming it after the very year when enslaved Africans first arrived in what would eventually become the United States?) It passed the House with bipartisan support. (It's interesting how Republicans and Democrats can all agree to help everybody else specifically except African Americans. That's the real Bipartisan Consensus: Keep Niggers Down!) When I first heard about it in November of 2021, it was being considered by the Senate Indian Affairs Committee. It has since been signed into law.[216][217]

This bill will give land rights and money to members of the Catawba Nation in North Carolina. There's nothing wrong with that. They deserve it because of the genocide that was committed against them by the United States Government and by White North Carolinians.[218] However, so do the American Descendants of Slavery (ADOS) also known as African Americans or Black

Americans. We deserve much more than a national hymn.[219] We deserve Reparations for Slavery, Segregation, and Ongoing Racial Discrimination in the form of cash payments, lands, other assets, tax breaks and subsidies, jobs and contracts, housing, education, legal protection from violence and discrimination, healthcare, mental health services, exemption from military service, autonomy, and a whole host of remedies for the hell we have endured and continue to endure. But, James Clyburn and Black misleaders like him could care less as long as they're getting their biscuits buttered.

Ironically, you have a descendant of slaves, James Clyburn, fighting hard for the descendants of slavecatchers, the Catawba Nation.[216] The Catawba were known as fierce slavecatchers.[216] So much so, that Whites paid them handsome sums of money to capture runaways.[216] Because of their fearsome reputation, runaway slaves preferred being captured by Whites than by these Indians.[216][220] James Clyburn loves to share how much he knows about South Carolina history and the travails of Blacks there. But, he won't fight for Black people like the Gullah/Geechee who have lost millions of acres of land to unscrupulous Whites.[216] He has no problem going to bat for people who if they had their way, would make him a slave. Jim, you got some 'splainin' to do.

He's secured over $1 billion in research grants for the Medical University of South Carolina and the University of South Carolina,[205] but what has he done for South Carolina State University, the state's only HBCU and his alma mater? What other Blacks, besides his daughter, has he helped get a federal job or a contract? How many roads, bridges, highways, federal buildings, courthouses, schools, hospitals, and clinics has he gotten funding for in the 6th District? If the answer is none or even a few, then why is he even in Washington? Black folks don't need representatives who won't bring home any bacon.

Score

Because Jim Clyburn was elected to the House of Representatives at the age of 52; then, proceeded to rapidly move up the ranks; and became the House Majority Whip twice during his 30-year career, he receives a 3.7 for ascending to the highest levels of <u>Leadership</u> in the Federal Legislature. James Clyburn is a Black man who grew up in the Segregated South. He knows his history and knows where he came from. He's a walking encyclopedia on Black history and culture. He is a descendant of slaves and therefore, he speaks with a certain authenticity and authority that many of today's Black politicos lack. However, he's used that authority to promote laws, like his so-called the 10-20-30 Plan, that primarily help rural and suburban whites to the exclusion of Blacks, be they urban, suburban, or rural.[206][207][213][214] Then, he has the nerve to call it Reparations.[206][207][213][214] You're calling money set aside in this program Reparations for Slavery, but you're giving it to White People?[206][207][213][214] Kneegrow, Please!!!

The seat he sits in was perfectly designed for someone like him. Unfortunately, he's forgotten why he was called to leadership in the first place. He was called to serve the Black masses not shake hands and rub shoulders with White America's elite. He was sent to Congress to ruffle feathers and "to make good trouble" on behalf of his people, but because his duplicitous self hasn't done so in 30 years, he receives a 0.9 for <u>Race Pride</u>.

He was a husband, an educator, and an activist. He's a father and a grandfather. He's a Black man who wears a suit; speaks English properly; and stays out of trouble. Therefore, he is a role model for Blacks both young and old, particularly his fellow Congresspersons. But, because he's only been concerned about making White people comfortable with him so he could climb the ladder of success, he receives a 0.9 for his efforts at being a <u>Role Model</u>.

Because Jim Clyburn has spent most of his over 50 years in public life focusing on improving his family's lot in life largely to the detriment of other Black people in South Carolina and the rest of the country, his <u>Impact on the Race</u> has been minimal. He receives a 0.8 in this category. His overall score is a 1.26, or a D. (3.7 + 0.9 + 0.9 + 0.8 = 6.3. 6.3/5 = 1.26.)

Kamala Harris

Kamala Devi Harris was born on October 20, 1964, in Oakland, California.[221] Her father Donald J. Harris, an economics professor, was from Jamaica. Her mother, Shyamala Gopalan, was a research biologist who specialized in oncology and was born in India.[221] Ms. Harris is the 49th Vice President of the United States and the first person of African or Asian ancestry elected to that position.[221] Previously, she was a US Senator from California, and before that, she had been elected California's Attorney and the District Attorney for San Francisco County. She has a younger sister named Maya, who is an attorney and pundit.[221] She is married to entertainment lawyer, Doug Emhoff, who is the first-ever Second Gentleman of the United States (SGOTUS.) The couple shares his two children from a previous marriage. [221]

Childhood and Youth

As a young child, Kamala lived in a mostly Black neighborhood and she attended both a Baptist church and a Hindu temple.[221] Although her parents divorced when she was 7, Kamala and her sister lived in Berkeley until she was 12.[221] After her mother received a job at McGill University, Kamala and her sister moved to Montreal, Quebec, Canada.[221] She attended three schools while there including the French-speaking Notre-Dame-des-Neiges.[221] After high school, Kamala went to Howard University in Washington, D.C. where she graduated in 1986 with a degree in Political Science and Economics.[221] She went on to earn her law degree from the University of California at Hastings.[221]

Early Work

Kamala Harris began her legal career as a Deputy District Attorney for Alameda County in 1990.[221] Four years later, she was also appointed to the state Unemployment Insurance Appeals Board and the California Medical Insurance Board by her boyfriend, the Speaker of the California Assembly, Willie Brown,[221] who was married. Later in 1994, she was hired by the San Francisco County District Attorney's Office as an Assistant District Attorney.[221] After getting into a dispute with a supervisor that led to her demotion, Harris left the DA's Office to work for the San Francisco City Attorney.[221] She ran the Division of Family and Children's Services.[221]

Race for District Attorney

In 2003, Kamala Harris ran against Bill Fazio and her former boss, Terence Hallinan, to become San Francisco County's District Attorney.[221] Although Hallinan had recruited her to work in his Office, Harris portrayed him as weak, incompetent, and "soft on crime" during her campaign.[221] She especially harped on his Office's felony conviction rate which was significantly below the state average. She conveniently left out the fact that most of these cases involved nonviolent crimes that were referred to rehabilitation and pre-trial diversion instead of trial and imprisonment. Today, prosecutors routinely offer nonviolent offenders these options instead of incarceration because both politicians and the public have realized that 30 years of getting 'tough on crime" and 50 years of fighting a "War on Drugs" have made our society worse not better. Mr. Hallinan was getting the job done. Overall crime was down sharply and violent crimes were down by 60%.[222] But, in the 1990s and the early 2000s, it didn't matter. Such crime-fighting methods were seen as sacrilegious by the media and law enforcement.

Harris was able to out-fundraise Hallinan by a 2-to-1 margin because her "tough on crime" message resonated with the city's wealthy and law enforcement unions.[222] She also received the backdoor endorsement of San Francisco's Mayor and her former lover, Willie Brown.[222] Finally, she received the endorsement of the conservative <u>San Francisco Chronicle</u>.[222] After being bombarded by the Harris campaign's media blitz, the voters were swayed. The upstart Harris defeated the incumbent Hallinan in the runoff election by almost 13%.[222]

Tenure as DA

Kamala Harris served as San Francisco's District Attorney from 2004 to 2011.[221] During that time, she spearheaded several initiatives and continued the work of her predecessor, Terence Hallinan.[222] Her office hardly pursued offenders possessing small amounts of marijuana and when it did they rarely faced jail time.[221] She "extended the light-touch approach to most medical marijuana dispensaries and promoted drug-diversion programs."[222] The new District Attorney was tough on violent criminals, however. She sought higher bail amounts for suspects who had guns and pursued the maximum sentences allowed for those convicted of gun-related crimes.[221] During her first two years in office, she had "an 87% conviction rate for homicides and a 90% conviction rate" for crimes involving the use of a firearm.[221]

Harris styled herself as a reformer. She added three new units to the DA's Office: Environmental Crimes, Gun Crimes, and Hate Crimes.[221] The last one emphasized the protection of victims who were from the LGBT+ Community.[221] She instituted three major reforms during her tenure: not pursuing the death penalty, the Back on Track Initiative, and her Anti-Truancy Program.[221] During her first campaign, she vowed never to seek the death penalty and kept her pledge even in the face of fierce criticism from several high-profile California politicians and local police.[221] The Back on Track Initiative was an anti-recidivism program for first-time nonviolent offenders that offered them a clean slate if they agreed to be supervised by a judge for 18 to 22 months; stayed sober or sought drug treatment; performed community service; and received a high school diploma or GED if they didn't already have one.[221]

The program was so successful that the State copied it five years later.[221]

Her third reform program was the Anti-Truancy Initiative which was developed in 2006.[221] Harris claimed that there was a strong link between truancy, dropping out, imprisonment, and homicide and that her program was the solution.[221] Families were given letters and brochures about the program from the DA's Office and seminars were held on campuses in the Autumn of 2006 to inform them of the changes and the legal consequences of failing to adhere to the new attendance policy.[221] Parents weren't immediately prosecuted for failing to follow the new rules.[221] It was a months-long process where local schools would remind parents by phone and mail that their children had not been attending school and were in danger of being truant.[221] Then, there would be meetings on campus and hearings held by the Board of Attendance.[221] If parents still failed to participate by ensuring their kids attended school, they were brought to court where they faced tickets, arrests, and sentences of up to one year in jail and a $2,500 fine if they were found guilty.[221] The results were immediate. 12% fewer elementary students were truant between 2006 and 2007; 32% fewer elementary students were truant between 2007 and 2008; and 23% fewer elementary students were truant between 2008 and 2009.[221] Harris claimed that only seven parents were taken to court and none went to jail.[221]

Harris' tenure wasn't scandal-free, however. During her second term as District Attorney, she faced a scandal of epic proportions. In March of 2010, the San Francisco Police Department admitted that there was tainted evidence in their crime lab.[223] An employee, with a criminal record, had stolen drugs from the lab and had failed to report to court to testify.[223] Harris, who was running for California's Attorney General, claimed it was the first time she had heard of the problem, but an Assistant DA named Sharon Woo had reported problems with this lab employee to her superiors.[223] However, nothing was done about it.[223] By law, prosecutors are supposed to share information with defense attorneys if it can be

160

used to prove their clients' innocence.[223] Ms. Harris claimed to know nothing about it and blamed the police.[223] But, it was her responsibility as the District Attorney, not the police.[223] Also, after six years in office, she still hadn't written rules that regulated the sharing of exculpatory evidence with defendants and their legal counsel.[223] After a judge ruled against her office, Harris threw out almost 1,000 convictions.[223] Despite her reputation taking a hit, she was elected the State's new AG later in the year.[223]

Kamala Harris has this tendency to blame others for her failures and to pass the buck. She even lies – sometimes needlessly. She also is disorganized; lacks a tight enough grip on her subordinates; doesn't inspire loyalty from her troops; and relies on them too much to make decisions. She carried these poor leadership traits with her into her tenure as California AG. They showed up, again, during her failed presidential campaign and perhaps, they're resurfacing now during her term as Vice President. Kamala enjoys the spotlight, but she doesn't enjoy getting her hands dirty. She claims to have learned from the crime lab scandal. In an interview with The Washington Post, she said the following, "You cannot run an office without designating folks and giving them authority."[223] She told The Post that after the scandal, she developed an open door policy with her top subordinates saying, "Hey, I need to know these things. It will not be bothering me. . . . My name is on the door. And I took an oath."[223] Only time will tell whether or not Harris has truly learned from her experience with the crime lab scandal. But, it appears that the Vice President has a lot of growing to do, and soon if she ever wants to become President.

Tenure as California Attorney General

Kamala Harris' tenure as California AG was similar to her stint as San Francisco's District Attorney. She pushed initiatives and laws that addressed recidivism, LGBT+ Rights, truancy, the environment, law enforcement, women's rights, and gang violence.[221] However, some of the same issues that dogged her during her time as District Attorney like how she dealt with wrongful convictions, her criminalizing of truancy, and her bias in favor of law enforcement became front and center, again, during her term as Attorney General. Harris also forced inmates, who were eligible for parole, to stay locked up to help fight fires because of a firefighter shortage. Then, she also blamed her employees for the situation; and later, lied about it.

Harris' anti-truancy initiative in San Francisco became the model for a 2010 state law that for the first time criminalized the parents of truant children.[224] They faced a maximum penalty of one year in the county jail and a $2,000 fine.[224] She pushed for the passage of Senate Bill 1317 both during her term as DA and during her campaign for Attorney General.[224] She denied jailing parents was her intent when asked about it in 2019 by CNN during her presidential campaign, but she previously admitted it when she took the AG's office in January 2011.[224] During her swearing-in, she said, "we are putting parents on notice. If you fail in your responsibility to your kids, we are going to work to make sure you face the full force and consequences of the law."[224] It appears that Ms. Harris had been caught in a lie.[224] She was even filmed laughing about sending parents to jail over their truant kids while she spoke before the Commonwealth Club of California on January 12, 2010.[225]

Of course, the group most negatively impacted by this new law Kamala championed were Blacks. But, it was not because their kids were the most truant. It was because White parents were able to pay those tickets and fines. Black parents, like Black people in general, are much less likely to be able to pay their way out of jail. On top of that, they were targeted. (When Kamala was San Francisco's DA, it was her representatives that held those seminars about the anti-truancy program in schools serving low-income areas.) Cheree' Peoples, an African American mother of two in Orange County, became the face of truancy because of a law that Kamala Harris, another Black woman, pushed. "On the morning of April 18, 2013, in the Los Angeles suburb of Buena Park, a throng of photographers positioned themselves on a street curb and watched as two police officers entered a squat townhouse. Minutes later, their cameras began clicking. The officers had re-emerged with a weary-looking woman in pajamas and handcuffs, and the photographers were jostling to capture her every step." [226][227]

Ms. Peoples, a mother of a child with Sickle-Cell Anemia, never should've been arrested.[226][227] All of her daughter's absences from school were excused and covered under Section 504 of the Rehabilitation Act which addresses servicing individuals with disabilities in schools, the workplace, and in the public.[227] Her daughter had a 504 plan developed by her mother and the school because she was hospitalized often.[227] But, that didn't matter to the prosecutors and school administrators in Orange County. They just wanted to lock Ms. Peoples up so they could earn additional money from the state if they did so. This whole "anti-truancy" scheme was a ploy by local governments for more money. The employees of local school districts, DA's offices, courts, child protective services, and jails, to name a few, all got paid from the tickets, fees, court costs, state funds, and incarceration of parents, who were virtually all Black, much like the rest of the criminal justice system. Not only did Ms. Peoples needlessly have to go through the embarrassment and distress of being arrested, but she also lost her job; couldn't find another job because she had an arrest record; and was evicted from her home as a result.[227] On top of that, Ms. Peoples' daughter had a stroke from all the stress both she and her mother endured after her mother's arrest. [226][227] An 11-year-old child has a stroke, and Kamala Harris wants to talk about unintended consequences.[227]

Attorney General Harris fought against DNA testing of evidence that might have freed a Black man, Kevin Cooper, who claims he was framed, from death row.[228] She also fought to preserve the conviction of 79-year-old George Gage for molesting his stepdaughter.[228] The victim had lied to police multiple times and her mother, Gage's ex-wife, said, "the daughter was a pathological liar."[228] A judge ruled against Harris stating that her office should

163

have turned over evidence that might have exonerated the defendant.[228] She also fought against compensation for the wrongful conviction of Rafael Madrigal who served seven years of a 25-year sentence for a crime he didn't commit.[229] Finally, AG Harris blocked the release of Daniel Larsen who was convicted of possession of an illegal knife in 1998.[229] A judge ordered him released in 2010, but the Attorney General fought his being released for years and when he finally got out, she appealed the case claiming he missed a filing deadline.[229] Apparently, she's more interested in upholding convictions than seeking justice. How many thousands of Blacks, both male and female, are languishing in prison because of the overzealousness of a Prosecutor Harris?

Senate Race & Mitrice Richardson

In January of 2015, Barbara Boxer announced that she would not be seeking re-election to the US Senate in 2016.[221] Kamala Harris announced that she would be running to replace her 7 days later.[221] She was immediately the front-runner.[221] She received 40% of the vote in the Democratic Primary and because it had a top-two format, her nearest competitor, Congresswoman Loretta Sanchez, would also appear on the November ballot.[221] With the endorsement of Governor Jerry Brown and President Obama, Kamala cruised to a landslide victory winning more than 60% of the vote.[221]

On September 17, 2009, a beautiful, young college graduate named Mitrice Richardson suffered a mental health episode at Geoffrey's, a fancy restaurant in suburban Los Angeles.[230][231] She was arrested by LA County Sheriff's deputies for marijuana possession and defrauding an innkeeper when she allegedly attempted to leave without paying.[230][231] She was taken to the Lost Hills station where she was booked and then, inexplicably released after midnight into the heavily wooded area that surrounded the station.[230][231] A year later, her remains were found in the forest nearby.[230][231]

On October 6, 2015, California AG and US Senate candidate Kamala Harris was asked by Richardson family friend, Dr. Ronda Hampton, to investigate the LA County Sheriff's Office for its role in her disappearance and death.[232] The AG's responded to the complaint on November 15, 2015, by stating "after careful evaluation, my inquiry warranted no formal action and that 'The records you provided do not create a reasonable inference that the actions of the Los Angeles Sheriff's Department or its employees violated the law.' "[232] Dr. Hampton alleged that Ms. Harris declined to find any evidence of wrongdoing because the Sheriff at the time, Jim McDonnell, was an ally of hers and she wanted to spare him any embarrassment.[232] Michael Richardson, Mitrice's father, requested in December 2015, that she reconsider investigating his daughter's death.[232] Two months later, Kamala Harris agreed.[232] During her Senate race, she touted her efforts in looking at Mitrice's case.[230][232] It was even on her Wikipedia page.[232] But, a month after the race was over and she won her Senate seat, Kamala Harris, again closed her investigation into Ms. Richardson's disappearance and death by saying there was insufficient evidence of wrongdoing on the part of the Sheriff's Office.[232] She had no intention of seeking justice for Mitrice Richardson. She just rode on this Black woman's death to get elected and she has to answer for that. She also has to answer for the wrongful arrest of Cheree' Peoples and the thousands of others whom she unjustly prosecuted.

Senate Term

Kamala Harris served in the Senate from 2017 to 2021 until she was sworn in as the 49th Vice President. She had an unremarkable Senate career. She spent most of her time playing to cameras by dressing down Republican nominees during confirmation hearings. She didn't sponsor or co-sponsor much in the way of legislation, either. The only bill that was noteworthy was an anti-lynching bill that she co-sponsored with Senator Cory Booker of New Jersey. Of course, it was a hundred years too late. If this had been 1919 when there had been a "Red Summer" where thousands of Blacks were lynched and their homes, businesses, churches, neighborhoods, and towns were burned down by racist and envious Whites, such a bill would have made sense. Now as then, we have cops and vigilantes killing Blacks with impunity. But in addition to that, today we have "stand your ground" and "castle doctrine" laws that virtually deputize Whites and others to take the law into their own hands and kill Black people. We also have mandatory minimum sentences, three-strikes you're out laws, sentencing disparities between crack and powder cocaine, stop-and-frisk, and legal doctrines like "qualified immunity" which I call "qualified impunity." We need laws to address this new, more sophisticated form of racist violence and oppression as well as the old forms. As a Senator, Kamala Harris was in a position to at least advocate for this type of reform. She just didn't care to do it. Instead, she spent most of her time in the Capitol soaking up the spotlight and running for President.

2020 Presidential Race

I remember reading an article in December of 2018 about male members of the CBC, James Clyburn included, saying that Kamala Harris would make an excellent Vice President and I remember thinking that wasn't fair. She hadn't even announced that she was running for President. Why pigeon-hole her like that? But, as it turned out, they were right. She did become Vice President.

On Monday, January 21, 2019, Martin Luther King Day, Sen. Harris announced her candidacy for President at Howard University, her alma mater. The significance of her launching her campaign on the King holiday at an HBCU was not lost on me. She was playing on the symbolism of the moment by tying herself to Martin Luther King and the role that Historically Black Colleges and Universities have played in developing Black leaders like Dr. King and herself as well as countless others. She was also signaling towards the historic significance of her possibly being the First (Black) Woman President. However, she didn't want to play up her Blackness too much. So, when a reporter asked her thoughts about the importance of being the First Black Woman President, she responded, "I'm American." She did what many ambitious Blacks do. They trade on their Blackness to get in the door. However, after getting in, they suddenly don't want to be Black anymore. They want to be known as an American, an actor, a doctor, a lawyer, a businessman, or hell, just a human being. But, aren't Black people human beings? By running from her Blackness, she was running away from part of her humanity.

After she made her announcement and held a rally, she quickly became the frontrunner. She began making her rounds on radio and TV shows particularly those that serve Black audiences like the Tom Joyner Morning Show and The Breakfast Club to shore up Black support. On Tom Joyner's show, she skillfully avoided answering any questions about what she would do specifically for Blacks, and on The Breakfast Club, she talked about smoking marijuana because she was Jamaican and listening to Snoop and Tupac when she was in college. This story didn't add up because neither Tupac nor Snoop were recording artists in the 1980s when she attended Howard. But, as usual, Kamala was able to able to smile and slide her way on by after telling a fib or two.

Kamala Harris is not in favor of Reparations

During an interview with theGrio, an online publication, Sen. Harris was asked by a reporter what her agenda was for the Black Community.[233] In addition to a lot of headshaking and saying, "Right. Right. That's right."[233] like she was in church, she gave a response that included a list of standard, cookie-cutter programs that are designed to help everybody. She said, "Well, the first step is to understand that the needs of Black Folks are the needs of everyone and the needs of everyone are the needs of Black Folks."[233] The Senator acknowledged, however, that there were disparities between Blacks and Whites because of Slavery, Segregation, and Ongoing Discrimination.[233] Nevertheless, like a good Democrat, she still proposed race-neutral solutions to race-based problems.[233] She mentioned the high number of Black women dying during childbirth and blamed it on health professionals not listening to Black women.[233] She even referred to Serena Williams and the difficulties she faced when giving birth to further make her point.[233] She glibly mentioned HBCUs, and talked about how she got more funding for their landmarks.[233] Then, she vaguely spoke about STEM[233] which stands for Science, Technology, Engineering, and Math. She claimed that her LIFT Act, which would save families making $100,000 or less a year $500 a month, "would lift up 60% of Black families out of poverty."[233] How does receiving an extra $6,000 a year lift anyone out of poverty, Sen. Harris?

But, the most telling part of the interview or should I say the most damning part was when the good Senator was asked about Reparations.[234]

Interviewer: "Do you support Reparations for Black people?"

Sen. Harris: "Well, listen. Again, we had over 200 years of Slavery. We had Jim Crow for almost a century. We had legalized discrimination, Segregation, and now, we have segregation and discrimination that is not legal but still exists and is a barrier to progress. We have disparities around housing. We have disparities around education. We have disparities around income. And we have to recognize that everybody did not start out on an equal footing in this country. And in particular, Black people have not. And so, we have got to recognize that and do something about that and give folks a lift up. That's why, for example, I'm proposing the Lift Act. Give people who are making a hundred thousand dollars or less as a family a tax credit which will benefit and uplift 60% of Black families who are in poverty."

Interviewer: So, by default, it affects Black families. But, there's not a particular policy for African Americans that you would support?

Sen. Harris: But, no, if you look at the reality of who will benefit from certain policies. When you take into account that they're not starting at the same place and they're not starting on equal footing, it will directly benefit Black children, Black families, Black homeowners because the disparities are so significant. So, if we focus on the specific issues that have resulted in the greatest disparities and we understand that that's part of why we're doing it. Listen – the reality also is this – any policy that will benefit Black People will benefit all of society. Let's be clear about that. Let's really be clear about that! So, I'm not going to sit here and say I'm going to do something that's only going to benefit Black people. No! 'Cause whatever benefits that Black family will benefit that community and society as a whole and the country. Right?"[234]

It's interesting to see how much Kamala Harris contradicted herself in that interview. She acknowledged the specific wrongs done to Black people. But, then, she offers a general remedy. She tried to fool the listener into believing that if you just cast a wide enough net, you can solve the vast majority of Black people's problems. And that's just not true. Something specifically was done to harm Black people and something specifically must be done to help Black people. You have to use race-based solutions to remedy race-based problems. In other words, you have to go through race in order to get through race. Kamala Harris, Barack Obama, and other politicians know this. They're just hoping we'll be naïve enough to believe their lies to the contrary.

Kamala Harris has no problem creating laws, policies, and benefits that only go to specific groups of people. For example, the Biden-Harris Administration has given Native Americans $31 billion, Asian Americans $50 million and an anti-discrimination law just for them, Latino immigrants a new immigration bill that has $4 billion attached to it in addition to the billions they'll receive from the American Recovery Plan, and executive orders that protect and give money to LGBT+ Americans, during its first 100 days. [235][236][237][238] Plus, President Biden signed an executive order that increases the number of H-1B visas that would allow computer programmers and other highly educated professionals to immigrate to the United States from India, China, and Vietnam. In 2018, it was reported that almost 75% of H-1B visa holders were from India.[239] So, Kamala can do something specific for her Indian half, but not her Black half? Hmmm?

Her comments exemplify a sophisticated form of "bait and switch" that today's politicians do when speaking to Black people. They will share with a Black audience a litany of examples of where Black folks, specifically, were harmed by the system to elicit our support after pulling on our heartstrings. But, then, they propose generalized, one-size-fits-all solutions that ensure that Whites are the primary beneficiaries of whatever government program (e.g., civil rights, voting rights, Affirmative Action, tax credits, mortgage assistance, and student loan forgiveness) that comes about. "A rising tide lifts all boats." No, it does it, especially if you're in a rickety, little boat with a hole in it which is where many, if not most, Blacks find themselves. The majority of "progressive" proposals that Democrats talk about are simply stabilization programs for Whites to ensure that they at least stay middle class and don't fall below Blacks and other racial and ethnic minorities. The sad thing is in this conservative climate most of these so-called race-neutral proposals never actually get drafted into bills let alone become law because centrist Democrats like Kamala are just as opposed to them as the Republicans are. The American people, especially Black American people, are being played here.

Her Democratic Primary Campaign

During a CNN town hall meeting in January of 2019, Candidate Harris said she was in favor of Medicare for All and ending private health insurance. But, previously, she said Americans could keep their private insurance if they wanted it. After she received criticism from Republicans and saw opinion polls that said Americans wanted to keep their current healthcare plans, Sen. Harris backtracked to her previous position of expanding Medicare and maintaining private health insurance.[240]

Debate Performance

During the first Democratic Primary Debate for President, Kamala Harris scored major points against her opponents. Many in the media said she won that debate in late June of 2019.[241] Her biggest moment of the night was when she attacked then former Vice President Joe Biden for praising segregationists that he worked with in the Senate weeks earlier on the campaign trail and his opposition to school desegregation by bussing.[241][242] She implied that his opposition to desegregation harmed her as a little girl who was bussed to desegregate her elementary school. Biden was stunned! The next day, Senator Harris capitalized on the moment by setting fundraising records and selling t-shirts of her as a cute little girl wearing pigtails. Her stock soared after that debate and she became the frontrunner in the race.

Biden hammered back during the next debate. Both, he and Congresswoman Tulsi Gabbard attacked her record as California's Attorney General. But, it was Gabbard who made the more strident attack when she said the following, "She blocked evidence that would have freed an innocent man from death row until the courts forced her to do so. She kept people in prisons beyond their sentences to use them as cheap labor for the State of California. She put over 1,500 people in jail for marijuana violations and then, laughed about it when she was asked if she smoked marijuana."[243] Harris had no answer. She offered no rebuttal. All she did was smile. She never recovered from that attack. Her poll numbers cratered in the months that followed and she was never seen as a serious contender, again.

Her Presidential Run Ends Prematurely

November 2019 was a very tough month for Kamala Harris. Both, Politico and The New York Times published scathing articles about the state of her campaign.[244][245] On top of that, there were massive layoffs and her State Operations Director, Kelly Mehlenbacher, abruptly quit.[244] Her resignation letter was later published in The Times.[244] In it, she complained about layoffs without notice and the staff being treated horribly.[244] On December

3, 2019, Senator Kamala Harris dropped out of the race for President.[245] The one-time presidential hopeful blamed self-funding billionaires like Michael Bloomberg for her woes and an inability to raise money to compete.[244] But, she raised over $26 million? How was she already out of the race before a single primary or caucus began? Clearly, she was not ready for primetime.

Early on, Kamala Harris made some very bad choices starting with the structure of her campaign.[244] She appointed her sister, Maya, campaign chair, and she appointed as her campaign manager, Juan Rodriguez, a man "who could not be replaced without likely triggering the resignations of the candidate's consulting team."[244] Neither one had any experience running a presidential campaign and because one was her sister and the other her campaign manager, no one knew who really was in charge.[244]

In addition to being divided between two factions: Maya's and Juan's, Harris' team was divided between two coasts.[244] The headquarters was split between Baltimore and San Francisco.[244] "The setup cost Ms. Harris opportunities to recruit some of her party's most sought-after outside strategists and left her reliant on a team less experienced in national politics than in California…"[244] According to Dan Sena, a top Washington fundraiser, Kamala & Co. relied too heavily "on political thinking shaped in California…"[244]

Sen. Harris also did not listen to Washington veterans like Congresswoman Marcia Fudge who told her that she had to take charge of her campaign and fire her campaign manager.[244] The Senator failed to manage her subordinates properly just as she did when she was San Francisco's District Attorney and California's Attorney General. She had no idea that her campaign was hemorrhaging money nor that her campaign manager, Juan Rodriguez, had laid off staff until it had occurred.[244] How many times are these lapses going to occur until a change in behavior takes place? "You can't run the country if you can't run your campaign," said Gil Duran, a former aide to Ms. Harris.[244]

But, the candidate's biggest problem was her messaging or lack thereof.[244] At first, she was " a progressive prosecutor." She backed off that after facing criticism. When she saw that Bernie Sanders and Elizabeth Warren were getting all the ooh's and ah's, she was for Medicare-for-All. When reminded by the press of her previous position, she hedged her bet and said she was for Medicare for All and private insurance. Kamala went in whatever direction the wind blew and when she finally staked out a position, she lacked specifics. Her advisers complained that she "struggles to carry a message beyond the initial script."[244] and that's her chief problem. She refuses to study and prepare and thus, she often sounds unprepared. This is why one voter, after hearing her speak, said, "I guess she lost me today."[244] Is Kamala Harris ready for primetime? The evidence suggests she is not.

Vice Presidential Campaign

MoveOn.org activist and MSNBC contributor, Karine Jean Pierre, came to Kamala's defense after she was selected to be Ms. Harris' Chief of Staff by declaring that she, too, was "an ambitious woman" after it had been reported in July of 2020 that some of Joe Biden's allies described Kamala Harris as "too ambitious" to be Vice President.[246][247][248] But, that's the chief knock on her: that she's full of naked ambition, but has no policy prescriptions or vision for the future. She just wants to be President, but can't tell us why. She's just an "empty skirt" like a lot of ambitious men are just "empty suits."

In July and August, Black leaders and influencers were demanding that Joe Biden select a Black woman as his running mate. 100 Black Men and 200 Black Women wrote letters to the Democrats' presumptive nominee.[249][250] Senator Amy Klobuchar (D-MN,) Congresswoman Karen Bass (D-CA,) Congresswoman Val Demings (D-FL,) former UN Ambassador Susan Rice, and Senator Tammy Duckworth (D-WI) among others were mentioned as possible running mates, but everyone knew that Kamala Harris was going to get the VP nomination.

After she was selected to be Joe Biden's running mate, there was this tremendous push by the Democrats, the CBC, Black media personalities, and celebrities to get Black voters to support Joe Biden because of her. Former MTV host and actress Amanda Seales went on a rant on social media telling Black People that she didn't want to hear about policy, a Black Agenda, or Reparations and that they had better just go out and vote for Joe Biden and Kamala Harris. Former ESPN reporter Jemele Hill produced an online commercial targeting Black men that appeared on Facebook called "Get Your Booty to the Poll" which featured strippers. Alpha Kappa Alpha, Harris' sorority, and other Black Greek organizations, collectively known as the "Divine 9," campaigned for the Biden-Harris ticket. The Breakfast Club's Charlamagne Tha God said he was voting for Kamala Harris, not Joe Biden. So, you're voting for the bottom of the ticket, but not the top of the ticket? Number 2, but not number 1? Now, what sense does that make? She wasn't running for President. He was. A Biden Presidency was not going to be Obama 2.0, Black people. Nevertheless, Joe and Kamala were victorious in November 2020 largely on the strength of the Black Vote.

Performance as VP Thus Far

Is Kamala Harris ready to be President? Her performance as Vice President, thus far, suggests she is not. In February of 2021, Vice President Kamala Harris and Treasury Secretary Janet Yellen met with US Black Chambers, Inc., a trade association of Black chambers of commerce around the country, to discuss President Biden's almost $2 trillion economic stimulus package called the American Rescue Plan.[251] When one of the Chamber's representatives asked when his members can expect targeted assistance from the Biden-Harris Administration, Madam Vice President stammered and stuttered and looked down and around

174

before she gave a very long-winded answer that didn't remotely answer the man's question.

Mr. O'Neal: "What can we expect from the Administration in terms of ongoing, targeted support for the businesses we represent?"

Vice-President Harris: (stammering) "That's an excellent point, Mr. O'Neal. Um, and thank you for your leadership. So, we have. We need to get this rescue plan passed and the reason I was in the Senate, now as the President of the Senate to break the tie was so we can get that moving along. To get that relief to families and to small businesses as quickly as possible. Uh, to deal with the immediate issues including what cannot be overlooked – even since December when the last package was passed almost a hundred thousand people died. Right. So, when we think about this moment we're in – you know the way I think of it and you'll appreciate it (being) from Texas. Think of it as a hurricane. Right. Sometimes, we tend to think we now need to clean up after the hurricane. No, we're still in the hurricane and it's picking up speed. Right. So, that as much as anything is the motivation and the spirit behind the (American) Rescue Plan, which is people are hurting, right now…"[251]

The very White Treasury Secretary Yellen just looked and smiled. She probably thought to herself, "Ooh, I'm glad I didn't have to answer that question." She probably also thought to herself, "You niggers (know you) ain't getting nothing. So, why are you asking?"

Now, Kamala spent over a minute and a half blathering on about nothing because she didn't want to answer the question. Not only did she not want to answer the question, but she also wasn't prepared to answer it. But, she should've been. She knew it was coming. After all, she was speaking to the Black Chamber of Commerce. Plus, throughout her Democratic Primary run and during the General Election both she and Joe Biden were asked pointedly what they were going to do specifically for Black people. Hell, Biden even said after he won the White House, "the African

175

American community has always had my back and I'm going to have theirs!" A halfway decent politician would have delineated all the policies and programs in the American Rescue Plan that would have a positive impact on Black people. Then, he/she would've promised to get back with his/her audience with more information as soon as possible. Kamala Harris is the Vice President, not the President. She doesn't make the decisions, nor does she set the agenda. The President does. But, she does have influence in the White House, or at least she should. It's up to her to use it on our behalf. Hell, on her behalf, if she wants to ever become President! What's the purpose of having her there if she's not going to represent us?

Politicians, and the reporters that cover them, are always looking toward the next election. Six months into the Biden-Harris Administration and you already had stories focusing on the 2024 and the 2028 Presidential Elections. There are those in Democratic circles already wondering if Kamala Harris "is ready to be the Democratic Party's standard-bearer, should Joe Biden not run for re-election or after he has completed two terms. One thing that might inhibit her from succeeding Joe Biden is her public perception, or how voters and donors see her. On two separate occasions, the Vice President laughed and made a sarcastic remark when she was asked about when she would be visiting the US-Mexico border. If it were just these two instances, it could be ignored. But, Kamala always laughs, inappropriately, or plays dumb whenever she is asked a tough question, particularly one she is not prepared for. This is not going to fly for a Vice President. She's got to learn how to think quickly on her feet and she can't just give glib answers, either. She has to be able to quickly give answers that show she's thought seriously about the issue she's being asked to address. Kamala led poorly managed offices when she was a District Attorney, an Attorney General, a Senator, a Presidential candidate, and now, a Vice President.[252][253] This is a deeply disturbing pattern of behavior with Ms. Harris. One she has got to break if she wants any chance at becoming President.

Score

Ms. Harris receives 3.75 points in the <u>Leadership</u> category for becoming the first Black Vice President of the United States. That's a heck of a feat and she did it! Kamala Harris gets a 1.0 for <u>Race Pride</u> because she's always used her Blackness to get herself in the door whether it was going to an HBCU; joining a sorority; being admitted into law school; or winning elected office. But, once she's gotten where she wanted to go, she eschews, or downplays her Blackness as she did by identifying solely as an American and not a Black American while announcing her run for President at an HBCU on Martin Luther King Day. She also trades in Black stereotypes such as Jamaicans smoking ganja or using Rap as a link to the Black Community. We all know you don't listen to Cardi B, Kamala!

Her reaching the second-highest office in the land does make her a <u>Role Model</u> to little Black girls and boys. She's even a role for aspiring Black teens and adults. Unfortunately, those youths and young adults might emulate her using Blackness to get ahead and eschewing it when it's disadvantageous. Therefore, she gets a 1.0 in that category.

Kamala's <u>Impact on the Race</u> should primarily be looked at during her time as a prosecutor. I understand that it's a prosecutor's job to put people in jail. But, Kamala created new ways to put people there with her anti-truancy initiative and because she cared more about her win-loss record, she fought very hard to keep people in jail even when there was evidence that could have proven their innocence. Many, if not most, of those people were BLACK. But, Ms. Harris didn't care. She was too busy climbing the ladder of success off other people's backs.

It's unlikely that Ms. Harris will succeed Obama as the Second Black President of the United States. She doesn't have the polish, the political acumen, the work ethic, or the common sense not to show such open contempt for as valuable a constituency as Blacks are to her as well as the Democratic Party. We are her most loyal

177

constituents. We got her ass in the Vice President's Office in the first place. Obama never would've just glibly declared that "…I'm not going to sit here and say I'm going to do something that's only going to benefit Black people. No!" He would have and has given more thoughtful no answers to Black aspirations than that like when he told Ta-Nehisi Coates that Reparations weren't politically feasible. She gets a 0.8 because her Impact on the Race will not be positive, nor will it be long-lasting. At best, it will negligible when the history books will be written about her. This book is the first. Her overall score as a Black leader is a 1.31, or a D. (3.75 +1.0+1.0+0.8 = 6.55/5 =1.31)

Barack Obama

Barack Hussein Obama II was born on August 4, 1961, in Honolulu, Hawaii. He became the first and only Black person ever elected President on Tuesday, November 4, 2008. He first came to national prominence when he delivered a keynote speech at the 2004 Democratic National Convention where he said, "There's not a liberal America or a conservative America. There's only a United States of America!" Two years later, he was elected to the United States Senate from the State of Illinois. When he ran for President in 2007 and 2008, there was a tremendous amount of hope that he would be a champion of Progressivism and that Black people would have finally "arrived" and be made part of the American Mainstream. Obama ran on "hope and change." Sadly, by the end of his Presidency, there was very little hope because very little had changed.

Why I Voted for Obama

Barack Obama was not the first Black person to run for President. That honor belongs to Congresswoman Shirley Chisholm (D-NY) who ran in 1972. Jesse Jackson ran twice in 1984 and 1988. Even Al Sharpton ran in 2004. Although most Blacks were very skeptical about Obama's chances of winning the Democratic nomination until his victory during the Iowa Caucuses, I felt it was important that Black Americans support his candidacy first if he was going to have a chance. The logic being if his own people didn't support him, why should anybody else? Blacks had a right to be skeptical after getting behind Jesse Jackson's two spectacular, but failed runs for the White House. Both, Shirley Chisholm and Al Sharpton never had a real chance. Plus, the

Congressional Black Caucus, to which Obama belonged, never really got behind him. They backed the person whom they thought was the safer choice: the White Senator from New York, Hillary Clinton. Civil Rights leader and former Mayor of Atlanta, Andrew Young openly mocked him when he said Bill Clinton was as Black as Barack Obama.[254]

But, what made me get on the Obama bandwagon was the speech he gave at the National Constitution Center in Philadelphia on March 18, 2008, entitled, "A More Perfect Union."[255][256] That speech made a huge impression on me and is probably the largest reason that I am disappointed in Obama because no presidential candidate before him had ever talked about "the wealth and income gap"[255][256] between Blacks and Whites. Silly me, I honestly thought he was going to do something to close it. During his eight years in the White House, he did more to expand it by doing nothing about the foreclosure crisis and created millions of new White millionaires through Quantitative Easing which boosted the stock market while millions of homeowners, many of them Black, lost their homes.[257][258]

Senator Obama was forced to make that speech during the Democratic Primary in response to criticism by politicians and the media that tied him to some comments made by his pastor, Dr. Jeremiah Wright, that seemingly condemned America for its racism. Obama was surging in the polls after having just won Iowa the month before and he had to respond to this latest crisis to keep his campaign from derailing. The part of the speech that caught most of my attention was where he explained why Rev. Wright and most Black Americans feel frustrated with their plight in America. Obama said, "…we do need to remind ourselves that so many of the disparities that exist in the African-American community today can be directly traced to inequalities passed on from an earlier generation that suffered under the brutal legacy of slavery and Jim Crow."[255][256] Then, he proceeded to outline the following four ways of how these disparities between Blacks and Whites came about: 1.) segregated schools; 2.) legalized discrimination; 3.) a lack of opportunity among Black Men and the deleterious effect of Welfare on the Black Family; and 4.) the lack of basic services in so many urban Black neighborhoods.[255][256] After eloquently stating the case against institutional racism, he pivots and began pandering to Whites by comparing White rage to Black rage as if they were equally justified.[255][256] <u>My critique of Obama's effectiveness as a Black leader will center on how well he as President fought to close the wealth gap between Blacks and Whites by eliminating or reducing the 4 causes of the disparities that he outlined in his speech and how he reacted to and addressed racism.</u>

Segregated Schools

Barack Obama did absolutely nothing to address school segregation. In fact, he increased it by supporting the growth of charter schools and implementing his Race to Top program. At the start of his Presidency, only 39% of Black students attended an integrated school and roughly 60% of them attended schools where the overwhelming majority of students lived in poverty according to the Civil Rights Project at the University of California.[258] Three reasons for the increase in school segregation cited in the study were: the shrinking percentage of school-age students that are White; the 2007 Supreme Court ruling that eased government pressure on school districts to desegregate; and the lack of Federal enforcement of housing desegregation.[259]

Here's how Obama contributed further to school segregation. First, he appointed former Chicago Public Schools Superintendent, Arne Duncan, as his Education Secretary. Duncan, a notorious public school privatizer, who in 2010 gleefully remarked that Hurricane Katrina was the "best thing that happened to the education system in New Orleans!"[260] New Orleans' school district became the first in the country to have all charter schools in 2014.[261] Next, he supported the 2009 renewal of the dreadful No Child Left Behind Act, an odious piece of legislation passed by Congress in 2001 and promoted by his predecessor, George W. Bush. This law accelerated both the high-stakes testing regime that our students are still under and the privatization of public schools. Third, he proposed the "Race to the Top" program that linked federal funding of school districts to student test scores and the closing of "failed schools."[262]

Race to the Top or "Race to the Bottom" as I call it worked like this: 1.) school transformations; 2.) school turnarounds; 3.) school restarts; and 4.) school closures.[262] "Failing schools" were "transformed" by firing the administrators and upwards of half of its faculty.[262] They were replaced by new teachers, substitutes, and consultants.[262] Teachers maintained their jobs by focusing on test scores.[262] " 'Transformed' schools tie teachers' jobs to test scores (that's what caused the national epidemic of cheating scandals,) lengthening school days with no extra pay, cutting wages and benefits, and of course, lots more costly and useless tests."[262] School turnarounds emphasized testing even more and required at least 50% of the previous year's teachers to be fired and the new hires have to come from teacher mills like "Teach for America."[262] School restarts consisted of a charter school taking over the building that had previously housed a public school.[262] "Charters of course can use public money to hire even less qualified teachers; pick and choose the students (they) serve; and often generate handsome profits."[262] The final step was school closure.[262] Parents and students were left to find another school usually farther away and the community was scarred by another shuttered building.[262] Those districts that emphasized transformations, restarts, and closures received their slice of the additional $4 billion in federal funding.[262] Those that didn't, didn't.[262]

The President acknowledged that segregated neighborhoods lead to segregated schools during a 2009 address to Congress when he said, "In this country, the success of our children cannot depend more on where they live than on their potential."[263] Regrettably, he did nothing to improve this situation. Obama, like his predecessor George Bush, was a major proponent of charter schools and the biggest beneficiaries of this government largesse were charter school operators such as the Eli Broad Foundation, the Bill and Melinda Gates Foundation, the Walton Foundation, and KIPP Academy.

For-profit public schools also known as charter schools because they are given a charter to operate by the states they do business in, are much more segregated than regular public schools. Despite the explosive growth in the number, scope, and size of charter schools, they made up only 6.5% of all public school students as of the 2018-2019 school year.[264] They were also concentrated in only 9 states.[265][266] That's only up slightly from 2.6% of public school students and 5 states in 2009 the same year that Obama took office.[264][265][266]

Because they are located mostly in cities, charters have a higher proportion of Black students than regular public schools do. Black students are more likely than any other group to attend a charter school that is overwhelmingly Black. "While segregation for Blacks among all public school students has been increasing for nearly two decades, Black students in charter schools are far more likely than their traditional public school counterparts to be educated in intensely segregated settings. At the national level, seventy percent of Black charter school students attend intensely segregated minority charter schools (which enroll 90-100% of students from under-represented minority backgrounds,) or twice as many as the share of intensely segregated Black students in traditional public schools. Some charter schools enrolled populations where 99% of the students were from under-represented minority backgrounds. Forty-three percent of Black charter school students attended these extremely segregated minority schools, a percentage that was, by far, the highest of any racial group, and nearly three times as high as Black students in traditional schools."[263]

Testing and privatizing schools were the only solutions that the first Black President proposed to improve the educational opportunities for Black children at the start of his Presidency. So, what could he have done to remedy the situation? His Education Department could have revised the civil rights rules for charter schools.[263] It could have also put more emphasis on the hugely successful magnet schools model that had been widely implemented for decades and that already offers parents many choices to meet their children's educational needs.[263] He could have pushed for new laws that required the federal government to gather enough data on charters "so that we can monitor student access and outcomes by race, class, and language ability."[263] As ESEA (Elementary and Secondary Education Act) is reauthorized, it should be amended to include students' socioeconomic status as part of the annual evaluation of charter school enrollment."[263]

Sadly, Barack Obama was hostile towards Historically Black Colleges and Universities (HBCUs.) He didn't seem to understand nor care about their value nor did he acknowledge the indirect role that they played in his getting an education and employment because of the high-caliber graduates they have produced over the last century and a half. During his Administration, their funding was cut in two separate budgets. It was only after radio host, Tom Joyner, talked to him about it, not once but twice, that he restored their funding. It was probably from these talks with Mr. Joiner that Mr. Obama thought it would at least look good for public relations' sake to create a White House Initiative on Historically Black Colleges and Universities. But, despite this new initiative, he cut their funding a third time. This time indirectly when his Education Department made the criteria for qualifying for a Parent PLUS Loan more stringent. Since 90% of HBCU students depend on student loans to pay for their education, many were unable to attend and there was a sharp drop in enrollment as a result. The situation got so bad that the presidents of HBCUs had to take the Obama Administration and the Department of Education to court to reverse the damage.

Legalized Discrimination

Barack Obama ran as a candidate for change. His campaign's slogan was "Change We Can Believe In." After eight years of suffering under the ineptitude of George Walker Bush, Americans were desperate for change. (It was ABB: Anybody But Bush!) Compared to the Republican nominee John McCain, Obama represented change. He was young; McCain was old. Obama was Black; McCain was White. (Up to this point in American History, no Black candidate had ever made it out of the primaries.) Obama was an electrifying speaker; McCain was not. Obama was against the Iraq War; McCain voted for it. Finally, Obama had a plan to rescue the economy; McCain shockingly admitted that he didn't. Candidate Obama became President-Elect Obama on November 4, 2008. History was made when America elected its first Black President. But did President Obama turn out to be the agent of change that Candidate Obama claimed to be? Let's see.

One glaring area in American society that needed to be changed was the wealth gap between Blacks and Whites. Obama even addressed this issue, the first presidential candidate that I ever recall doing so, when he gave the "A More Perfect Union" speech in Philadelphia in March of 2008. When I heard him articulate so succinctly the Black-White Economic Divide, I became excited. I just knew he was going to do something to fix it. Before we look at what President Obama did or did not do to address the Racial Wealth Gap, let's examine what it is and what causes it.

A February 2013 study entitled, "The Roots of the Widening Racial Wealth Gap: Explaining the Black-White Economic Divide" written by Thomas Shapiro, Tatijana Meschede, and Sam Osoro for the Institute on Assets and Social Policy, defined what the Racial Wealth Gap was; explained how it came into existence and why it continues to persist; and offered policymakers like President Obama suggestions on how to solve the problem.[267] Wealth, also known as net worth, is defined as a person's assets minus his/her liabilities or as the Study's authors put it "what we own minus what we owe."[267] In 2009, the same year Obama took office, "the median wealth of white families was $113,149 compared with \$6,325 for Latino families and \$5,677 for black families."[267] According to this study, the four major causes for this disparity are homeownership, income, education, and inheritance.[267]

The study's authors proposed commonsense and tried-and-true solutions to address the causes of the Black-White Wealth Gap. First, housing, mortgage, and lending regulations must be enforced and expanded "so that the legacy of residential segregation no longer confers greater wealth opportunities to white homeowners than it does to black homeowners."[267] Second, they argue "raising the minimum wage, enforcing equal pay provisions, and strengthening employer-based retirement plans and other benefits."[267] Third, daycare needs to be affordable and an emphasis needs to be placed on getting children ready for school.[267] Education is a public right, not a private investment.[267] Colleges and universities need to be made affordable and students shouldn't be saddled with loans.[267]

Finally, governments local, state, and federal need to reduce the disparate impact that inheritances cause between workers and the wealthy.[267] "If we truly value merit and not unearned preferences, then we need to diminish the advantages passed along to a small number of families. Preferential tax treatment for large estates costs taxpayers and provides huge benefits to less than 1 percent of the population while diverting vital resources from schools, housing, infrastructure, and jobs. Preferential tax treatment for dividends and interests are weighted toward wealthy investors as is the home mortgage deduction and tax shielding benefits from retirement savings. It is time for a portfolio shift in public investment to grow wealth for all, not just a tiny minority. Without that shift the wealth gap between white and black households has little prospect of significantly narrowing. A healthy, fair, and equitable society cannot continue to follow such an economically unsustainable trajectory."[267]

In his "A More Perfect Union" speech, Candidate Obama talked about how Blacks were denied loans for homeownership and business development for decades,[255][256] but President Obama did little to nothing to change this. He was actually worse than Bush on this front.[258] The 7a Program is the Small Business Administration's main program that the federal government uses to lend money to small businesses.[268] Despite promising in 2009 to offer more loans via this plan, the SBA lent 47% fewer loans to Black businesses while giving Asian businesses 21% more in 2011.[268] Another SBA program known as 8a offers loans specifically to business owners from "socially and economically disadvantaged" groups (i.e., minorities and women.) Here again, the Obama Administration failed to help struggling Black business owners. By September 30, 2012, the SBA had lent Black borrowers 1.7% of the $23 billion it had set aside for minority and women-owned businesses.[258] That was down sharply from the 8.2% that Black borrowers had received in 2008 the last year of the Bush Administration.[258] It would seem that all his talk in 2008 about Blacks being locked out of generational wealth because they were denied business loans was just Obama paying lip service.

Black wealth declined under Obama. 12 years after the Great Recession of 2008-2010, Blacks were the only group that has not recovered and it's only gotten worse since the Coronavirus Pandemic of 2020 which caused a massive economic shutdown. These economic crises are on top of the Recessions of 2001 and 2003 that had a deleterious effect on Black Wealth.

Not only did Black wealth decline under Barack Obama, he actively destroyed it with his mortgage-rescue plan known as the Home Affordable Modification Plan (HAMP.)[257] During the 2008 Campaign, he promised to help struggling homeowners stay in their homes.[269] "I will change our bankruptcy laws to make it easier for families to stay in their homes," Obama told supporters at a Colorado rally on September 16, 2008, the same day as the bailout of AIG."[269] After he became President, he performed another bait-and-switch doing all he could to rescue the banks and leaving homeowners to fend for themselves. HAMP was a program that the Obama Administration created that was based on a provision in the Troubled Asset Relief Program (TARP) of 2008 that authorized "an unspecified appropriation to 'prevent avoidable foreclosures.' "[257] $75 Billion was ultimately the amount approved.[257] Needless to say, it didn't work because it wasn't supposed to. "Protecting the banks was the actual goal," according to Neil Barofsky, Special United States Treasury Inspector General for TARP from 2008 to 2011.[257] Obama even admitted as much when he told a group of Wall Street executives in March of 2009, "My Administration is the only thing between you and the pitchforks."[270]

HAMP worked like this: the Government would pay mortgage servicers, or the companies that process documents and payments for lenders, to modify home loans for the benefit of borrowers.[257] Despite potentially receiving up to $4,000 per loan, servicers had even more motivation not to modify their loans and to even foreclose on them because they can receive a share of the outstanding balances, or money from the sale of the homes.[269] As a result, many of these companies decided to forego receiving modification payments from the Government in favor of higher payments from the banks.[269] In many cases, servicers would "double-dip" by taking payments from the Government and the banks.[269]

To make things even worse for homeowners, the Obama Administration didn't enforce the law or its own regulations.[257] Servicers would often play a variety of games with a borrower such as "lose his documents" in order to obtain a few more payments and fees until they were ready to foreclose on the person's home.[257] The Administration "didn't bother to seriously investigate these abuses. The Treasury Department didn't even permanently claw back a single one of its payments from abusive servicers."[257]

Due to little enforcement by the President, The Home Affordable Modification Plan (HAMP) essentially gave mortgage companies the green light to steal from borrowers. "Its re-default rate—the fraction of people who got a modification and later defaulted out of the program—was 22 percent as of 2013. Only about $15 billion of the original $75 billion appropriation was spent by mid-2016."[257]

"Out of an initial promised 4 million mortgage modifications—itself a drastic underestimate—by the end of 2016 only 2.7 million had even been started. Out of that number, only 1.7 million made it to permanent modification, and of those, 558,000 eventually washed out of the program...All told, some 9.3 million homeowners lost their homes. It was the greatest destruction of middle-class wealth since the Great Depression at least."[257]

Black homeowners were hurt much worse than others because most of our net worth is tied to our homes. Also, we were more likely than others to be steered towards risky subprime loans even when we qualified for prime loans by predatory lenders.[257] The rate of homeownership under Obama fell to its lowest level since 1965 to 64% in 2015 and for Blacks that rate was 43% in 2015.[257] Black homeownership has always been lower than it has been for Whites and it went even lower after the Housing Bubble burst. There was no increase in Black homeownership "from 2013-2016."[257]

The overall homeownership rate doesn't tell the whole story, though. Also, included in it is negative equity which is worse than having no equity, or ownership in a property.[257] It's like leasing a car because you're borrowing money to rent the vehicle rather than to own it. That makes absolutely no sense! But, that's where a lot of borrowers found themselves during the Great Recession. Black homeowners were more likely to find themselves in this predicament than any others. "After the crisis, the percentage of black homeowners with negative equity exploded by twenty-fold, from 0.7 percent to 14.2 percent—and unlike white families, did not reach its peak until 2013."[257]

Because Whites are more likely to be wealthy and middle-class than Blacks, a much smaller percentage of their wealth is tied to their homes while a much larger percentage of their wealth is tied to financial investments like stocks and bonds.[257] By bailing out the banks with the Troubled Asset Relief Program and inflating the stock market with Quantitative Easing, or keeping interest rates for corporations and wealthy borrowers extremely low, the Obama Administration and the Federal Reserve made the rich even richer and turned the Racial Wealth Gap into a chasm.

What could President Obama have done differently? Firstly, he could have modeled HAMP after a New Deal-era program called the Home Owners' Loan Corporation (HOLC.) This "program bought up mortgages in default, and refinanced them with a lower interest rate and with a longer, fully amortized repayment period— a great help because there were no such mortgages at the time."[257] Principal, or the amount originally borrowed could also be reduced under this program.[257]

Secondly, he could've kept his promise to change bankruptcy laws to help struggling borrowers through a process called cramdown.[257][269] This is where the bankruptcy court judge could reduce the outstanding loan balance; reduce the interest rates; and extend the life of a mortgage on a primary residence so that borrowers have more time to repay it.[269] (This is already legal on almost every type of loan including those for vacation homes.)[269] Obama declined on four separate occasions to support cramdowns: once as a candidate and three times as President.[269]

Thirdly, he could have prosecuted those lenders guilty of mortgage fraud and taxed 100% of their profits.[257] The prospect of jail time and zero profits would have made bankers much more willing to assist distressed borrowers.[257] Fourthly, he could have followed the advice of Federal Depository Insurance Corporation (FDIC) Chair, Sheila Bair, by making "the banks and servicers to write down to face value any underwater mortgage that was more than sixty days delinquent."[257]

So, why didn't Obama create a better recovery plan for the homeowners? Well, as he said it was his job to protect the bankers from the borrowers. As a result, homeowners, particularly Black ones, suffered the most during the Great Recession.

Lack of opportunity for Black Men and Welfare's Effect on the Black Family

At the start of Obama's Presidency, African Americans were experiencing financial collapse. In response, civil rights leaders asked the President to do something to specifically address the extremely high levels of Black unemployment. The President replied, "I have a special responsibility to look out for the interests of every American. That's my job as president of the United States. And I wake up every morning trying to promote the kinds of policies that are going to make the biggest difference for the most number of people so that they can live out their American dream."[271] Yes, Mr. President that is your job, but not all Americans are going through what Black Americans are going through and you have on numerous occasions during your political career helped specific groups of non-Black Americans with no qualms, hesitations, or excuses made about it.

In March of 2009, two months into his Presidency, Black male unemployment stood at 15.4%.[272] This was the highest unemployment rate for any group and it "was more than twice that of White men and up almost 7 percentage points from a year earlier."[272] During a recession, jobless claims spike up. However, Blacks are less likely than Whites to receive unemployment insurance because they are more likely to work part-time and low-paying jobs. [272] They are the most likely group to be unemployed after their unemployment benefits have expired and they account for a quarter of those unemployed for a long time.[272] The Great Recession worsened the decades-long trends affecting Black men's unemployment such as the decline in manufacturing jobs, the increased volatility in the US auto industry, the decline in the unionization of the workforce, high unemployment in the best of times, and racial discrimination.[272] Obama did nothing to eliminate or reduce the losses suffered by American workers let alone those suffered by Black ones.

High unemployment leads to poverty. Poverty leads to crime. Crime leads to incarceration. Incarceration leads to the breakup of families. Ex-convicts have a high chance of being repeat offenders because they have few employment and educational opportunities.[272] It's just a vicious cycle that repeats itself in poor and Black communities. The first Black President should have been sensitive to this situation and done something to alleviate it.

There were several things President Obama could have done to reduce Black male unemployment. Firstly, he should have fought employment discrimination vigorously.[272] His Justice Department, Labor Department, and Equal Employment Opportunity Commission should have enforced all laws and regulations against racial discrimination in the workplace.[272] He also could have urged Congress to change the Reagan era law that places more of the burden of proof on the person alleging discrimination than the employer denying the allegation.

Secondly, he could have made it easier for part-time and low-wage workers to qualify for unemployment insurance.[272] This race-neutral policy would have helped Black men because they disproportionately make up part-time and low-wage workers.[272] Thirdly, he could have expanded unionization across the American workforce by supporting the Employee Free Choice Act, which would have made it easier for workers to organize, as he said he would.[272] Fourthly, he could have created and funded training and employment programs for high school students and young adults.[272] My Brother's Keeper was a good idea, but it should have been developed at the very start of his Presidency, not at the very end. Fifthly, he should have recruited more Blacks to work in the federal government and offered more opportunities for contracts for Black suppliers and vendors. During the transition period between his election and his swearing-in, he had promised to offer temporary jobs to hundreds of thousands of people willing to clean up the national parks. Unfortunately, he did not follow through. Temporary jobs during the middle of a recession would have helped those out of work and lowered the unemployment rate. He could have also promoted and offered Green jobs in Black Communities.[272] These jobs pay well and people with low to medium skills would qualify for them. Lastly, the Obama Administration along with state and local partners could have developed plans to reduce recidivism among former prisoners and developed ways to prevent Black men and boys from ever entering the criminal justice system.[272]

The Lack of Services in Black Neighborhoods

Wikipedia defines urban blight as "the sociological process by which a previously functioning city, or part of a city, falls into disrepair and decrepitude. It may feature deindustrialization, depopulation or deurbanization, economic restructuring, abandoned buildings and infrastructure, high local unemployment, increased poverty, fragmented families, low overall living standards and quality of life, political disenfranchisement, crime, elevated levels of pollution, and a desolate cityscape, known as a greyfield or urban prairies."[273] For the past 50 years, urban blight has been a serious problem in American cities, especially in the Northeast and the Midwest.[273] Think Detroit, St. Louis, Newark, and Baltimore.

What did Obama do to combat urban blight? He could have fought for more funding for cities, housing, education, healthcare (i.e., clinics,) and infrastructure. Use the Community Redevelopment Act to actually develop communities for residents not gentrify them for investors. If he would have punished the banks for their illegal foreclosures and bailed out homeowners, there would have been less blight. If he had tried to save Detroit, Flint, Benton Harbor, and Saginaw; stopped Michigan Gov. Snyder from taking over these Black towns and their school districts; and intervened to prevent the Flint Water Crisis, maybe there would be less blight in those communities. Finally, he could have gotten Congress to move away from giving states and localities Block Grants, which the federal government has less control over once they've been paid out, and increased federal mandates with federal money. These grants, especially those found in the 2009 Stimulus Package, should have been targeted for individuals and families and given to local governments who would have targeted these funds towards individuals and families. Instead, most of the Black Grants went to shore up state budgets in jeopardy of running deficits. This did nothing to get money into people's pockets which would have spurred demand which would have jumpstarted the economy and lowered unemployment.

How Obama Reacted to and Perpetuated Racism

When Barack Obama entered office on January 20, 2009, he had an approval rating of nearly 70%.[274] He had the wind at his back and the Republicans were shaking in their boots. So much so, that former Speaker of the House Newt Gingrinch and Republican leaders were regularly plotting in secret his downfall.[275] At no other time during his Presidency was he as popular and as powerful as he was at the start. But, he quickly squandered his political capital by making a series of early blunders and gaffes; creating a subpar stimulus package and housing market recovery plan that served the interests of Corporate America over those of Middle America; focusing on healthcare over jobs; promoting Bipartisanship over Principles; always wanting to be loved rather than feared; and being too fearful to grab the reins of power.

The Beer Summit

Presidential buddy and Harvard historian, Henry Louis "Skip" Gates got himself arrested on the night of July 16, 2009, for breaking into his own home and talking smack to the police. The arresting officer was Sgt. James Crowley of the Cambridge, Massachusetts Police.[276] A few days later, President Obama was asked during a press conference what he thought about the incident. Although he was caught off by the question, he went

194

ahead and replied, "I don't know, not having been there and not seeing all the facts, what role race played in that. But I think it's fair to say, number one, any of us would be pretty angry; number two, that the Cambridge police *acted stupidly* in arresting somebody when there was already proof that they were in their own home, and, number three, what I think we know separate and apart from this incident is that there's a long history in this country of African Americans and Latinos being stopped by law enforcement disproportionately."[276] After he was roundly criticized by law enforcement, the media, and White folks in general, Obama walked backed his statements and called the situation "a teachable moment."

Barack Obama, Mr. Obsequious, thought bringing the two men together to have a beer at the White House would diffuse the situation and get him back in the good graces of White America. It was dubbed the "Beer Summit" by the press. The President, Vice President, Prof. Gates, and Sgt. Crowley all talked it over beers in front of the cameras but away from the microphones. It was a complete disaster! Despite receiving some heavy-duty Presidential ass-kissing, Sgt. Crowley continued to say he was justified in arresting Skip Gates and made no apologies. Both, President Obama and Prof. Gates walked away from the situation with egg on their faces. James Crowley walked away a hero to White Supremacists everywhere because he, a Podunk cop, stood up to the "Nigger President." From that point on, Barack Obama never criticized the police or said much about racism, again. He avoided it like the Plague! I fault Obama for letting a reporter goad him into such an obvious trap in the first place. I fault him even more for not sticking to his original position. He never should've answered the question or made a statement on such an inflammatory subject if he wasn't prepared to accept the inevitable backlash that was coming and "stand his ground." This incident would be the first of many where the most powerful person in the world would knuckle under the thumb of White racists, both large and small.

195

Pastor Calls for His Death

In August of 2009, the pastor of Faithful Word Baptist Church, Stephen Anderson of Tempe, Arizona, called for the death of the President in a sermon entitled, <u>Why I Hate Barack Obama</u>.[277][278] He quoted Psalms 109:9 when he said the following, "May his children be fatherless and his wife a widow." Under the United States Code Title 18, Section 871, calling for the death of a president is the same as threatening him and is a Class D felony.[279] The maximum penalty is a five-year sentence, a $250,000 fine, a $100 special assessment, and three years of supervised release.[279] The Secret Service may have spoken to Rev. Anderson. I don't know. But, Barack Obama neither did nor said anything about the threat made against his life.

Congressman Joe Wilson Calls Him a Liar Before Congress

On September 9, 2009, South Carolina Congressman Joe Wilson shouted, "You lie!" as President Barack Obama addressed a Joint Session of Congress.[280][281] He made his outburst right after the President said that his health care plan does not insure undocumented immigrants. What did Obama say in response to this GOP Congressman's disrespectful outburst? He simply smiled and said, "That's not true." Everybody else in the House was howling and booing! Obama did not even have the self-respect to shout down Rep. Wilson and tell him he was out of order. If I were President, I would have ordered the Secret Service to arrest him immediately. Then, he would be subject to interrogation and incarceration until trial for his Treasonous Disrespect. I would have demanded that Speaker of the House Nancy Pelosi do the following: 1.) call for a vote to censure him immediately; 2.) have the House Ethics Committee investigate him for wrongdoing; 3.) call for a vote to expel him from the House Representatives; and 4.) take away his pension. If Obama had demanded that Wilson be removed from the House Chamber in cuffs, Republicans would have been terrified and they never would have crossed him as frequently and as disrespectfully as they did. Obama never understood that for a President "it is better to be feared than loved."[282]

The Firings of Van Jones and Shirley Sherrod

On Saturday, September 5, 2009, the President fired his Green Jobs Czar, Van Jones, after receiving weeks of condemnation for hiring this man from the conservative commentator, Glenn Beck.[283] Because he was afraid of Fox News, Obama left this brilliant young lawyer and activist out to dry. (Jones is a co-founder of ColorofChange.org.)[283] Allegedly, Mr. Jones was forced to resign because he signed a petition that questions the veracity of the September 11, 2001 attacks and he called Republicans mean names.[283] The real reason was racism. Beck and other racists couldn't stand to see another young, confident, and polished Black man in the White House. "Bad enough we got one nigger in there. We can't have two!" Or so the thought goes. President Obama and his Administration should have defended Van Jones, period. But, I guess I shouldn't have been surprised since Barack Obama was too scared to defend himself.

Shirley Sherrod, the Georgia State Director of Rural Development for the U.S. Agriculture Department, was forced to stop on the side of the road and was fired over the phone on July 19, 2010, by Agriculture Secretary Tom Vilsack at the behest of the President although Administration officials denied it.[284][285] The reason given for her firing by the Secretary was her comments at an NAACP event "damaged her effectiveness at a time when USDA was working to improve its previous civil rights abuses."[284] A heavily edited video of Ms. Sherrod's speech was released by the conservative journalist, Andrew Breitbart. It made her appear to be a "reverse racist" when she talked about referring a White farmer to a White lawyer after he refused her help because she was Black. It turned out that the White lawyer was a crook who tried to rip off his White brother. A few days later, the White farmer whose name is Roger Spooner[284][285] returned begging for Ms. Sherrod's help.

On the unedited tape, she is shown saying that she helped him save his farm and they became friends which Mr. Spooner acknowledged during an interview on CNN.[284] Tom Vilsack, not President Obama, eventually apologized to Ms. Sherrod and even offered her a better job which she graciously turned down.[284][285] The whole sad, sorry episode could have been avoided if Mr. Obama wasn't so scared of White people.

Obama's in the White House Hidin'

One December evening, I was watching cable news and I see Senator Orrin Hatch (R-Utah) gleefully howl, "Obama's in the White House hidin'!" At least, that's what it sounded like to me. What he actually said was, "All we need [is] a president who will step up and start to lead and quit acting like some scaredy-cat hiding in some closet in the White House." He went on to say, "He doesn't lead. He gets pushed around by one or the other huge factions in the Democratic Party."[286] The Senator was right about Obama allowing himself to be pushed around, but he was being dishonest about who was pushing the President around. It was the Republicans. It had been 13 months since the GOP took back the House in November 2010 and during that time, they had whipped the President. I mean just beat him down and there was still more butt whoopin' to come. In August of 2011, they made the Obama sign into law the Budget Control Act of 2011 which led to Sequestration, or automatic budget cuts. House Speaker John Boehner even bragged about it.

It was very unsettling to see the Senator mock the President like that, but he was right. President Obama was hiding! He was criticizing him for dragging his feet on approving the Keystone XL Pipeline.[286] But, in the weeks prior, there had been no public sightings of the President. It wasn't until months into 2012 did you see the President much, again, and that was because he was running for re-election.

The Press Briefing with President Obama and President Clinton

198

On December 10, 2010, President Obama held a "joint" press conference with former President Bill Clinton.[287] It was more like Obama introduced the "President" and then, walked off. He starts the meeting off jokingly by saying, "I thought it was a slow news day, so I thought I'd bring the other guy in." Out pops Bill Clinton the former President! It was almost like he had never left. A minute and thirty-six seconds into the presser, the President stepped away from the podium and allowed Mr. Clinton to speak.[287] Immediately, the ex-President jumped back into form, holding court while speaking and addressing the press. It was surreal seeing the current President standing beside the former President listening to him speak like he was a Secret Service Agent or some other functionary. The reporters there played right along and began asking Clinton questions about what he and the President talked about as if Obama wasn't standing there. The ex-President wisely didn't reveal what they had discussed only saying that he would not reveal anything unless he had President Obama's permission.

Eleven minutes and nine seconds into the briefing, Obama said he had kept the First Lady waiting for 30 minutes and that he had to leave, now, to go with her to a Christmas Party.[287] He shook the former President's hand and left the stage. Bill Clinton proceeded to spend the next 20 minutes answering questions from reporters talking about the budget agreement between the White House and Congressional Republicans as if he were the President.[287] I sat and watched incredulously as the current President handed off the reins of power, although briefly, to one of his predecessors. Barack Obama literally before our very eyes shirked one of his most important responsibilities as President which is to address the American people. Even the host of Comedy Central's The Daily Show, Jon Stewart, said, "It was a mistake!"[288]

One person I talked to about it later said it was embarrassing and that he made it seem like Black people were incompetent by allowing the former President, who is White, to take over a press conference on his behalf. I agree. Mr. Obama, why was it necessary for Bill Clinton to speak about the payroll tax cut deal that you struck with the Republicans? The first Black President said it was because Clinton had presided over one of the greatest economies in the history of the country that he was qualified to speak on the current situation. This remark just proves my friend's point that Obama's extremely insecure vis-à-vis White people. That's why he brought Bill Clinton in to speak to the Press Corps. That's why he selected Hillary Clinton to be his Secretary of State. Mr. Obama, you beat them; you don't need them! You're the President; you don't need anybody else to speak for you. The buck stops with you! But, passing the buck, especially when it came to Black issues, became a familiar theme during Obama's Presidency.

If you had to be somewhere and you didn't want to speak to the press, why didn't you have one of your press secretaries speak to them, Mr. Obama? This was unprecedented. No president before or since has allowed a former President to hold a press conference on his behalf. Obama seemed to be oblivious or unconcerned about the optics or the message he was sending about himself or Black people. It wasn't "a good look, Barack."[66] I hope the next Black President never does this.

Obama Lectures Black People

It was on Sunday, June 15, 2008, Father's Day, when presidential candidate Barack Obama felt it necessary to lecture Black men about fatherhood. The Democrats' likely nominee gave a sermon at Apostolic Church of GOD on the southside of Chicago. It was billed by Democratic strategists and consultants as Obama's pivot towards the mainstream and the General Election where he would go on to face Republican John McCain.[289]

During his speech, Obama presented the usual tropes about Black men being deadbeat dads and how "they're acting like boys instead of men."[289] He went on to say, "Any fool can have a child. That doesn't make you a father. It's the courage to raise a child that makes you a father."[289] Comic strip writer, Aaron McGruder later parodied these remarks during an episode of his animated series

200

The Boondocks.[290] Obama was so eager to be embraced by White America that he even threw his own father under the bus.[288]

There is a fatherhood problem in the country and there is one among African Africans, but it's an outright lie to portray it as a "Black thang" or to say that Black men are not fathers. Black men are fathers and they're damn good ones! In a 2013 report by the Centers for Disease Control and Infection (CDC,) it was found that Black dads spent more time daily with their children than men of other races.[291] Also, the Pew Center for Research found that 67% of Black men who did not live with their children saw them at least once a month compared to 59% for White men and 32% for Hispanic men.[291] Now, why don't we hear these stats being blared out all over the news? Why didn't Obama celebrate Black fathers like himself instead of lumping them in with the handful of deadbeats?

There were numerous instances during Obama's Presidency when he wagged his finger at Black people. But, his commencement speech at Morehouse was for me the most irksome. Obama has never been shy about his antipathy towards HBCUs. Mr. Ivy League cut their funding three times during his Presidency while increasing federal funds for Predominantly White Institutions (PWIs.)

Instead of congratulating these young men on a job well done and exhorting them to go even higher, Obama took this sacred and solemn occasion to lecture them about not making excuses. (Pardon me, but who was making excuses, Mr. President?) The President said, "We've got no time for excuses – not because the bitter legacies of slavery and segregation have vanished entirely; they have not. Not because racism and discrimination no longer exist; we know those are still out there. It's just that in today's hyperconnected, hypercompetitive world, with millions of young people from China and India and Brazil – many of whom started with a whole lot less than all of you did – all of them entering the global workforce alongside you, nobody is going to give you anything that you have not earned."[292]

It was as if because they were Black, he assumed they were going to make excuses. That's racist and I don't care that the President is Black what he said was racist. Black people are as much indoctrinated by anti-Black racism and White Supremacy as any other group in American society. Self-hatred is rampant among our group. But, my question to him would be, why did you go to Morehouse College, of all places, to lecture its graduates about making excuses? It was like he didn't do any research about this Institution that has for over a century and a half produced leaders in every human endeavor imaginable. Plus, the President of the College at the time of his address, John S. Wilson, had previously worked for his Administration as the Director of the White House Initiative on HBCUs. Did the President lecture these Morehouse graduates solely because they attended a College for Black men? I don't know. But, I do know that everybody feels they have the right to berate Black men and I'm sick of it. Would he have gone to Wellesley and told those White women not to make excuses? Would he have gone to Spelman or Bennett and lectured those Black women? Would he have gone Wabash and lectured those White men? I don't think so. This was just another instance where Obama felt the need to talk down to Blacks for the consumption of Whites and his own need to feel smug and superior to other Blacks.

Young Black men making excuses for failure wasn't the only ASSumption that Barack Obama made on that third Sunday in May. He also ASSumed that college students born in India, Brazil, or China must've had it rougher than Black college students born in the US. That's not necessarily true. It's more likely that they had it easier than those young Black men at Morehouse because it is much more likely that they were born into their country's elite. Unlike in the US and other so-called developed nations, education in most parts of the world is a privilege not a right. K-12 education is not free. Most people in the so-called developing world drop out long before they're high school age if they go at all. Obama, ever the American Exceptionalist, just ASSumed that just because someone was born in a developing country they must be poor. Because of their elite backgrounds, college graduates from India, Brazil, and China are much more connected to their societies. Their nations work to include them. Our nation works to exclude Blacks.

Lastly, the President said he felt a duty to help those Blacks who were left behind because they didn't have the opportunities that he had.[292] He said that's what "motivates" him.[291] Well, if that were truly the case, why didn't we see any of that "motivation" in the form of policies and laws that would have fought racial discrimination and expanded opportunities for Black men and Black people in general?

AFRICOM

AFRICOM, or the United States Africa Command was founded on October 1, 2007[293] by the George W. Bush Administration in response to China's growing influence on the Continent. It's based in Stuttgart, Germany.[293] (How do you have an African Command in Europe?) Under Obama, this Unified Combatant Command metastasized. The United States Government claims our military is in Africa to advise and train African militaries on how to maintain stability and fight terrorism.[294] But, in the 16 years since AFRICOM was established, there has been more instability, more wars, more terrorist attacks, more coups, more corruption, more slavery, and more narcotics trafficking. On top of that, China's influence has grown there exponentially. One country has conquered an entire continent and has done so without firing a single shot.

Obama not only maintained the Africa Command, but he also expanded it. It operates in 53 of 55 of Africa's countries and engages in training, logistics, supplies, weapons, drone strikes, intelligence gathering, and combat missions.[293] AFRICOM has a drone base and special forces troops in Niger. It has been involved in drone strikes against Al-Shabaab in Somalia and assisted the Federal Government of Nigeria in its fight against Boko Haram. But, no single mission has had as devastating an impact on Africa as Operation Odyssey Dawn also known as the 2011 invasion of Libya.[295] In fact, the Libyan invasion was Obama's second-biggest foreign policy blunder after he engineered the 2014 coup in Ukraine that was led by Confederate flag-waving Ukrainian rebels. (His decision to foment a coup there nine years ago is why we are all paying higher gas prices in 2023 and the reason why Ukrainians are dying.)

The US-Allied invasion of Libya not only led to the overthrow and assassination of Colonel Muammar Gaddafi, the nation's President, but to a civil war between armed militants from both the Western and Eastern parts of the country. Not only were tens of thousands of people killed from the fighting, which is ongoing, but thousands more were enslaved and sold to buyers throughout the Islamic world. The victims of human trafficking were Blacks who either originated in Libya's southern region or were immigrants from West Africa. Genocide was committed against the Black Southerners of Libya.

The fallout was not limited to Libya's borders. Many of the Libyan military's weapons ended up in the hands of terrorists like Boko Haram throughout the Sahel region of Africa, especially in the Western part. Jihadists from Libya and other parts of Northwest Africa have made their way into Mali, Niger, Chad, and Nigeria causing death, destruction, and displacement. Parts of the ancient city of Timbuktu in Mali were destroyed by Tuareg raiders and the country has had two coups since 2014. The President of Chad, Idris Deby was killed in May 2021 while fighting with Islamic militants. In Nigeria, Africa's largest and most prosperous country, Boko Haram and other terrorist groups have killed hundreds of thousands of people and displaced millions. It's one of the most underreported stories in the world. Even Barack Obama admitted that the invasion of Libya was his greatest mistake.[296] For me as a

Black man and a descendant of enslaved Africans, I don't understand how a "Son of Africa" could betray his people so.

Obama's Post-Presidency

Since Barack Obama left office in 2017, he has remained in the mode of a sheepdog who barks at and chases after sheep (voters) until they have been safely corralled into the pens of the Democratic Party. Bill Clinton, Hillary Clinton, Al Gore, and Bernie Sanders all have performed this role. Black elected officials, activists, journalists, and celebrities have all herded Black voters over the last three decades on behalf of the Democrats. Jesse Jackson, Al Sharpton, the Congressional Black Caucus, the NAACP, the Urban League, Roland Martin, Sean "Puffy" Combs, and Charlamagne Tha God have all served in this role. But, when it comes to keeping Black voters in line, in check, and voting "blue no matter who," Barack Obama is the Vote-Herder-in-Chief. In the following paragraphs, I am going to provide three examples of when he as the former President criticized Black voters for not voting Democratic; patronized them by telling them to remain hopeful and resilient in the face of crushing racism; and when he intervened on behalf of Corporate America to kill a nascent movement for Black freedom.

On Sunday, August 23, 2020, Jacob Blake, a Black man from Kenosha, Wisconsin, was shot in the back by a local police officer. The cop held Mr. Blake by his shirt as he pumped seven bullets into him. There were protests in Kenosha and all over the country and this was the latest incident in a summer of unrest over police brutality that was kicked off by the murder of George Floyd on live camera by Minneapolis Police Officer Derek Chauvin.

Three days later the Milwaukee Bucks decided to forfeit Game 5 of their playoff match up with the Orlando Magic by sitting out the game in protest of Mr. Blake's shooting. The Orlando Magic declined to accept the win and also agreed to sit out the game. Four other teams that were playing that night followed suit and the NBA Players Strike began on Wednesday, August 26, 2020.[297][298]

Because all the remaining playoff teams were located at the same place, Walt Disney World in Orlando, Florida, players from those teams were able to meet together Wednesday night to decide what to do next. They had a stark choice to make: 1.) continue the playoffs or 2.) strike until the NBA's owners used their considerable influence over politicians to do something about racism and police brutality. A tremendous weight was on these players' shoulders. Not only would the League suffer financially from a boycott after already losing hundreds of millions of dollars due to the National Quarantine caused by the Coronavirus Pandemic, but the players' salaries would be cut if they didn't play. That's on top of the salary cuts that they had already suffered from games being canceled because of the Quarantine.

At first, only two teams agreed to cancel the season: the Lakers and the Clippers.[299] But, those teams were the two most popular teams in the League and a playoff matchup between the two was highly coveted.[299] As the Lakers and Clippers went, so went the rest of the teams. The strike was on or so we thought when we went to bed Wednesday night.

Shortly after the players met, LA Lakers star LeBron James and Oklahoma City Thunder star and NBA Player Rep. Chris Paul received a call from Barack Obama.[297][298] The former President told them that it would be in everyone's best interests if they convinced the other players to end the strike.[297][298] The next morning it was announced that games would resume on Saturday and there would be a "social justice committee" formed by the NBA to address the concerns raised by the players.[297][298] In addition, NBA arenas would be used as polling places during the 2020 Election.[297][298] Awe, ain't that nice?

Instead of encouraging these stars to continue to fight for justice, Barack Obama used his cache' as the First Black President to tell them to throw in the towel in the face of racism and injustice in exchange for a large check, more voting locations, Black Lives Matter painted on basketball courts, taking a knee, and placing hashtags on their jerseys. I guess that's "change we can believe in." Not! Even the White writers of the articles I've cited, knew better and seemed to care more about racial justice than the former President. Christian Rivas of the <u>Silver Screen and Roll</u> podcast said, "...these players have already been through so much — from the death of Kobe Bryant to a global pandemic that has forced them to be away from their families for almost two months now. If enough is enough for them, then we shouldn't be the ones to judge their decision. Right now, they deserve nothing less than our support."[299] Ricky O'Donnell of <u>SB Nation</u> was even more powerful when he said, "NBA players took an incredible stand to strike. It would have been even more powerful if they walked away completely, but it also would have been costly. Obama helped convince them to return, which had been criticized by some as a move to break a unionized strike."[298]

Obama's a union buster! Maybe that's why he didn't push for the Employee Free Choice Act to become law when he was President despite campaigning for it as a candidate. If the 2020 NBA Players strike had been allowed to continue, it would have had a tremendous impact on both race and labor relations. Because of their lost profits, the NBA's billionaire owners would have felt compelled to pressure the politicians who serve them to change discriminatory laws and policies that allow police brutality to go unchecked and unpunished. You would have seen chokeholds, no-knock warrants, and qualified immunity abolished almost immediately. You also would have seen more grand jury indictments of crooked cops by district attorneys who need donations from the wealthy in order to get re-elected. Activists would have been inspired to push for even more change. Ordinary rank-and-file workers and consumers of all races would have been inspired to use their political muscle by striking, protesting, boycotting, and yes, lobbying their representatives for change. It would have been a sea change in the way business was done in this country. It would have been "no more business as usual." Barack Obama, ever the servant of White Capital, made sure that was never going to happen on his watch. Perhaps, that's why the NBA's owners made him a strategic partner in their African league.[202]

On Friday, June 18, 2021, former President Obama appeared on the ABC News special entitled "Juneteenth: Together We Triumph." He was interviewed by former NFL lineman and Good Morning, America host, Michael Strahan.[300] After Mr. Strahan gave him reasons why many Americans, particularly African Americans, have lost hope in the years since his election, Mr. Obama replied, "You get hope back from, for me at least, taking the long view. Recognizing that resilience, determination, the ability to deal with setbacks and disappointments and keep going. Those are qualities that can carry us forward and no one has exhibited that more historically in this country than African Americans."[300] Now, everything he said was true. Each person, both as an individual and as a member of a group, has a responsibility to him/herself to take control of his/her life as much as humanly possible and to meet the challenges he/she may face. But, that doesn't negate the fact that they are powerful individuals and groups in society who seek to harm and oppress us. People need a life jacket to keep afloat in deep water and they need a sturdy boat to navigate the ocean's currents. But, politicians like Obama only seem to want to give their constituents, particularly Blacks, pep talks about personal responsibility instead of policies that would improve all of our lives. That's just not going to cut it, anymore. Politicians are either going to strive to be public servants or they don't deserve our votes anymore. I know many other people who feel the same way. No more business as usual! Yvette Carnell is right. "Politics is an exchange."

In the November 15, 2020 edition of The Atlantic, former President Obama was interviewed for an article entitled, "Why Obama Fears for Our Democracy."[301] Although he wasn't asked by the interviewer, Jeffrey Goldberg, for his thoughts on why more Black men voted for Trump in 2020 than they did in 2016, the ex-President decided to give his take anyway. He said, "It's interesting—people are writing about the fact that Trump increased his support among Black men [in the 2020 presidential election], and the occasional rapper who supported Trump. I have to remind myself that if you listen to rap music, it's all about the bling, the women, the money. A lot of rap videos are using the same measures of what it means to be successful as Donald Trump is. Everything is gold-plated. That insinuates itself and seeps into the culture."[301]

It's interesting to note that Trump almost doubled his support among Black women in 2020 to 8% up from 4.5% in 2016 according to pollsters with Edison.[302][303] But, it shouldn't be surprising that this little inconvenient truth went unreported by the mainstream media. It's because it doesn't fit the Democrats' narrative that Black women are the backbone of the Democratic Party and it's only those pesky Black men who have gone off the reservation. Democrats have told this same lie over and over since Doug Jones defeated Roy Moore in 2017.

Obama casted aspersions on the characters of those Black men who voted for Trump by using racist stereotypes and tropes that compared these men to materialistic, amoral rappers. This is dangerous for two reasons. First, it gives license to Whites and other non-Blacks, who already believe these falsehoods, to feel justified in believing in and spreading them because a Black person agrees with them. Second, it reinforces negative stereotypes that Blacks have about themselves among themselves which is self-destructive. On both counts, an educated Black man like Obama is wrong for perpetuating these stereotypes about his own people. The fact that he did it after becoming the President of the United States made it criminal.

What Obama Did Right

While there were many things that Obama did wrong, there were some things he did right. The first thing he did right was run for President. He was not the first Black to run for President or even Vice President, but he was the first to win. That was a big deal! It gave me and millions and perhaps billions of other Blacks around the world hope that the world was going to be a better place and things were finally going to turn around for our race. His election to the highest office in the land inspired Black children into believing that they, too, could one day grow up to be President. It inspired Black women. Kamala Harris would not be Vice President today if Barack Obama hadn't first become President. It renewed Black people's faith in America. Millions of elderly and not so elderly Black People "died happy" because they had lived to see a Black man become President.

His Presidency also established a positive image of Blacks in the minds of others. I remember arriving at an elementary school for an interview and a little Hispanic boy, out of the blue, just waved and said to me, "Good Morning, Mr. President!" as he walked by. I remember feeling touched by his words. Later that evening, I thought about how Barack Obama, a Black man, was the only president this child has known in his very short life, so he associated any Black man wearing a suit with the Presidency. It certainly wasn't that way when I was growing up and sadly, it's not that way, now. For a very brief period in history, a Black Man symbolized the power and the prestige of the United States.

The second thing he did right was keeping both his personal life and his public life scandal-free. Despite everything the Republicans and the press threw at him, we never heard about any mistresses, any unwanted children, bribes, indictments, convictions, or even any appearances of impropriety on his part or any member of his Administration's part. In other words, he didn't embarrass us.

The third thing he did right was introducing us to his lovely family. His wife Michelle was as fine a First Lady as there has ever been. It was a pleasure seeing his young daughters grow up into young women. I was happy to see that his mother-in-law, Marian Shields Robinson, decided to live with them in the White House. I can only imagine what she feels like as a Black woman who grew up during

Segregation to live to see a Black man become President. On top of that, he's her son-in-law. We got to know his brother-in-law, Craig Robinson as well the President's sister and his extended family. He has a few uncles and aunts who are siblings of his father, Barack H. Obama I, who also live in the US.

Score

"...I would hope that you would not just be Blacks in Government. But, in the next century that you would be Blacks Over Government."[304] – Min. Louis Farrakhan

Well, for eight years, we had "Blacks Over Government." How did we do? **How did he do?** As President, Obama gets a B-/C+. He was an effective leader. He got the country out of a recession and managed the numerous crises he faced (e.g., the BP Oil Spill.) He was a great campaigner, and his oratory was second to none. He would have gotten higher marks from me if he would have stood up to the Republicans; reduced both economic inequalities and racial disparities; gotten us out of Iraq and Afghanistan; never invaded Libya; and never expanded AFRICOM.

As a Black leader, however, he receives much lower marks. Mr. Obama received four points in the <u>Leadership</u> category for becoming the President of the United States and for being the first Black to do so. He gets a 1.0 for <u>Race Pride</u> because despite all of his swag, coolness, and racial appeals, Obama more often than not threw Black people under the bus whenever it suited him. He traded in on Black stereotypes and used his Blackness as a bridge to mainstream success. In other words, he used Black people to get to White people so he could get ahead. This is a strategy employed by innumerable Black politicians, activists, entertainers, and others to achieve the success and acceptance they crave from White America. Lastly, he often openly displayed his contempt for Blacks as individuals and as a group in speeches, interviews, and most importantly in his policies.

Although Barack Obama was educated, clean-cut, and professional, he receives a 1.0 in the Role Model department because he demonstrated too much meekness and obsequiousness in the face of his opponents who were openly racist and hostile towards him. He reinforced over and over again the lesson that Blacks already know which is to "turn the other cheek" in the face of racism. Had Obama just stood up for himself, he would have been a much stronger, more effective, and more revered President and leader. In this respect, his Presidency was a lost opportunity for both him and us.

Finally, Barack Obama's Impact on the Race was a very mixed bag. On the one hand, he was inspirational because he showed that a Black person could become President. But, on the other hand, he showed that that same Black person has to surrender to racists and accept junior level status if he/she wants to stay President. I've never seen or even read about another President having to accept the kind of abuse and disrespect that Barack Obama did. Furthermore, he was in the unique position to make some significant policy changes for the benefit of all Americans, but particularly Black Americans, if he would've only been willing to wield the levers of Presidential Power. His hands were not tied! For example, he could've used the President's "Bully Pulpit," to enforce existing laws; issue signing statements; and write executive orders. Instead, he often deferred and kowtowed to a racist and recalcitrant Congress. Since Mr. Obama preferred to be "an interested observer, a thoughtful interlocutor between African Americans and the country as a whole, rather than a (President) with the political influence to effect the changes of which he spoke,"[271] he gets a 1.0 for his Impact on the Race. Therefore, his overall score is a 1.4 or a D. (4+1+1+1 = 7.7 divided by 5 = 1.4.)

Afterword

I often look at the Obama Presidency as a cruel joke or a cruel hoax played on Black people. We thought we had finally made it only to find out that we had moved backward. The word that best describes his two terms for Black folks is bittersweet. It was sweet because one of us reached the top of the pyramid and for eight years we got to bask in his and his family's glow from the White House. It's bitter, however, because we lost so much to get him in there and to keep him in there. Blacks are far worse off after Obama left than before he went in. Black wealth has cratered; we're the only group that still hasn't recovered from the Great Recession; racists have been emboldened to attack us; and internally we're a mess. Homicide, suicide, drug abuse, crime, health disparities, and every other negative statistical category that you can use to describe a people's condition are up. The only one that's down is life expectancy. Barack Obama is not responsible for these things, but he was responsible for addressing these things to the best of his ability. Blacks voted for him largely because we expected him to be our champion and to improve our lives. But, he just didn't try. And to those Black apologists who said all through his two terms and since that he was the President of America not the President of Black America, I ask the following question: Are Black Americans not Americans? If we're Americans, then why should we accept less than any other American would? You're siding with racists if you say that we should.

Other races, ethnicities, demographics, constituencies, and even individuals petition their government for specific requests and remedies and get them. Why shouldn't we? Because Black leaders have long since taught that we should only fight for equality and we shouldn't fight for specific redress for our problems we've spent almost 60 years endorsing our own oppression and running with our hands tied behind our backs in this race. Every other group fights not only for equal opportunity and due process under the law, but also for specific remedies that not only make them equal but will give them advantages in this so-called free enterprise system. How can you expect some poor Black kid from the ghetto, who might be smart, to compete with some White trust fund kid, smart or not, whose family members have always gone to college? You can't. That's why you have to have Affirmative Action to ensure that Blacks get admitted to colleges and find jobs in the workplace and get opportunities to bid for government and corporate contracts. Otherwise, the people who already have will get even more because they have all the advantages.

I knew Obama wasn't going to end racism or poverty. But, I did expect after eight years we'd be on the road to reducing them. I certainly didn't expect us to suffer the losses that we did. Racist police and vigilantes killed Black people with impunity and the First Black President acted like he couldn't do anything about it. But, if the Republican George H.W. Bush was able to convict the cops who beat Rodney King for violating his civil rights, why the hell couldn't Obama at least prosecute the killers of Trayvon Martin, Mike Brown, Eric Garner, and Sandra Bland? I certainly didn't expect to see a terrorist quietly and calmly stroll into a Black church's Bible study and massacre nine people in Charleston, South Carolina. I didn't need the President to sing "Amazing Grace." I needed him to prosecute both the triggerman and his associates. Barack Obama could've and should've set the tone by letting racists know that their bigotry and violence would no longer be tolerated. By being weak in the face of anti-Black bigotry and White Supremacy, he made all of us Blacks sitting ducks.

Maybe, deep down I was a little like The Boondocks character, Riley Freeman, and I expected Obama to "save us!"[66] In 2010, the Black scholar Sara Suten Seti admonished us for being "a Messiah-prone people. Always looking for a savior!"[192] Obama did nothing to disabuse us of this notion that he was a Black Messiah. He even joked about it during his remarks at the 2008 Al Smith Dinner when he said, "Contrary to the rumors you have heard, I was not born in a manger (like Jesus.) I was actually born on Krypton and sent here by my father, Jor-El, to save the planet Earth."[305]

After eight miserable years of Bush, people were excited to buy "the change" Obama was selling. If he was indeed the Messiah, then I've got buyer's remorse because I didn't get what I bargained for. Now, I understand why the crowd in Jerusalem said, "Give us Barabbas!"[306] after Pontius Pilate asked them, "Which of them do you want me to release to you?"[306] It's because they expected Jesus to lead a revolution against the hated Romans and establish a new, independent Jewish kingdom. But, instead, they got "turn the other cheek"[307] and "love your enemies…and pray for those which despitefully use you."[308] On top of that, they heard sermons filled with nebulous ideas like a "Kingdom of Heaven"[309] for the righteous which would be established at the end of the world. They weren't interested in that. They wanted their freedom, right now! In the same vein, Obama would often admonish Blacks to remain patient, resilient, and hopeful because someday they, too, would live the American Dream.

Barabbas, on the other hand, was a zealot, or freedom fighter, who fought against the Romans and their Jewish collaborators. He only robbed and killed them not his own people. So, in the minds of the crowd, his actions were justified. Barack Obama, like Jesus, let his enemies mock and abuse him. He let them treat him with scorn and derision. But, Jesus, unlike Barack, loved his people and he never deceived them. Never mistreated them. Never mocked nor abused them. Never abandoned them to the wolves. Never sold them out! He was even willing to die for them. Now, I didn't expect Obama to die for us, but I did expect him to lead this country in a better direction and leave it better off than when he found it. I expected him to fight racism, poverty, injustice, inequality, and other societal ills. I expected that we would have at least made headway in those areas as did many other people. That's why we voted for him. We thought he'd be different from the Presidents before him

215

in outlook as well as complexion. We were expecting a Progressive because that's what he ran as. But, that never happened because Barack Obama never wanted it to happen. We have more racism, more discrimination, more inequality, more poverty, more crime and violence, and more disunity after he left than when he went in.

Black America certainly got the worst of it. I feel like Black people after Obama are like the guy in the New Testament who had been exercised of one demon only to be repossessed by that same demon and seven of his buddies.[310] Of course, the man was much worse off than he was before with eight demons tormenting him. We're worse off after Obama than we were before him in every quality of life category with some new ones like the highest rates of coronavirus infections and deaths,[310] a spike in suicides, especially among children and men,[311][312] and now, higher rates of drug overdoses than Whites.[313]

But, it wasn't all Obama's fault. Black people, his followers, also didn't "make him do it!" Leaders come from the people and if the leaders are bad, then the people are bad as well. The late Reverend Dr. E.V. Hill once posed two very important questions to us. The first was "Will this generation of Negroes or African Americans, as you prefer to be called, ever become a people, again?"[314] Then, he asked, "Will this generation of African Americans, new Negroes, prove (they) have what it takes to make (the) leaders among us great?"[314]

In answering his first question, we have to acknowledge that Blacks today are not a people. We're a collection of talented individuals each going in his or her own direction. A people are a collection of individuals some talented and some not so talented each going in the same direction. If Blacks saw themselves as a group, a group they wanted to belong to, then, each Black individual would always consider what's in their group's interest in addition to what's in their individual interest. Because he belongs to a group that sees itself as a people and who wants to be a people, a White President understands and appreciates that he must serve White people. He has no problem walking and chewing gum at the same time. Because there's little sense of peoplehood and little sense of obligation towards one another among Blacks, individual Blacks consider primarily what's in their individual self-interest even if it's detrimental to the group's self-interest.

So, it was in Barack Obama's self-interest to protect the bankers from the wrath of the American people in 2009 while doing nothing to save millions of homeowners, a good chunk of whom were Black, from foreclosure. So, while it was in the former President's interest that NBA players end their strike, it wasn't in those players' interest nor was it in the ordinary, everyday Black person's interest that they did. Because he looked out only for himself, he's seen as a hero by the bankers, executives, and lobbyists and they've rewarded him with $400,000 a pop speaking engagements and strategic partnerships, while the people who opened the doors of opportunity for him are shutout.

My answer to Dr. Hill's second question is good followers make good leaders and the leaders come from the people. If the people are morally bankrupt, their leaders will be, too. If people don't follow their leaders, their leaders won't succeed. Most importantly, if the people don't hold their leaders accountable, they won't deliver on their promises or meet the people's expectations. Barack Obama didn't succeed at improving the lives of Black Americans because we lacked integrity or we didn't support him. He failed because as he said once we didn't "make him do it." I don't know why we had to "make him do it" since we gave him the power to do it by electing him, President. This is Barack Obama once again, shirking his responsibility and passing the buck by blaming us for not holding him accountable. A leader with any integrity would simply honor his obligations to his supporters.

We didn't hold the First Black President accountable by making demands of him and securing commitments from him when he first ran as a candidate in 2008 and then, again when he ran for re-election in 2012. Instead of trying to protect him from racists and critics, we should've been demanding that he protect us from them. We also should've protested in the streets against his policies and put even more pressure on him by taking out ads in the national newspapers; engaged in letter-writing and social media campaigns; boycotted his corporate donors; and even voted Republican, in some instances, just to send a message. Ultimately, we could've voted him out by electing not to re-elect him by simply sitting out the election. That definitely would've sent both him and the Democrats the message to NOT take us for granted.

What are some ways we can develop our leaders? First, we must develop a sense of race pride, self-respect, obligation, and peoplehood among ourselves. "Treat my brother or sister as I treat myself." Second, we have to develop a code of conduct or ethics that dictates how each of us deals with one another regardless of whether we like each other or not and it must be adhered to regardless of the situation we find ourselves in as individuals. Third, we as Black adults have to teach our children our history and culture. We also have to teach them to love and respect themselves and those like them. We have to model the behavior we expect in our children. We have to foster healthy relationships among ourselves and develop nonviolent and non-destructive ways of conflict resolution.

Fourth, we have to groom our children to be leaders early on in life. They have to learn to value hard work and responsibility. Scouting and rites of passage programs provide plenty of opportunities to teach these values. Fifth, we have to stop embracing celebrities and other individuals anointed by the press as our leaders. Our leaders should be homegrown and come from grassroots organizations, civic groups, churches, fraternal organizations, and HBCUs. These organizations should have a formal and rigid application process that involves interviews, references, and background checks so that they are not infiltrated by police, government agents, or reporters. Existing members of the organization have to be able to vouch for prospective members of the organization. Otherwise, they can't join.

Lastly, no candidate for elected office will receive the Black vote without first being voted for in the "People's Primary." What is a "People's Primary," you say? It's an informal process where individuals, families, activists, and community members vet a potential candidate for office. If the individual running office references check out; he/she has a track record of service to the Black Community; and he/she has personally and publicly made the case to us for why we should consider his/her candidacy, then, we'll throw our support behind him/her. He/she will be free to run in the party's primary of his/her choosing and we'll support him/her in that primary and/or general election. This way no (Black) candidate claiming to represent the Black Community will have our vote unless he/she has been first vetted by Our Community. He/she can still run without it, but he/she just won't have our support.

Why is it important that we have a formal process by which to choose our leaders? Because currently, we choose our leaders informally based on subjective criteria like their personal charm (e.g., Jesse Jackson,) their celebrity (e.g., Oprah Winfrey,) or their status within mainstream society (e.g., Condoleezza Rice.) Very often, the media chooses them for us (e.g., Colin Powell or Barack Obama.) Very few become our leaders based on what they've done for us. But, hopefully, that will change as Blacks adopt the Leadership Scorecard because it provides a standard, independent method for grading Black leaders that individuals, families, and organizations can use.

Bibliography

1. "Oprah Winfrey." Wikipedia 8 January 2022
   https://en.wikipedia.org/wiki/Oprah_Winfrey
2. Lane, Randall. "Inside the $126 Billion Forbes Cover."
   Forbes 18 September 2012. 8 January 2022
   https://www.forbes.com/sites/randalllane/2012/09/18/inside
   -the-126-billion-forbes-cover/?sh=1f1295307a97 2/3
3. Berg, Madeline. "Oprah Winfrey Just Sold Most Of Her
   Stake In Her OWN Cable Network." Forbes 22 December
   2020. 9 January 2022
   https://www.forbes.com/sites/maddieberg/2020/12/22/opra
   h-winfrey-just-sold-most-of-her-stake-in-her-own-cable-
   network/?sh=55cdf5672546 2/5
4. "Recy Taylor." Wikipedia 8 January 20
   https://en.wikipedia.org/wiki/Recy_Taylor
5. Chuba, Kirsten. "Seal Accuses Oprah of Knowing About
   Harvey Weinstein's Sexual Misconduct." Variety 11
   January 2018. 8 January 2022
   https://variety.com/2018/music/news/seal-accuses-oprah-
   knowing-about-weinstein-misconduct-1202661226/ 2/15
   REX/Shutterstock/NBC
6. PNL. "Mo'Nique Blasts Oprah for Giving Different
   Treatment to White Alleged Abusers Like Harvey
   Weinstein." COMPLEX 4 February 2020. 8 January 2022
7. Levine, Jon. "Gayle King Refuses to Abandon Charlie
   Rose Despite 27 New Accusers: 'I Still Consider Him a
   Friend' (Video.)" The Wrap 3 May 2018. 8 January 2022
   https://www.thewrap.com/gayle-king-refuses-to-abandon-
   charlie-rose-despite-27-new-accusers-i-still-consider-him-
   a-friend/ 2/11
8. Since Wikipedia did not have it, I did a Google search for
   Kimberle' Crenshaw's exact date of birth, and May 4, 1959

popped up. But, no related articles that were generated from this search had this information. The Wikipedia article has since been updated to say her birthdate is May 5, 1959.

9. "Kimberle' Williams Crenshaw." Wikipedia 5 January 2022 https://en.wikipedia.org/wiki/Kimberl%C3%A9_Crenshaw

10. Crenshaw, Kimberle'. Interview National Association of Independent Schools (NAIS) 22 June 2018 30 December 2021. <https://www.youtube.com/watch?v=ViDtnfQ9FHc>

11. Crenshaw, Kimberle'. "The urgency of intersectionality." TED 7 December 2016 https://www.youtube.com/watch?v=akOe5-UsQ2o

12. "Intersectionality." Wikipedia 2 January 2022 https://en.wikipedia.org/wiki/Intersectionality

13. Curry, Tommy J. "Decolonizing the Intersection." Critical Psychology Praxis pp. 132-154 February 2021 5 January 2022. p. 147 paragraph 3. https://www.researchgate.net/publication/349589709_Decolonizing_the_Intersection_Black_Male_Studies_as_a_Critique_of_Intersectionality's_Indebtedness_to_Subculture_of_Violence_Theory/link/6037765c4585158939ca7020/download

14. Curry, Tommy J. "Decolonizing the Intersection." Critical Psychology Praxis pp. 132-154 February 2021 5 January 2022. p. 148 paragraph 3. https://www.researchgate.net/publication/349589709_Decolonizing_the_Intersection_Black_Male_Studies_as_a_Critique_of_Intersectionality's_Indebtedness_to_Subculture_of_Violence_Theory/link/6037765c4585158939ca7020/download

15. Moore, Antonio. "Intersectionality and the Gender Divide in Black American Explained." ToneTalks. 9 April 2021 30 December 2021. https://www.youtube.com/watch?v=t6g6D3Cc-Wc

16. Westcott, Diane Nilsen. "Blacks in the 1970's : Did they scale the job ladder?" <u>Monthly Labor Review</u> June 1982 p. 2 & 4. 30 December 2021. https://stats.bls.gov/opub/mlr/1982/06/art5full.pdf

17. "Social Dominance Theory." <u>Wikipedia</u> 2 January 2022 https://en.wikipedia.org/wiki/Social_dominance_theory

18. Little, Becky. "The Massive, Overlooked Role of Female Slave Owners." <u>The History Channel</u>. 12 March 2019 4 January 2022. https://www.history.com/news/white-women-slaveowners-they-were-her-property

19. Bucholz, Katherine. "The Gender Pay Gap Visualized." <u>Statista</u>. 22 October 2021 31 December 2021. https://www.statista.com/chart/3958/gender-pay-gap-by-ethnicity/

20. Leonhardt, David. "The Black-White Wage Gap Is as Big as It Was in 1950." <u>The New York Times</u>. 25 June 2020 31 December 2021. https://www.nytimes.com/2020/06/25/opinion/sunday/race-wage-gap.html?searchResultPosition=2

21. Lamont Hill, Marc. "Tarana Burke and Dr. Brittany Cooper Talk Impact Cosby's Overturned Conviction Black Community." <u>Black News Tonight</u>. Black News Channel. 30 June 2021 2 July 2021. https://www.youtube.com/watch?v=YfVxuZCD8cI

22. <u>Fact Sheet: Intimate Partner Violence in the African American Community</u>. Institute on Domestic Violence in the African American Community. University of Minnesota. http://www.ncdsv.org/images/IDVAAC_IPVintheAfricanAmericanCommunity.pdf

23. Langhinrichsen-Rohling, Jennifer, Tiffany A. Misra, Candice Selwyn, & Martin L. Rohling. "#3 Rates of Bi-directional versus Uni-directional Intimate Partner Violence Across Samples, Sexual Orientations, and Race/Ethnicities: A Comprehensive Review." <u>Partner Abuse</u> Volume 3, Issue 2, April 2012 pp.1-2(2)

https://www.researchgate.net/publication/309528062_3_Rates_of_Bi-directional_versus_Uni-directional_Intimate_Partner_Violence_Across_Samples_Sexual_Orientations_and_RaceEthnicities_A_Comprehensive_Review

24. Glover, Alex. "Uncomfortable Racial Preferences Revealed by Online Dating." Meetville.com. 27 May 2021. https://meetville.com/blog/interracial-dating/the-uncomfortable-racial-preferences-revealed-by-online-dating

25. Brown, Ashley. " 'Least Desirable'? How Racial Discrimination Plays Out In" Online Dating." NPR. 9 January 2018 https://www.npr.org/2018/01/09/575352051/least-desirable-how-racial-discrimination-plays-out-in-online-dating

26. Peters, Adele. "Black women will get no-strings-attached monthly checks in this new guaranteed income experiment." Fast Company. 3 January 2022.

27. Crenshaw, Kimberle'. Interview "Kimberle' Crenshaw Discusses 'Intersectional Feminism.' " Lafayette College 15 October 2015 30 December 2021. https://www.youtube.com/watch?v=ROwquxC_Gxc

28. Crenshaw, Kimberle'. "On Intersectionality." Women of the World (WOW) Conference 14 March 2016 30 December 2021. https://www.youtube.com/watch?v=-DW4HLgYPlA

29. "Richard Pryor." Wikipedia. 28 December 2021. https://en.wikipedia.org/wiki/Richard_Pryor

30. McPherson, James. "The new comic style of Richard Pryor." New York Times 27 April 1975 28 December 2021. < https://www.nytimes.com/1975/04/27/archives/the-new-comic-style-of-richard-pryor-i-know-what-i-wont-do-says-the.html?searchResultPosition=1>

31. A Tribe Called Quest. "Sucka Nigga." Midnight Marauders. 1993.

223

32. Maynard, Joyce. "Richard Pryor, King of the Scene-Stealers." New York Times 9 January 1977 29 December 2021. < https://www.nytimes.com/1977/01/09/archives/richard-pryor-king-of-the-scenestealers-richard-pryor.html?searchResultPosition=1>

33. Jackson, Derrick Z. "The N-word and Richard Pryor." New York Times 15 December 2005 29 December 2021. < https://www.nytimes.com/2005/12/15/opinion/the-nwordand-richard-pryor.html?searchResultPosition=2>

34. "Jay-Z." Wikipedia 10 November 2021. https://en.wikipedia.org/wiki/Jay-Z

35. Mr. Davey D. "Payola: The Dirty Industry Practice That's Ruining Hip Hop." Hip Hop and Politics 2 December 2012 13 November 2021. < http://hiphopandpolitics.com/2012/12/02/payola-the-dirty-industry-practice-thats-ruining-hip-hop/>

36. Golianopoulos, Thomas. "The Rap Pact: How Jay Z and Hot 97 Combined Forces to Take Over Hip-Hop." Pitchfork 14 February 2017 25 November 2021. < https://pitchfork.com/features/article/10021-the-rap-pact-how-jay-z-and-hot-97-combined-forces-to-take-over-hip-hop/>

37. Trap Lore Ross. "How Jay Z Finessed Dame Dash for $29m+ (The Roc Story.)" Trap Lore Ross 19 December 2019. < https://www.youtube.com/watch?v=E6I6JWWd_F0>

38. Hale, Kori. "Jay-Z's Roc Nation Gets Iconix Lawsuit Dismissed For $15 Million." Forbes magazine 24 November 2019 25 November 2021. < https://www.forbes.com/sites/korihale/2019/11/24/jay-zs-roc-nation-gets-iconix-lawsuit-dismissed-for-15m/?sh=6a8559606e29>

39. Toxsique Diamond. "Jay Z Pleads Innocent And Get UP SET And Loud In C OUR T." Toxsique Diamond

Productions LLC 30 October 2021 25 November 2021. < https://www.youtube.com/watch?v=hlF4bCWgm4M>

40. DeGregory, Priscilla. "Jay-Z calls perfume company's work 'lazy,' 'crappy,' at contract trial." New York Post 1 November 2021 25 November 2021. < https://nypost.com/2021/11/01/jay-z-calls-perfume-companys-work-lazy-at-contract-trial/>

41. Rosman, Katherine and Vanessa Friedman. "Jay-Z and LVMH, Two of the World's Biggest Brands, Go Into Business." New York Times 22 February 2021 25 November 2021. https://www.nytimes.com/2021/02/22/style/jay-z-lvmh-ace-of-spades-champagne.html

42. Greenberg, Zack O'Malley. "The Real Story Behind Jay Z's Champagne Deal." Forbes 6 November 2014 9 November 2021. < https://www.forbes.com/sites/zackomalleygreenburg/2014/11/06/why-jay-zs-champagne-news-isnt-so-new/?sh=7e0a63717528>

43. Freeman, Abigail. "Here's How Much Jay-Z Made On His Ace Of Spades Deal—And How It Stacks Up Against Other Celebrity Cashouts." Forbes 26 February 2021 25 November 2021. < https://www.forbes.com/sites/abigailfreeman/2021/02/26/heres-how-much-jay-z-made-on-his-ace-of-spades-deal-and-how-it-stacks-up-against-kylie-jenner-kim-kardashian-george-clooney-rihanna--cashouts/?sh=2d25cd41679c>

44. "Tidal (Service.)" Wikipedia 26 November 2021. https://en.wikipedia.org/wiki/Tidal_(service)

45. Jones, Rhian. "WHY DID SPRINT PAY $200M FOR TIDAL?" Music Business Worldwide https://www.musicbusinessworldwide.com 1 February 2017 7 December 2021. < https://www.musicbusinessworldwide.com/sprint-pay-200m-

tidal/#:~:text=Now%20we%20know%3A%20because%20
Sprint,gap%20on%20rivals%20like%20AT%26T.>

46. Halperin, Shirley. "Kanye West Takes Jay-Z's Tidal to Task Over Money Owed." Variety 5 July 2017 7 December 2021. < https://variety.com/2017/music/news/kanye-west-jay-z-tidal-money-owed-1202487355/>

47. Greenberg, Zack O'Malley. "Artist, Icon, Billionaire: How Jay-Z Created His $1 Billion Fortune." Forbes 3 June 2019 11 December 2021. < https://www.forbes.com/sites/zackomalleygreenburg/2019/06/03/jay-z-billionaire-worth/?sh=1b59e9733a5f>

48. Fridson, Martin S. HOW TO BE A BILLIONAIRE. p. 23-26 & p. 178-181 New York. John Wiley & Sons, Inc., 2000.

49. Fridson, Martin S. HOW TO BE A BILLIONAIRE. p. 16-17 & p. 179 New York. John Wiley & Sons, Inc., 2000.

50. "Project Panther Bidco." Wikipedia 7 December 2021. < https://en.wikipedia.org/wiki/Project_Panther_Bidco>

51. Oder, Norman. "Jay-Z's hip-hop of distraction." Salon 25 October 2011 21 December 2021. < https://www.salon.com/2011/10/25/the_jay_z_distraction/>

52. Oder, Norman. "Net gain to Ratner, loss to public: IBO says developer saves $726M on arena; city loses $40M plus another $180M in opportunity costs." 20 September 2009 21 December 2021. < https://atlanticyardsreport.blogspot.com/2009/09/net-gain-to-ratner-loss-to-public-ibo.html>

53. Mlynar, Phillip. "Point: Jay-Z Sold Out Brooklyn." The Village Voice 8 October 2012 21 December 2021. <· https://www.villagevoice.com/2012/10/08/point-jay-z-sold-out-brooklyn/>

54. Net Income. "The Jay-Z rule"-- NBA raises bar for team ownership" Nets Daily 30 January 2015 20 December 2021. < https://www.netsdaily.com/2015/1/30/7952347/the-jay-z-rule-nba-raises-bar-for-team-ownership>

55. Moore, Antonio. "The Decadent Veil: Black America's Wealth Illusion" <u>Huffington Post</u> 5 August 2014 and updated on 6 December 2017 30 November 2021. < <u>https://www.huffpost.com/entry/the-decadent-veil-black-income-inequality_b_5646472</u>>

56. Fuchs, Hailey and Laura Barron-Lopez. "Black lawmakers threaten to cut off K St. unless it diversifies." <u>Politico</u> 19 December 2021 19 December 2021. < <u>https://www.politico.com/news/2021/12/19/black-lawmakers-diversity-lobbying-firms-525362</u>>

57. Russell, Chris. "Jay-Z To Buy Ownership In Washington Football Team?" <u>Sports Illustrated</u> 26 May 2021 30 November 2021. < <u>https://www.si.com/nfl/washingtonfootball/news/jay-z-buy-washington-football-team-nfl-ownership</u>>

58. Giacomazzo, Bernandette. "Is Jay-Z Buying The Denver Broncos With Jeff Bezos?" <u>Afrotech</u> 14 September 2021 20 December 2021. < <u>https://afrotech.com/jay-z-jeff-bezos-amazon-denver-broncos</u>>

59. BlackBusiness.com. "Jay-Z Invests in Company That Tracks Parolees With GPS Software." <u>Black Business.com</u> 30 May 2019 30 November 2021 <u>https://www.blackbusiness.com/2019/05/jayz-invests-promise-company-tracks-parolees-gps-software.html</u>

60. Rose, Sandra. "Outrage: Jay-Z Criticized for Investing In Company That Sells GPS Software to Track Parolees." 26 May 2019 22 December 2021. <u>https://sandrarose.com/2019/05/outrage-jay-z-criticized-for-investing-in-company-that-sells-gps-software-to-track-parolees/</u>

61. Kentucky Ave. "Gentrify your own hood before these people do it." – HOV. <u>Kentucky Ave.</u> 27 April 2019 22 December 2021. < <u>https://www.youtube.com/watch?v=bZbLbqsXU5M</u>>

62. Audacy Originals "JAY-Z Stops Concert To Tell 9-Year-Old Girl: You Got Potential To Be President." <u>Audacy</u>

<u>Originals</u> 21 November 2017 22 December 2021. <
https://www.youtube.com/watch?v=4vMEkuhPtA4>

63. Federal Bureau of Investigation. "Rape Offender vs. Victim Demographics." <u>Crime Data Explorer</u> 2020 3 February 2022. < https://crime-data-explorer.app.cloud.gov/#>

64. Greg Hengler. "Jay-Z: 'My Presence is Charity Just Like Obama's'. " <u>Greg Hengler</u> 31 July 2013 22 December 2021. < https://www.youtube.com/watch?v=94GnMlAZ1mg>

65. b/60. "Jay Z Declares 'My Presence Is Charity,' Compares Himself to Obama." <u>b/60</u> 29 July 2013 22 December 2021. < https://www.youtube.com/watch?v=JKLo2yEmAbl>

66. McGruder, Aaron. "It's a Black President, Huey Freeman." <u>The Boondocks</u> Sony Pictures Television. Cartoon Network 2 May 2010.

67. CNN staff. "Beyonce', Jay-Z, and the Obamas: Inside a Friendship." CNN 4 August 2020 23 December 2021. https://www.cnn.com/ampstories/entertainment/beyonce-jay-z-and-the-obamas-inside-a-friendship)

68. Rolling Stone. "Beyonce, Jay-Z Raise Money for Obama." <u>Rolling Stone</u> 19 September 2012 23 December 2021. < https://www.rollingstone.com/music/music-news/beyonce-jay-z-raise-money-for-obama-174723/>

69. Krol, Charlotte. "Barack Obama inducts Jay-Z into Rock and Roll Hall of Fame: 'I've turned to Jay's words at different points in my life.' " <u>NME</u> 31 October 2021 23 December 2021. https://www.nme.com/news/music/barack-obama-inducts-jay-z-into-rock-roll-hall-of-fame-ive-turned-to-jay-zs-words-at-different-points-in-my-life-3083375

70. Roc Nation. "ROC NATION ENTERS INTO LONG-TERM PARTNERSHIP WITH NFL" A video uploaded by <u>Roc Nation</u> 16 August 2019 23 December 2021. https://www.youtube.com/watch?v=ph2XnPekWJU

71. Bromwich, Jonah. "Counterpoint: Jay-Z Saved Brooklyn" <u>Village Voice</u> 8 October 2012 21 December 2021. <

https://www.villagevoice.com/2012/10/08/counterpoint-jay-z-saved-brooklyn/>

72. Florio, Mike. "Robert Kraft played key role in NFL, Jay-Z deal." Pro Football Talk NBC Sports 14 August 2019 30 November 2021. < https://profootballtalk.nbcsports.com/2019/08/14/robert-kraft-played-key-role-in-nfl-jay-z-deal/>

73. NBC Sports. "Robert Kraft addressing role in facilitating Jay-Z, NFL Partnership." NBC Sports 21 August 2019 30 November 2021. <https://www.nbcsports.com/boston/patriots/robert-kraft-addresses-role-facilitating-jay-z-nfl-partnership#:~:text=In%20an%20interview%20Wednesday%20on,New%20England%20Patriots%20owner%20said.>

74. Google Search of Carolina Panthers Owner of David Tepper 9 February 2022.

75. Wallace, Julia. "Jay-Z Is Wrong: White Supremacy and Capitalism Cause Police Brutality—Not Absent Fathers." Left Voice 3 September 2019 23 December 2021 < https://www.leftvoice.org/jay-z-white-supremacy-and-capitalism-cause-police-brutality-not-absent-fathers/>

76. Evans, Will. Interview. "Jay Z: 'I Still Experience Racism Even As A Billionaire." Will Evans on his channel 3 November 2021 23 December 2021. < https://www.youtube.com/watch?v=w5gjmQ_tETM>

77. Jay-Z. "The Story of OJ." 4:44 2017.

78. Delerme, Tony. "Jay-Z Recruited By New York Governor Kathy Hochul To Convince Black Americans To Get 'You Know What.' " TD Hip Hop Media 28 September 2021 24 December 2021. https://www.youtube.com/watch?v=PyAKNW7x-lg

79. TMZ. "JAY Z & BEYONCE BLACK RAGE OVER WHITEOUT AT TIDAL." TMZ 28 May 2015 30 November 2021. < https://www.tmz.com/2015/05/28/jay-z-beyonce-tidal-staff-photo-white-people/>

80. Watkins, Boyce. "Jay-Z, Harry Belafonte is a MAN –
    Don't you ever call him a 'Boy' " New Pittsburgh Courier
    20 July 2013 24 December 2021. <
    https://newpittsburghcourier.com/2013/07/20/jay-z-harry-
    belafonte-is-a-man-don-t-you-ever-call-him-a-
    boy/#:~:text=Opinion-
    ,Jay%2DZ%2C%20Harry%20Belafonte%20is%20a%20M
    AN%20%E2%80%93%20Don',ever%20call%20him%20a
    %20%E2%80%9CBoy%E2%80%9D&text=(YourBlackW
    orld.net)%20%2DI,with%20entertainment%20legend%20
    Harry%20Belafonte.>

81. Addison, Nathan. "Nets Owner Clara Wu Tsai Almost
    Caused Jay Z to Spill His Drink at Game" for Black Sports
    Online 28 October 2021 20 December 2021. <
    https://blacksportsonline.com/2021/10/nets-owner-clara-
    wu-tsai-almost-caused-jay-z-to-spill-his-drink-at-game/>

82. "Al Sharpton." Wikipedia 3 November 2021.
    https://en.wikipedia.org/wiki/Al_Sharpton

83. Gumbel, Bryant. Real Sports with Bryant Gumbel HBO 23
    July 2002.

84. "Al Sharpton." Wikipedia 3 November 2021. <
    https://en.wikipedia.org/wiki/Al_Sharpton>

85. Sharpton, Al. Interview 60 Minutes CBS 22 May 2011 5
    October 2021.
    https://www.youtube.com/watch?v=UHoMXLSjlDo

86. McQuiston, John T. "After 6 Hours, Jury Acquits Sharpton
    of All Charges." New York Times 3 July 1990 27 October
    2021. <
    https://www.nytimes.com/1990/07/03/nyregion/after-6-
    hours-jury-acquits-sharpton-of-all-charges.html>

87. Kaplan, Sarah. "Lawsuit accuses Comcast, Al Sharpton of
    discriminating against black-owned media." Washington
    Post 24 February 2015 29 October 2021. <
    https://www.washingtonpost.com/news/morning-
    mix/wp/2015/02/24/lawsuit-accuses-comcast-al-sharpton-
    of-discriminating-against-black-owned-media/>

88. REVOLT. "Diddy releases statement regarding Comcast, Byron Allen's discrimination lawsuit against the media company." REVOLT 21 November 2019 29 October 2021. < https://www.revolt.tv/2019/11/21/20975492/diddy-statement-byron-allen-comcast-lawsuit>

89. Porter, Dawn. Interview. "Film Preview and Panel Discussion." Vernon Jordan: Make It Plain WETA PBS App December 16 2020 8 October 2021.

90. Mawelu Onwuku "Critical Thinking and Planning In Confronting The New World Order." Mawelu Onwuku 3 March 2015 8 October 2021 < https://www.youtube.com/watch?v=sYOeilUSRLU>

91. The Council on Black Internal Affairs. "Vernon Jordan." The American Directory of Certified Uncle Toms p. 268 second paragraph. CBIA Publishing 2002.

92. Newsweek. "Black and White in America." Newsweek p. 21. 7 March 1988.

93. "Vernon Jordan." Wikipedia 21 September 2021 https://en.wikipedia.org/wiki/Vernon_Jordan

94. Gerth, Jeff. "THE FIRST FRIEND -- A special report.; Being Intimate With Power, Vernon Jordan Can Wield It." New York Times 14 July 1996 26 September 2021. < https://www.nytimes.com/1996/07/14/us/first-friend-special-report-being-intimate-with-power-vernon-jordan-can-wield-it.html>

95. Wilkins, Roger. "Vernon Jordan And the Issues Vital to Blacks." New York Times 22 November 1977 1 October 2021. < https://www.nytimes.com/1977/11/22/archives/vernon-jordan-and-the-issues-vital-to-blacks.html>

96. Gailey, Phil. "VERNON JORDAN'S NEW CAREER HAS TRACES OF THE OLD." 20 May 1983 18 September 2021. < https://www.nytimes.com/1983/05/20/us/vernon-jordan-s-new-career-has-traces-of-the-old.html>

97. Clymer, Adam. "PRESIDENT REJECTS JORDAN'S CRITICISM." New York Times 26 July 1977 20

September 2021. <
https://www.nytimes.com/1977/07/26/archives/president-rejects-jordans-criticism-says-attacks-on-his-record-hurt.html>

98. Wicker, Tom. "Carter and Jordan" New York Times 29 July 1977 18 September 2021. <
https://www.nytimes.com/1977/07/29/archives/carter-and-jordan.html?searchResultPosition=1>

99. New York Times. "Jordan Praises F. B. I. Choice." New York Times 19 July 1977 2 October 2021. <
https://www.nytimes.com/1977/08/19/archives/jordan-praises-fbi-choice.html?searchResultPosition=1>

100.   New York Times. "Vernon Jordan Tells Black Elks to Give Leadership." New York Times 14 August 1979 21 September 2021. <
https://www.nytimes.com/1979/08/14/archives/vernon-jordan-tells-black-elks-to-give-leadership.html?searchResultPosition=1>

101.   UPI . "Jordan to Let Reagan Act, Then Judge Him on Rights." New York Times 1 December 1980 2 October 2021. <
https://www.nytimes.com/1980/12/01/archives/jordan-to-let-reagan-act-then-judge-him-on-rights-reagans.html?searchResultPosition=1>

102.   Barron, James. "MONDALE ENDORSED BY VERNON JORDAN" New York Times 31 July 1984 23 September 2021. <
https://www.nytimes.com/1984/07/31/us/mondale-endoresed-by-vernon-jordan.html?searchResultPosition=1>

103.   "Jordan Urges Blacks to Use Their Political Strength." Sheila Rule New York Times 8 August 1980 2 October 2021. <
https://www.nytimes.com/1980/08/08/archives/jordan-urges-blacks-to-use-their-political-strength-last-years.html?searchResultPosition=1>

104.   Apple, Jr., R.W. "THE PRESIDENT UNDER FIRE: THE POWER BROKER; Jordan Trades Stories With Clinton, and Offers Counsel." New York Times 25 January 1998 26 September 2021. < https://www.nytimes.com/1998/01/25/us/president-under-fire-power-broker-jordan-trades-stories-with-clinton-offers.html?searchResultPosition=1>

105.   The Council on Black Internal Affairs. "Vernon Jordan." The American Directory of Certified Uncle Toms p. 268 second and fourth paragraphs. CBIA Publishing 2002.

106.   Abramson, Jill. "TESTING OF A PRESIDENT: POLITICAL MEMO; For Jordan, Lewinsky Matter Tests a Friendship." New York Times 22 February 1998 25 September 2021. < https://www.nytimes.com/1998/02/22/us/testing-president-political-memo-for-jordan-lewinsky-matter-tests-friendship.html?searchResultPosition=1>

107.   "Zoe Baird." Wikipedia 2 October 2021 13 February 2022. https://en.wikipedia.org/wiki/Zo%C3%AB_Baird

108.   The Council on Black Internal Affairs. "Vernon Jordan." The American Directory of Certified Uncle Toms p. 270 first paragraph. CBIA Publishing 2002.

109.   Farrakhan, Louis. "Message to the American Association of Black Corporate Professionals" Final Call, Inc. 15 August 1980.

110.   The Council on Black Internal Affairs. "Vernon Jordan." The American Directory of Certified Uncle Toms p. 269 second paragraph. CBIA Publishing 2002.

111.   Robinson, Randall. Defending the Spirit p. 271 New York: Penguin Group, Dutton 1998.

112.   New York Times. "PRIVATE SECTOR; All in the (Jordan) Family." New York Times 28 February 1999 23 September 2021. <

https://www.nytimes.com/1999/02/28/business/private-sector-all-in-the-jordan-family.html>

113.   Berkman, Johanna. "The Way We Live Now: 7-16-00: Questions for Vernon Jordan; The Insider." New York Times 16 July 2000 26 September 2021 < https://www.nytimes.com/2000/07/16/magazine/the-way-we-live-now-7-16-00-questions-for-vernon-jordan-the-insider.html?searchResultPosition=1>

114.   Leder, Michelle. "Vernon Jordan Gets a Big Payday From Lazard." New York Times 15 March 2010 25 September 2021. < https://dealbook.nytimes.com/2010/03/15/vernon-jordan-gets-a-big-payday-from-lazard/?searchResultPosition=1>

115.   The Council on Black Internal Affairs. "Vernon Jordan." The American Directory of Certified Uncle Toms p. 269 first paragraph. CBIA Publishing 2002.

116.   Robinson, Randall. Defending the Spirit p. 265-266 New York: Penguin Group, Dutton 1998.

117.   The Council on Black Internal Affairs. "Vernon Jordan." The American Directory of Certified Uncle Toms p. 268 third paragraph first sentence. CBIA Publishing 2002.

118.   Sorkin Andrew Ross, Jason Karaian, Michael J. de la Merced, Lauren Hirsch and Ephrat Livni. "The Rosa Parks of Wallstreet: Remembering Vernon Jordan, the civil rights leader turned corporate power broker." New York Times 3 March 2021 24 September 2021. < https://www.nytimes.com/2021/03/03/business/dealbook/vernon-jordan-dead.html>

119.   Maynard. Dir. Sam Pollard. Auburn Avenue Films and Two Dollars and a Dream production, 2017. 8 September 2021 < https://www.youtube.com/watch?v=K2r88mM5Pbs>

120.   New York Times. "Negro Will Challenge Talmadge in Georgia Primary." New York Times 3 August 1968 1 September 2021. <

https://www.nytimes.com/1968/08/04/archives/negro-will-challenge-talmadge-for-senate-in-georgia-primary.html>

121. "Maynard Jackson." Wikipedia 12 September 2021. https://en.wikipedia.org/wiki/Maynard_Jackson

122. Nordheimer, Jon. "Atlanta Next Mayor Maynard Holbrooke Jackson." New York Times 18 October 1973 8 September 2021. < https://www.nytimes.com/1973/10/18/archives/atlantas-next-mayor-maynard-holbrook-jackson.html>

123. New York Times. "Negro to Oppose Talmadge." New York Times 5 June 1968 31 August 2021. < https://www.nytimes.com/1968/06/06/archives/negro-to-oppose-talmadge.html?searchResultPosition=1>

124. New York Times. "Talmadge Defeats Negro Opponent in Georgia Vote." New York Times 12 September 1968 1 September 2021. < https://www.nytimes.com/1968/09/12/archives/talmadge-defeats-negro-opponent-in-georgia-vote.html?searchResultPosition=1>

125. Wooten, James T. "Two Whites in Atlanta Mayor Runoff." New York Times 8 October 1969 2 September 2021. < https://www.nytimes.com/1969/10/09/archives/two-whites-in-atlanta-mayor-runoff.html?searchResultPosition=1>

126. "Jew and Negro Take 2 Top Atlanta Jobs." New York Times 6 January 1970 2 September 2021. < https://www.nytimes.com/1970/01/06/archives/jew-and-negro-take-2-top-atlanta-jobs.html?searchResultPosition=1>

127. Nordheimer, Jon. "Race Is Factor in Runoff Vote For Atlanta Mayor Tomorrow." New York Times 15 October 1973 8 September 2021. https://www.nytimes.com/1973/10/15/archives/race-is-factor-in-runoff-vote-foratlanta-mayor-tomorrow-city-52-per.html?searchResultPosition=1

128.	New York Times. "Atlanta Installs Black Mayor, 35" New York Times 15 January 1974 8 September 2021. < https://www.nytimes.com/1974/01/08/archives/atlanta-installs-black-mayor-35-maynard-jackson-calls-on-crowd-of.html>

129.	Ayres, Jr., B. Drummond. "Atlanta Mayor Refuses to Oust Black." New York Times 18 April 1975 9 September 2021. < https://www.nytimes.com/1975/04/18/archives/atlanta-mayor-refuses-to-oust-black.html?searchResultPosition=1>

130.	Breasted, Mary. "Black Mayors Asking Arabs to Invest in Their Region." New York Times 1 February 1975 12 September 2021. <https://www.nytimes.com/1975/02/01/archives/black-southern-mayors-asking-arabs-to-invest-in-their-region.html?searchResultPosition=1>

131.	King, Wayne. "Mayor Jackson Favored as Atlanta Votes Tomorrow." New York Times 3 October 1977 12 September 2021. < https://www.nytimes.com/1977/10/03/archives/mayor-jackson-favored-as-atlanta-votes-tomorrow.html?searchResultPosition=1>

132.	New York Times. "Atlanta Mayor Orders Flags at Half Staff." New York Times 2 July 1974 9 September 2021. < https://www.nytimes.com/1974/07/02/archives/atlanta-mayor-orders-city-flags-at-half-staff.html?searchResultPosition=1>

133.	New York Times. "Conditions in Project Shock Atlanta Mayor." New York Times 21 October 1974 11 September 2021. < https://www.nytimes.com/1974/10/21/archives/conditions-in-project-shock-atlanta-mayor.html?searchResultPosition=1>

134.	"Sanitation Protest in Atlanta." New York Times 20 July 1976 12 September 2021. <

https://www.nytimes.com/1976/07/20/archives/sanitation-protestin-atlanta.html?searchResultPosition=1>

135.   King, Wayne. "Municipal Workers' Union Open National Attack on Atlanta Mayor." New York Times 30 March 1977 12 September 2021. < https://www.nytimes.com/1977/03/30/archives/municipal-workers-union-opens-national-attack-on-atlanta-mayor.html?searchResultPosition=1>

136.   King, Wayne. "Mayor Appears to Have Crushed Strike by Atlanta Sanitation Men." New York Times 17 April 1977 12 September 2021. < https://www.nytimes.com/1977/04/17/archives/mayor-appears-to-have-crushed-strike-by-atlanta-sanitationmen-mayor.html?searchResultPosition=1>

137.   New York Times. "STRIKE IS CRITICIZED BY DR. KING'S FATHER." New York Times 5 April 1977 12 September 2021. < https://www.nytimes.com/1977/04/05/archives/strike-is-criticized-by-drkings-father-clergyman-backs-atlanta.html?searchResultPosition=1>

138.   Ayres Jr., B. Drummond. "Atlanta's Police Director Is Relieved' of Command." New York Times 8 March 1978 12 September 2021. < https://www.nytimes.com/1978/03/08/archives/atlantas-police-director-is-relieved-of-command-evidence-termed.html?searchResultPosition=1>

139.   New York Times. "Atlanta Mayor Raises Funds for Black Rebels." New York Times 18 May 1979 12 September 2021. < https://www.nytimes.com/1979/05/18/archives/atlanta-mayor-raises-funds-for-black-rebels.html?searchResultPosition=1>

140.   Raines, Howell. "Atlanta, Fearing for National Reputation, Mounts Urgent Fight on Crime." New York Times 15 August 1979 13 September 2021. < https://www.nytimes.com/1979/08/15/archives/atlanta-

fearing-for-national-reputation-mounts-urgent-fight-on.html?searchResultPosition=1>

141.   "Atlanta's Troubles." <u>New York Times</u> 19 August 1979 12 September 2021. <https://www.nytimes.com/1979/08/19/archives/atlantas-troubles.html?searchResultPosition=1>

142.   "Lee P. Brown." <u>Wikipedia</u> 14 September 2021. https://en.wikipedia.org/wiki/Lee_P._Brown

143.   New York Times. "Bell to Be Crime Aide For Mayor of Atlanta." <u>New York Times</u> 18 August 1979 14 September 2021. < https://www.nytimes.com/1979/08/18/archives/bell-to-be-crime-aide-for-mayor-of-atlanta.html?searchResultPosition=1>

144.   New York Times. "Atlanta Gets Curb on Pistols." <u>New York Times</u> 25 November 1979 14 September 2021. < https://www.nytimes.com/1979/11/25/archives/atlanta-gets-curb-on-pistols.html?searchResultPosition=1>

145.   Rawls, Jr., Wendell. "Atlanta Acts to Fight Crime After Spate of Slayings." <u>New York Times</u> 23 October 1979 14 September 2021. < https://www.nytimes.com/1979/10/23/archives/atlanta-acts-to-fight-crime-after-spate-of-slayings-sixmonth.html?searchResultPosition=1>

146.   The Associated Press (AP.) "AROUND THE NATION; Atlanta Mayor Asks Council For 160 More Police Officers." <u>New York Times</u> 3 February 1981 13 September 2021. < https://www.nytimes.com/1981/02/03/us/around-the-nation-atlanta-mayor-asks-council-for-160-more-police-officers.html?searchResultPosition=1>

147.   United Press International (UPI.) "AROUND THE NATION; Activists in Atlanta Vow To Begin Armed Patrols." <u>New York Times</u> 19 March 1981 13 September 2021. < https://www.nytimes.com/1981/03/19/us/around-

the-nation-activists-in-atlanta-vow-to-begin-armed-patrols.html?searchResultPosition=1>

148.   "Wayne Williams." Wikipedia 13 September 2021. https://en.wikipedia.org/wiki/Wayne_Williams

149.   Smothers, Ronald. "MAYNARD JACKSON WINS IN ATLANTA." New York Times 10/5/89

150.   O'Brien, Soledad. "CNN Special: Atlanta Child Murders." CNN 4 July 2011.

151.   Jackson, Maynard. "Mayors Care About the Undercounted." New York Times 27 August 1980 13 September 2021. < https://www.nytimes.com/1980/08/27/archives/letter-on-the-census-mayors-care-about-the-undercounted.html?searchResultPosition=1>

152.   AP. "Atlanta Sues the Census Bureau, Charging Population Undercount." New York Times 28 September 1980 13 September 2021. < https://www.nytimes.com/1980/09/28/archives/atlanta-sues-the-census-bureau-charging-population-undercount.html?searchResultPosition=1>

153.   Smothers, Ronald. "MAYNARD JACKSON WINS IN ATLANTA." New York Times 5 October 1989 14 September 2021. < https://www.nytimes.com/1989/10/05/us/maynard-jackson-wins-in-atlanta.html?searchResultPosition=1>

154.   Smothers, Ronald. "Styles Conflict in Atlanta Mayor Race." New York Times 24 July 1989 14 September 2021. < https://www.nytimes.com/1989/07/24/us/photo-michael-lomax-outgoing-fulton-county-commission-chairman-campaigning-for.html?searchResultPosition=1>

155.   AP. "New Atlanta Police Chief." New York Times 21 August 1990 14 September 2021. < https://www.nytimes.com/1990/08/21/us/new-atlanta-police-chief.html?searchResultPosition=1>

156.   Applebome, Peter. "THE NATION; As a Mayor Returns, Atlanta Is Rich and Poor." New York Times 7

January 1990 14 September 2021. <
https://www.nytimes.com/1990/01/07/weekinreview/the-
nation-as-a-mayor-returns-atlanta-is-rich-and-
poor.html?searchResultPosition=1>

157.   Smothers, Ronald. "Popular Mayor of Atlanta Will
Not Seek Fourth Term." New York Times 10 June 1993 14
September 2021. <
https://www.nytimes.com/1993/06/10/us/popular-mayor-
of-atlanta-will-not-seek-fourth-
term.html?searchResultPosition=1>

158.   Dingle, Derek. "Maynard Jackson: The Ultimate
Champion for Black Business." Black Enterprise 10
February 2009 14 September 2021. <
https://www.blackenterprise.com/maynard-jackson-the-
ultimate-champion-for-black-business/>

159.   Sack, Kevin. "Black Democrats to Contest Party
Leadership." New York Times 22 December 2000 14
September 2021. <
https://www.nytimes.com/2000/12/22/us/black-democrats-
to-contest-party-leadership.html?searchResultPosition=1>

160.   "Bill Campbell." Wikipedia 14 September 2021
<https://en.wikipedia.org/wiki/Bill_Campbell_(mayor)>

161.   "Embattled Atlanta mayor raises racial tension."
CNN.com 9 2000 October 19 2021. <
https://www.cnn.com/2000/ALLPOLITICS/stories/10/09/p
olitics.atlanta.reut/index.html>

162.   "Douglas Wilder." Wikipedia 17 August 2021. <
https://en.wikipedia.org/wiki/Douglas_Wilder>

163.   Ayres Jr., B. Drummond. "THE 1989 ELECTIONS:
The Virginia Contest MAN IN THE NEWS: Lawrence
Douglas Wilder; From Confrontation to Conciliation." New
York Times 8 November 1989 19 August 2021. <
https://www.nytimes.com/1989/11/08/nyregion/1989-
elections-virginia-contest-man-lawrence-douglas-wilder-
confrontation.html?searchResultPosition=1>

164.   "Wilder, Lawrence Douglas (1931-.)" Encyclopedia
Virginia 21 August 2021
https://encyclopediavirginia.org/entries/wilder-lawrence-douglas-1931/

165.   Gailey, Phil. "BLACK RAISES STAKES IN
VIRGINIA VOTE." New York Times 24 October 1985 21
August 2021. <
https://www.nytimes.com/1985/10/24/us/black-raises-stakes-in-virginia-vote.html?searchResultPosition=1>

166.   Oreskes, Michael. "A Black Candidate in Virginia
Runs for Office, Not History." New York Times 3
November 1989 21 August 2021. <
https://www.nytimes.com/1989/11/03/us/a-black-candidate-in-virginia-runs-for-office-not-history.html?searchResultPosition=1>

167.   "Allen Iverson." Wikipedia 18 August 2021. <
https://en.wikipedia.org/wiki/Allen_Iverson>

168.   Armstrong, Ken and Bob Kemper. "Dec. 31, 1993:
Gov. Wilder Grants Conditional Clemency to Iverson."
Daily Press 31 December 1993 21 August 2021 <
https://www.dailypress.com/sports/dp-spt-legal-clemency-20110119-story.html>

169.   The Council on Black Internal Affairs. "Political
Uncle Tomism: Shuckin' at the Top." The American
Directory of Certified Uncle Toms p. 129 second
paragraph. CBIA Publishing 2002.

170.   "John Lewis." Wikipedia 11 August 2021.
https://en.wikipedia.org/wiki/John_Lewis

171.   CNN. "John Lewis Fast Facts." CNN 28 July 2020
3 February 2022 5 August 2021. <
https://www.cnn.com/2013/02/22/us/john-lewis-fast-facts/index.html>

172.   Wilentz, Sean. "The Last Integrationist: John
Lewis' American Odyssey." The New Republic 1 July
1996 9 August 2021. <

https://newrepublic.com/article/158564/the-last-integrationist-congressman-john-lewis-1996>

173. ProPublica. "H.R. 4488: Gold Medal Technical Corrections Act of 2014." 2017 9 August 2021. <https://projects.propublica.org/represent/bills/113/hr4488>

174. ProPublica. "H.R. 267: Martin Luther King, Jr. National Historic Park Act of 2017." <https://projects.propublica.org/represent/bills/115/hr267>

175. The Council on Black Internal Affairs. "Political Uncle Tomism: Shuckin' at the Top." The American Directory of Certified Uncle Toms p. 125 second paragraph. CBIA Publishing 2002.

176. The Council on Black Internal Affairs. "Political Uncle Tomism: Shuckin' at the Top." The American Directory of Certified Uncle Toms p. 123 first paragraph last sentence. CBIA Publishing 2002.

177. The Council on Black Internal Affairs. "Political Uncle Tomism: Shuckin' at the Top." The American Directory of Certified Uncle Toms p. 123 the middle of the first paragraph. CBIA Publishing 2002.

178. Dixon, Bruce. "Black Lobbyists, Black Legislators Leverage Their Brands for Banksters, Military Contractors, Corporate Interests." Black Agenda Report 4 June 2014 10 August 2021. < https://blackagendareport.com/content/black-lobbyists-black-legislators-leverage-their-%E2%80%9Cbrands%E2%80%9D-banksters-military-contractors-cor>

179. Ford, Glen. "Black Caucus Sells Out Its Constituents Again – to the Cops." Black Agenda Report 23 May 2018 8 August 2021. < https://www.blackagendareport.com/black-caucus-sells-out-its-constituents-again-cops>

180. Daniels, Ron. "Congressman John Lewis Betrays Black Cherokee Freedmen." 22 September 2009 8 August

2021. <
https://blackagendareport.com/content/congressman-john-lewis-betrays-black-cherokee-freedmen>

181.   Carter, Lauren. "Representative John Lewis reflects on the 50th Anniversary of the March on Washington." theGrio 21 August 2013 5 August 2021. < https://thegrio.com/2013/08/21/rep-john-lewis-reflects-on-the-50th-anniversary-of-the-march-on-washington/>

182.   Guevara, Marina Walker. "Lobbyists Tag Along on Civil Rights Tour." Money and Democracy The Center for Public Integrity 8 June 2006 19 May 2014 5 August 2021. < https://publicintegrity.org/politics/lobbyists-tag-along-on-civil-rights-tour/>

183.   Faith and Politics Institute. "Statement From the Faith and Politics Institute's Board on the Passing of Congressman John Robert Lewis." 15 July 2021 2 August 2021. <
https://www.faithandpolitics.org/news/2021/7/15/statement-from-the-faith-amp-politics-institutes-board-of-directors-and-staff-on-the-passing-of-congressman-john-robert-lewis>

184.   "Colin Powell." Wikipedia 23 July 20211 1 February 2022 https://en.wikipedia.org/wiki/Colin_Powell

185.   The Council on Black Internal Affairs. "Colin Powell." The American Directory of Certified Uncle Toms p. 283-284. CBIA Publishing 2002.

186.   The Council on Black Internal Affairs. "Colin Powell." The American Directory of Certified Uncle Toms p. 284. CBIA Publishing 2002.

187.   CNN. "Colin Powell". CNN. 1996. Archived from the original on September 2, 2000. Retrieved December 7, 2012 26 July 2021. https://web.archive.org/web/20000902031325/http://cgi.cnn.com/ALLPOLITICS/1996/conventions/san.diego/players/powell.bio/

188.   The Council on Black Internal Affairs. "Colin Powell." <u>The American Directory of Certified Uncle Toms</u> p. 285-287. CBIA Publishing 2002.

189.   The Council on Black Internal Affairs. "Colin Powell." <u>The American Directory of Certified Uncle Toms</u> p. 287-288. CBIA Publishing 2002.

190.   The Council on Black Internal Affairs. "Vernon Jordan." <u>The American Directory of Certified Uncle Toms</u> p. 269. CBIA Publishing 2002.

191.   Robinson, Randall. <u>Defending the Spirit</u> p. 271. New York. Penguin Group, Dutton 1998.

192.   Sara Suten Seti. "OBAMA THE FACE OF IMPERIALISM PART 1." <u>GhettoScholarCollect</u> 4 November 2010 24 February 2022 < https://www.youtube.com/watch?v=3pcQHNOEyBg>

193.   "World Conference Against Racism 2001." <u>Wikipedia</u> 27 July 2021. < https://en.wikipedia.org/wiki/World_Conference_against_R acism_2001>

194.   The Council on Black Internal Affairs. "Colin Powell." <u>The American Directory of Certified Uncle Toms</u> p. 293. CBIA Publishing 2002.

195.   "Colin Powell's 13 Rules of Leadership." <u>Parade</u> 13 August 1989 (I'm citing <u>Wikipedia</u> here. They cited <u>Parade</u> magazine here as their source. I couldn't find the original <u>Parade</u> article, but I did find an article by Tim McClimon that also used the rules as it's subject on the Internet's Wayback Machine which is also cited in the <u>Wikipedia</u> article on Colin Powell. Here's the link: Read CSR Now! with Tim McClimon of AmericanExpress. This week: Colin Powell's 13 Rules of Leadership (archive.org))

196.   Fridson, Martin S. <u>HOW TO BE A BILLIONAIRE</u>. p. 7 New York. John Wiley & Sons, Inc., 2000.

197.   The Council on Black Internal Affairs. "Colin Powell." <u>The American Directory of Certified Uncle Toms</u> p. 287 paragraph two 1st Sentence. CBIA Publishing 2002.

198.   The Council on Black Internal Affairs. "Political Uncle Tomism: Shuckin' At The Top." The American Directory of Certified Uncle Toms p. 131. CBIA Publishing 2002.

199.   "Clifford Alexander, Jr." Wikipedia 28 July 2021. https://en.wikipedia.org/wiki/Clifford_Alexander_Jr.

200.   Callersten, Carlos Anta. "How Colin Powell became a four star general. Best Practices in Diversity Management." Consejos para encontrar tu lugar en el mercado laboral: Personal blog with tips to promote your professional career and find your place in the labour market. 28 July 2021.

201.   Bowens, Dan. "Clifford Alexander Helped Shape the History of Civil Rights in the US." Fox 5 New York 4 21 February 2018 26 February 2022. < https://www.youtube.com/watch?v=EjHvxwSU7zM>

202.   NBA.com. "Former President Barack Obama Joins NBA Africa as Strategic Partner." National Basketball Association 28 July 2021 26 February 2022 < https://www.nba.com/news/former-president-barack-obama-joins-nba-africa-as-strategic-partner>

203.   "Jim Clyburn." Wikipedia 20 July 2021. https://en.wikipedia.org/wiki/Jim_Clyburn

204.   Low Country Digital Library. "Aftermath -The Charleston Hospital Workers Movement 1968-1969." Low Country Digital History Initiative 21 July 2021. <http://ldhi.library.cofc.edu/exhibits/show/charleston_hospital_workers_mo/aftermath>

205.   Wildeman, Mary Katherine. "Clyburn has taken more than $1 million in pharma money in a decade, far surpassing peers." The Post and Courier 16 December 2018 20 July 2021. < https://www.postandcourier.com/health/clyburn-has-taken-more-than-1-million-in-pharma-money-in-a-decade-far-surpassing/article_62b10180-d956-11e8-9122-4f50316f66fa.html>

206.   Delerme, Tony. "Jim Clyburn Runs The Most Impoverished District In South Carolina Yet Sternly Opposes Reparations." TD Hip Hop Media 16 July 2021 21 July 2021. < https://www.youtube.com/watch?v=wxASmlUmKnk>

207.   Jan, Tracy. "Reparations, rebranded." The Washington Post 24 February 2020 21 July 2021. https://www.washingtonpost.com/business/2020/02/24/reparations-south-carolina-clyburn/

208.   "Reconstruction: America After the Civil War, episode 2" By Henry Louis Gates. PBS 9 April 2019.

209.   Scott, Phillip. "Jim Crow Clyburn Voted For The 1994 Crime Bill & Wants Credit For It." African Diaspora News Channel 14 November 2020 20 July 2021. < https://www.youtube.com/watch?v=IGemmeBd-Es>

210.   Washington Post. "I'm not giving Joe Biden cover': Rep. Clyburn explains his 1994 crime bill vote." The Washington Post 21 June 2019 20 July 2021. < https://www.youtube.com/watch?v=hDIG688dpks>

211.   Stephanopoulos, George. "Rep. Jim Clyburn discusses election-altering support for Biden." ABC News 7 November2020 20 July 2021. < https://www.youtube.com/watch?v=2sRHIU74KzI>

212.   Brodey, Sam. "Jim Clyburn Has Plenty of Power With Joe Biden. Is He Actually Using It?" The Daily Beast 6 July 2021 21 July 2021. < https://www.thedailybeast.com/jim-clyburn-has-plenty-of-power-is-he-actually-using-it>

213.   Yvette Carnell. "Clyburn Builds a World Where American Slavery Never Happened." Yvette Carnell 27 February 2020 21 July 2021. < https://www.youtube.com/watch?v=ZC2_w0KsS2g>

214.   Delerme, Tony. "Hispanic Politicians Are Demanding Policy While Jim Clyburn Sells Out Black America and Reparations." TD Hip Hop Media 12 July

2021 21 July 2021. < https://www.youtube.com/watch?v=vqFascB8Xb8>

215.   Scott, Phillip. "Jim Crow Clyburn Proved Once Again He Can Careless About The Economic Future of Black America." African Diaspora News Channel 15 July 2021 21 July 2021. < https://www.youtube.com/watch?v=vqFascB8Xb8>

216.   Delerme, Tony. "Jim Clyburn Secures Land For Catawba Nation While Gullah Geechee Descendants of Slaves Lose Theirs." TD Hip Hop Media 8 January 2022 22 January 2022. < https://www.youtube.com/watch?v=2DhjNHCJTVQ>

217.   Battaglia, Danielle. "Defense bill authorizes Catawba Nation to operate its casino near Charlotte." The Charlotte Observer 23 December 2021 22 January 2021.

218.   Delerme, Tony. "Jim Clyburn Drops Reparations to Secure Historic Levels of Fund And Land For Native Americans." TD Hip Hop Media 25 November 2021 22 January 2022. < https://www.youtube.com/watch?v=ZrAdg9kDiBs>

219.   Delerme, Tony. "Disrespectfully Jim Clyburn & The Biden Admin. Roll Out More Symbolic Nonsense For Black America." TD Hip Hop Media 14 February 2022 16 February 2022. < https://www.youtube.com/watch?v=IRmGZoZD9N8>

220.   Bentley, Martha. "The Slavecatching Catawbas." South Carolina Historical Magazine Vol. 92, No. 2 ((Apr., 1991)), pp. 85-98 ((14 pages))

221.   "Kamala Harris." Wikipedia 7 July 2021. https://en.wikipedia.org/wiki/Kamala_Harris

222.   Fang, Lee. "Kamala Talked Tough on Crime to Win Her First Race." The Intercept 7 February 2019 3 July 2021. < https://theintercept.com/2019/02/07/kamala-harris-san-francisco-district-attorney-crime/>

223.   Kranish, Michael. "Crime lab scandal rocked Kamala Harris' term as San Francisco district attorney."

The Washington Post 6 March 2019 3 July 2021. <
https://www.washingtonpost.com/politics/crime-lab-
scandal-rocked-kamala-harriss-term-as-san-francisco-
district-attorney/2019/03/06/825df094-392b-11e9-a06c-
3ec8ed509d15_story.html>

224.   Kiely, Eugene. "Kamala Harris Spins Facts on
Truancy Law." FactCheck.org 14 May 2019 4 July 2021. <
https://www.factcheck.org/2019/05/kamala-harris-spins-
facts-on-truancy-law/>

225.   Martin, Roland S. "Video of Kamala Harris
Threatening Parents of Truant Children With Jail Sparks
Outrage." Roland Martin Unfiltered 30 January 2019 4 July
2021. <
https://www.youtube.com/watch?v=WDLANlZEicg>

226.   Moore, Antonio. "Kamala Harris Vice Presidential
Nominee Truancy Laws Explained – Interview Cheree
Peoples." Tonetalks 11 August 2020 2 July 2021. <
https://www.youtube.com/watch?v=redw6jD1QVU>

227.   Redden, Molly. "The Human Costs of Kamala
Harris' War on Truancy." Huffington Post 27 March 2019
2 July 2021. < https://www.huffpost.com/entry/kamala-
harris-truancy-arrests-2020-progressive-
prosecutor_n_5c995789e4b0f7bfa1b57d2e>

228.   Eustachewich, Lia. "Inside Kamala Harris'
polarizing record as a prosecutor." New York Post 12
August 2020 4 July 2021. <
https://nypost.com/2020/08/12/inside-kamala-harris-
polarizing-record-as-a-prosecutor/>

229.   Goodman, Alana. "Five times prosecutor Kamala
Harris got the wrong guy." The Washington Examiner 1
September 2019 4 July 2021. <
https://www.washingtonexaminer.com/tag/kamala-
harris?source=%2Fnews%2Ffive-times-prosecutor-kamala-
harris-got-the-wrong-guy>

230.   Yvette Carnell. "Mitrice Richardson's Father
Discusses Daughter, Kamala Harris." Yvette Carnell 1

February 2019 4 July 2021. <
https://www.youtube.com/watch?v=EteUEUb9xaI>

231. Kessler, Mike. "What Happened to Mitrice Richardson?" Los Angeles Magazine 1 September 2011 4 July 2021. < https://www.lamag.com/longform/what-happened-to-mitrice-richardson/>

232. Hampton, Ronda. "Kamala and Mitrice." LA Progressive 20 August 2020 4 July 2021. < https://www.laprogressive.com/kamala-and-mitrice/>

233. theGrio. "Sen. Kamala Harris shares her agenda for the Black community." theGrio 25 February 2019 4 July 2021. < https://www.youtube.com/watch?v=gF1NjRiUnWM>

234. theGrio. "#AskKamala: Does Kamala Harris support reparations for Black Americans." theGrio 25 February 2019 4 July 2021. https://www.youtube.com/watch?v=hsB6EWNUcyY

235. Delerme, Tony. "Native Americans Receive $31 Billon Under Biden Admin. But $0 For Black Americans That Voted For Him." TD Hip Hop Media 12 April 2021 6 July 2021. < https://www.youtube.com/watch?v=xNxNUzmuKiQ>

236. Delerme, Tony. "Joe Biden Commits $4 Billion for Immigration Issues But $0 For Black Americans Who Voted Him In." TD Hip Hop Media 29 January 2021 6 July 2021. < https://www.youtube.com/watch?v=eJ9bKgySG6A>

237. Gamboa, Suzanne. "Biden's Policies Have Benefitted Latinos, but There's Still a Hefty To-Do List, Group Says." NBC News 10 May 2021 6 July 2021. < https://www.nbcnews.com/news/latino/biden-impact-latinos-still-hefty-list-rcna871>

238. Yurcaba, Jo. "Undoing 4 Years of 'Damage': LGBTQ Advocates on Biden's first 100 days." NBC News 2 May 2021 6 July 2021. < https://www.nbcnews.com/feature/nbc-out/undoing-4-

years-damage-lgbtq-advocates-biden-s-first-100-n1266035>

239.   "Three-fourths of H1B holders in 2018 are India: US Report." The Economic Times NRI economictimes.indiantimes.com 20 October 2018 6 July 2018. < https://economictimes.indiatimes.com/nri/visa-and-immigration/three-fourths-of-h1b-visa-holders-in-2018-are-indians-us-report/articleshow/66289772.cms?from=mdr>

240.   Luhby, Tami and Gregory Krieg. "Harris backs 'Medicare-for-all' and eliminating private insurance as we know it." CNN politics 29 January 2019 7 July 2021. < https://www.cnn.com/2019/01/29/politics/harris-private-insurance-medicare/index.html>

241.   Wallace-Wells, Benjamin. "Democratic Debate 2019: Kamala Harris Won the Night." The New Yorker 28 June 2019 7 July 2021. < https://www.newyorker.com/news/current/democratic-debate-2019-kamala-harris-won-the-night>

242.   NBC New York. "Everything Kamala Harris Said at the Democratic Debate, From Food Fights to Busing." NBC New York 28 June 2019 7July 2021. < https://www.youtube.com/watch?v=iPyn3ozACz0>

243.   Stableford, Dylan. "Gabbard rips into Harris for her record on marijuana prosecutions and the death penalty." Yahoo!News 31 July 2019 7 July 2021. < https://www.yahoo.com/video/tulsi-gabbard-kamala-harris-record-as-prosecutor-on-marijuana-death-penalty-021423679.html>

244.   Martin, Johnathan, Astead W. Herndon, and Alexander Burns. "How Kamala Harris's Campaign Unraveled." The New York Times 29 November 2019 8 July 2021. < https://www.nytimes.com/2019/11/29/us/politics/kamala-harris-2020.html>

245.   Cadelago, Christopher and Caitlyn Oprysko. " 'One of the hardest decisions of my life': Kamala Harris ends

once-promising campaign." POLITICO 3 December 2019
8 July 2021.
https://www.politico.com/news/2019/12/03/kamala-harris-
drops-out-out-of-presidential-race-074902

246.   Greig, John. "Karine Jean-Pierre Is Kamala Harris'
Herstory-Making Chief Of Staff And 'Ambition' Is Her
Middle Name." Blavity 13 August 2020 6 July 2021.
https://blavity.com/karine-jean-pierre-is-kamala-harris-
herstory-making-chief-of-staff-and-ambition-is-her-middle-
name?category1=politics&category2=LGBT

247.   Schwartz, Brian. "Some Biden allies wage a
shadow campaign to stop Kamala Harris from becoming
vice president." CNBC 29 July 2020 6 July 2021.
https://www.cnbc.com/2020/07/29/biden-allies-move-to-
stop-kamala-harris-from-becoming-vice-president.html

248.   Schlitz, Hayley Taylor. "Calling Kamala Harris 'too
ambitious' is a lesson for young Black girls." theGrio 3
August 2020 6 July 2021.
https://thegrio.com/2020/08/03/kamala-harris-too-
ambitious-biden/

249.   Sullivan, Kate. "More than 100 Black men urge
Biden to pick Black woman as Vice President." CNN.com
10 August 2020 6 July 2021.
https://www.cnn.com/2020/08/10/politics/black-men-send-
letter-to-biden-vice-president/index.html

250.   Sullivan, Kate. "More than 200 black women urge
Biden to pick black woman as running mate." CNN.com 24
April 2020 6 July 2021.
https://www.cnn.com/2020/04/24/politics/black-women-
letter-joe-biden-running-mate/index.html

251.   Delerme, Tony. "Kamala Harris Benign Neglect
and the Myth of Black Businesses in America." TD Hip
Hop Media 15 February 2021 2 July 2021. <
https://www.youtube.com/watch?v=jYPmvoIL04A>

252.   " 'Not a healthy environment': Kamala Harris'
office rife with dissent." POLITICO 30 June 2021 9 July

2021. < https://www.politico.com/news/2021/06/30/kamala-harris-office-dissent-497290>

253.   Camerota, Alisyn. "Rising tension between staffs of Biden and Harris." CNN YouTube channel 2 July 2021 9 July 2021. < https://www.youtube.com/watch?v=IW-VLZA2_d0>

254.   Kirchik, James. "Andy Young, Barack Obama, and the Black Vote." 14 December 2007 7 June 2021. < https://newrepublic.com/article/38643/andy-young-barack-obama-and-the-black-vote>

255.   Obama, Barack. "A More Perfect Union." National Constitution Center, Philadelphia, PA. 18 March 2008.

256.   Obama for America. "A More Perfect Union." Change We Can Believe In p.223-225. New York. Three Rivers Press, Crown Publishing Group, Random House, Inc., 2008.

257.   Bruenig, Matt and Ryan Cooper. "How Barack Obama Destroyed Black Wealth." Jacobin 7 December 2017 16 June 2021. < https://jacobinmag.com/2017/12/obama-foreclosure-crisis-wealth-inequality>

258.   Curry, George. "Obama Worse than George Bush on SBA Loans." Black Press USA 24 March 2014 7 May 2021. < https://blackpressusa.com/obama-worse-than-george-w-bush-on-sba-loans/>

259.   Bigg, Matthew. "US school segregation on the rise: report." Reuters 14 January 2009 9 May 2021. < https://www.reuters.com/article/us-usa-segregation/u-s-school-segregation-on-the-rise-report-idUSTRE50D7CY20090114>

260.   Haiphong, Danny. "The Obama Legacy Part III: Destroying Education As We Know It." The Black Agenda Report 13 July 2016 8 June 2021. < https://blackagendareport.com/obama_legacy_III_privatization_schools>

261.   Mullins, Dexter. "New Orleans to be home to nation's first all-charter school district." Al Jazeera America 9 April 2014 8 June 2021. < http://america.aljazeera.com/articles/2014/4/4/new-orleans-charterschoolseducationreformracesegregation.html>

262.   Dixon, Bruce. "Obama's Race To Top Drives Nationwide Wave of School Closings, Teacher Firings." The Black Agenda Report 10 January 2013 8 June 2021. https://www.blackagendareport.com/content/obamas-race-top-drives-nationwide-wave-school-closings-teacher-firings

263.   Civil Rights Project of the University of California. "Choice Without Equity: Charter School Segregation and the Need for Civil Rights Standards." Civil Rights Project of the University of California 2009 8 June 2021. < https://www.civilrightsproject.ucla.edu/research/k-12-education/integration-and-diversity/choice-without-equity-2009-report>

264.   National Alliance for Public Charter Schools. "Charter School Data Dashboard." National Alliance for Public Charter Schools 8 June 2021. <data.publiccharters.org>

265.   White, Jamison and Jessica Snydman. "How Many Charter Schools Are There?" 13 November 2020 8 June 2021. < https://data.publiccharters.org/digest/charter-school-data-digest/how-many-charter-schools-and-students-are-there/>

266.   National Alliance for Public Charter Schools, "A Closer Look at the Charter School Movement." 27 June 2016 8 June 2021. < https://www.publiccharters.org/publications/charter-school-movement-2015-16>

267.   Shapiro, Thomas, Tatijana Meschede, and Sam Osoro. "The Roots of the Widening Racial Wealth Gap: Explaining the Black-White Economic Divide." The Institute on Assets and Social Policy February 2013 8 May 2021. < https://heller.brandeis.edu/iere/pdfs/racial-wealth-

equity/racial-wealth-gap/roots-widening-racial-wealth-gap.pdf>

268.   Bates, Tim and Alicia Robb. "Decline in SBA Loans to Blacks Raises Questions about Obama Administration's Commitment." Gazelle Index National Black Chamber of Commerce 12 June 2021. < https://www.nationalbcc.org/news/latest-news/1752-decline-in-sba-loans-to-blacks-raises-questions-about-obama-administrations-commitment>

269.   Kiel, Paul and Olga Pierce. "Dems: Obama Broke Pledge to Force Banks Help Homeowners." ProPublica 4 February 2011 16 June 2021. < https://www.propublica.org/article/dems-obama-broke-pledge-to-force-banks-to-help-homeowners>

270.   Scheiber, Noam. "Obama to Bankers: Beware the Pitchforks." The New Republic 2 April 2009 11 June 2021. < https://newrepublic.com/article/48854/obama-bankers-beware-the-pitchforks>

271.   Taylor, Keeanga-Yahmatta. "Barack Obama's Original Sin." The Guardian 13 January 2017 20 June 2021. < https://www.theguardian.com/us-news/2017/jan/13/barack-obama-legacy-racism-criminal-justice-system>

272.   "Weathering the Storm: Black Men in the Recession." Center for American Progress 15 April 2009 20 June 2021. < https://www.americanprogress.org/article/weathering-the-storm-black-men-in-the-recession/#:~:text=Black%20men%20lead%20the%20unemployment,the%20labor%20market%20are%20unemployed.>

273.   "Urban Decay." Wikipedia 13 May 2021. https://en.wikipedia.org/wiki/Urban_decay

274.   Jones, Jeffrey M. "Obama averages 47.9% Job Approval as President." Gallup 20 January 2017 22 May

2021. < https://news.gallup.com/poll/202742/obama-averages-job-approval-president.aspx>

275.　　MacAskill, Ewen. "Democrats Condemn GOP's Plot to Obstruct as "sad and appalling." The Guardian 26 April 2012 19 May 2021. < https://www.theguardian.com/world/2012/apr/26/democrats-gop-plot-obstruct-obama>

276.　　"Henry Louis Gates arrest controversy." Wikipedia 17 May 2021. < https://en.wikipedia.org/wiki/Henry_Louis_Gates_arrest_controversy>

277.　　Fox News. "Phoenix Pastor Draws Protests After Telling Church He Prays for Obama's Death." Fox News 31 August 2009 16 May 2021. < https://www.foxnews.com/politics/phoenix-pastor-draws-protests-after-telling-church-he-prays-for-obamas-death>

278.　　Associated Press. "Pastor's Prayer for Obama's Death Sparks Protest." Associated Press 7 September 2009 16 May 2021. < https://www.youtube.com/watch?v=pIW27p4BI_g>

279.　　"Threatening the president of the United States." Wikipedia 16 May 2021. < https://en.wikipedia.org/wiki/Threatening_the_president_of_the_United_States>

280.　　CNN Politics. "Rep. Wilson shouts, 'You Lie' to Obama during speech," CNN.com 9 September 2009 24 June 2021. < https://www.cnn.com/2009/POLITICS/09/09/joe.wilson/>

281.　　"Joe Wilson (American Politician.)" Wikipedia 20 May 2021. < https://en.wikipedia.org/wiki/Joe_Wilson_(American_politician)>

282.　　Machiavelli, Niccolo'. The Prince 1532

283.　　NPR. "Van Jones' Resignation Heaps Criticism Upon Obama." National Public Radio 8 September 2009 20 May 2021. <

https://www.npr.org/templates/story/story.php?storyId=112636478>

284.　"Firing of Shirley Sherrod." Wikipedia 24 June 2021. < https://en.wikipedia.org/wiki/Firing_of_Shirley_Sherrod>

285.　Stolberg, Sheryl Gay, Shaila Dewan, and Brian Stelter. "With Apology, Fired Official Is Offered a New Job." The New York Times 21 July 2010 22 May 2021. < https://www.nytimes.com/2010/07/22/us/politics/22sherrod.html>

286.　Lee, M.J. "Hatch – Obama is a 'scaredy cat.' " Politico 16 December 2011 25 May 2021. < https://www.politico.com/story/2011/12/hatch-obama-is-a-scaredy-cat-070557>

287.　The Obama White House. "Press Briefing with President Obama and President Clinton." The Obama White House 10 December 2010 25 May 2021. < https://www.youtube.com/watch?v=6Ac9uDLUdSs>

288.　Stewart, Jon. The Daily Show Comedy Central YouTube channel December 2010 25 May 2021.

289.　Hendren, John. "Obama Tells Black Men to Have the Courage to Be Fathers." ABC News 16 June 2008 5 June 2021. < https://abcnews.go.com/WN/Vote2008/story?id=5172580&page=1>

290.　McGruder, Aaron. "The Story of Lando Freeman." The Boondocks Sony Pictures Television. Cartoon Network 4 July 2010.

291.　Cadet, Daniel. "5 Lies We Should Stop Telling About Black Fatherhood." Huffington Post 13 June 2014 29 June 2021. https://www.huffpost.com/entry/black-fatherhood-statistics_n_5491980

292.　Morgenstein, Mark. "Obama to New Grads – No Time for Excuses." CNN.com 19 May 2013 5 June 2021. < https://www.cnn.com/2013/05/19/politics/obama-morehouse-commencement/index.html>

293.   "United States Africa Command." Wikipedia 5 June
2021.
https://en.wikipedia.org/wiki/United_States_Africa_Comm
and

294.   Volman, Daniel. "Obama Moves Ahead with
Africom." Pambazuka News 10 December 2009 5 June
2021. < https://www.pambazuka.org/governance/obama-
moves-ahead-africom>

295.   "2011 military intervention in Libya." Wikipedia 5
June 2021.
https://en.wikipedia.org/wiki/2011_military_intervention_i
n_Libya

296.   "The Libyan Crisis." Wikipedia 5 June 2021.
https://en.wikipedia.org/wiki/Libyan_Crisis_(2011%E2%8
0%93present)#First_civil_war

297.   Delerme, Tony. "Barack Obama Convinced LeBron
James To End NBA Players Strike." TD Hip Hop Media 2
September 2020 28 June 2021. <
https://www.youtube.com/watch?v=Xvbzb7yn-g4>

298.   O'Donnell, Ricky. "How Barack Obama helped
convince NBA players to end their strike and return to
play." SB Nation 29 August 2020 28 June 2021. <
https://www.sbnation.com/nba/2020/8/29/21406770/barack
-obama-nba-players-lebron-james-strike-chris-paul-
meeting-call>

299.   Rivas, Christian. "Lakers and Clippers both vote to
stop NBA season, most other teams want to continue." SB
Nation Silver Screen and Roll 26 August 2020 28 June
2021. <
https://www.silverscreenandroll.com/2020/8/26/21403640/l
akers-clippers-both-vote-stop-nba-playoffs>

300.   Obama, Barack. Interview with Michael Strahan.
"Juneteenth: Together We Triumph." ABC News 18 June
2021.

301.   Goldberg, Jeffrey. "Why Obama Fears for Our
Democracy." The Atlantic 15 November 2020 28 June

2021. <
https://www.theatlantic.com/ideas/archive/2020/11/why-obama-fears-for-our-democracy/617087/>

302.   Collins, Sean. "Trump made gains with Black voters in some states. Here's why." Vox 4 November 2020 28 June 2021. <
https://www.vox.com/2020/11/4/21537966/trump-black-voters-exit-polls>

303.   Mohdin, Aamna. "American women voted overwhelmingly for Clinton except the white ones." Quartz 9 November 2016 28 June 2021. <
https://qz.com/833003/election-2016-all-women-voted-overwhelmingly-for-clinton-except-the-white-ones/?

304.   Louis Farrakhan. "Message to the Blacks in Government." Annual Convention of Blacks in Government, Washington Hilton and Towers Hotel, Washington, D.C. 23 August 1997.

305.   Obama, Barack. "Al Smith Dinner 2008 (Full Video.)" C-SPAN 17 October 2008 4 March 2022. <
https://www.youtube.com/watch?v=pq4zrOoHXeg>

306.   Matthew 27:21-22. 4 March 2022.

307.   Matthew 5:39. 4 March 2022.

308.   Matthew 5:44. 4 March 2022.

309.   Matthew 5:10. 4 March 2022.

310.   Johnson, Carla K., Olga R. Rodriguez, and Angeliki Kastinis. "As US COVID-19 death toll nears 600,000, racial gaps persist." 14 June 2021 5 March 2022. <
https://apnews.com/article/baltimore-california-coronavirus-pandemic-race-and-ethnicity-health-341950a902affc651dc268dba6d83264>

311.   Caron, Christina and Julien James. "Why Are More Black Kids Suicidal? A Search for Answers." 18 November 2021 5 March 2022.
<https://www.nytimes.com/2021/11/18/well/mind/suicide-black-kids.html>

312.   Peters, LaMonica. 'No warning that this was on their agenda' | Black male suicide deaths are rising faster than any other racial groups." Author: KFMB CBS 8 28 January 2022 5 March 2022. <https://www.cbs8.com/article/news/local/black-male-suicide-deaths-rising-faster-than-other-racial-groups/509-1dea0383-e5d8-4ce2-95dd-12ee43b52b62>

313.   Mann, Brian. "Black Americans are now dying from drug overdoses at a higher rate than whites." All Things Considered NPR. 2 March 2022 5 March 2022 < https://www.npr.org/2022/03/02/1083838947/black-americans-dying-drug-overdoses>

314.   Dixon, James. "We Are Divided and Falling." If GOD IS SO GOOD, WHY ARE BLACKS DOING SO BAD? p. 155 fourth paragraph. Charlotte. LifeBridge Books, 2007